Mary Magdalen Taylor

**Religious Orders**

Or Sketches of Some of the Orders and Congregations of Women

Mary Magdalen Taylor

**Religious Orders**

*Or Sketches of Some of the Orders and Congregations of Women*

ISBN/EAN: 9783337279004

Printed in Europe, USA, Canada, Australia, Japan

Cover: Foto ©Lupo / pixelio.de

More available books at **www.hansebooks.com**

# RELIGIOUS ORDERS;

OR

## SKETCHES

OF SOME OF THE

### Orders and Congregations of Women.

BY THE AUTHOR OF "EASTERN HOSPITALS,"
ETC. ETC.

LONDON
BURNS AND LAMBERT,
17, PORTMAN STREET.
1862.

# PREFACE.

A VERY few words of introduction are necessary for this work. The subject of Religious Orders is always of such deep interest, and perhaps never more so than at the present moment, that it is hoped this volume will not be out of place.

The first and most obvious difficulty was the extent of the subject. The most complete work on Religious Orders is that of Père Helyot, which originally appeared in eight folio volumes. He died before the French Revolution; and the number of Orders and Congregations since that time alone can hardly be counted.

A new edition of Père Helyot's work was published by the Abbé Migne, with many additions; but still some names of modern communities are not to be found there. These works are in French, and in our own language no history on the subject exists.

It was necessary, then, to form a plan of selection for the present volume, and the author could only endeavour to choose for the first series those Orders which seem to occupy a peculiar place in the

Church; but it is her intention to continue the series, and thus gradually give, in English, the history of all the principal Orders and Congregations of Women. The author has been greatly indebted to the valuable assistance of Father Waterworth in revising the volume, and she cannot too gratefully acknowledge the benefit this has afforded her.

The work is entitled, " Orders and Congregations of Women." Strictly speaking, an Order is a community whose Rule has been confirmed by the Holy See, and whose members take solemn vows. A Congregation is a community whose Rule has been approved only by Rome, and who take simple vows, either for a fixed period or for life. If the latter, they can be dispensed with by the Bishop of the diocese; while in the case of solemn vows, they can be dispensed only by the Pope. In common parlance, however, the word *Order* is used in speaking of any religious body.

The subject of Religious Orders has excited so much interest, even among persons external to the Catholic Church, that of late years various imitations of them have been set on foot; and as may be naturally supposed, the members of these communities totally fail in grasping the true idea of religious life. They are unable to understand that the essence of this life consists in the vows that bind the religious to a close and solemn union with our Lord, and that these vows cannot be binding unless made under authority, and in compliance with the laws defined by the Church.

Religious costume, devotions, and rules, are only the external tokens of the solemn act that has been made, and without it, would be without use or meaning. Religious vows, even annual ones, to be binding, cannot be made at the will of an individual, or by the caprice of a Superior. If the requisite conditions are not complied with, the vows become null and void. Vows must be made under authority from Rome, either directly or through the Bishop of the diocese. They must be received by a Bishop, or a priest who is empowered by him to do so. One year and a day is the *shortest* time of noviciate allowed by the Church, and each candidate for vows must be seen privately by the Bishop or his delegate, in order that no coercion or persuasion of superiors may have induced her to take the step. Neither can any one exact obedience, or assume the office of Superior, without lawful authority. It is true, in cases of the foundation of new Orders the person who has been inspired with the idea must necessarily teach and govern their first followers; but during this time no vows can be taken, and the religious habit and name cannot be obtained till approbation be given from the Bishop; and when the new Institute begins to grow into form, a Superior must be canonically appointed, and then obedience, which would be servile if paid merely to a human being, becomes a noble and holy action when paid to the one Lord and Master, who is seen in the person of His servants. Thus carefully does the Church guard and protect the holy and sacred ties of religious life, rendering it, not an unwilling subjection or a bondage, but a life of true liberty in the joyful service of God.

# TABLE OF CONTENTS.

## INTRODUCTION.

PAGE

Foundation of Religious Life—The Early Christians—St. Mary Magdalene—Life of Our Blessed Lady—Traditions—The Virgins of the Early Church—Monastic Life—St. Antony—St. Syncletica—Her Mode of Life—The First Monasteries of Women—The Professions—St. Machrina—Nuns of St. Basil—Traces of different Convents in Early Ages—The true idea of Religious Life . . . . . . . . . . . . . . . . . . . 1

## RULE OF ST. AUGUSTINE.

Religious Life in Africa—Canonesses—Their Duties—St. Augustine's Counsels to them—His Letter—He draws up his Rule—Augustinian Religious—Form of Government—How the Rule is Divided—Its Spirit—Mutual Charity—Practice of Poverty—The Chapter on Prayer—The Vow of Chastity—On Humility—Dress of the Religious—Care of the Sick—Holy Obedience—Conduct of the Superioress—Study of the Rule—Spirit of St. Austin—Development of the Rule in after Years—Becomes a Monastic Code . . . . . . . . . . . . 7

## CANONESSES OF THE HOLY SEPULCHRE.

Traditions of the Order—St. James of Jerusalem—Melania—Fall of Jerusalem—St. Helen—Difficulty of tracing the Progress of the Order—Their Rule that of St. Austin—

The Comtesse de Chaligny enters the Order—Increase of Convents—Constitutions of the Order—The Convent in Paris—The Prioress Renée—Her Religious Virtues—Her Dying Advice—Circular Letters—Government of the Order—Its Obligations—Miss Hawley and Miss Cary—The Convent at Liège—The Community in England—Dress of the Order . . . . . . . . . . 12

## CANONESSES OF ST. JOHN OF JERUSALEM.

Date of Foundation—Hospital at Jerusalem—Convent at Saragossa—Rule Confirmed—Their Alliance with the Order of the Knights of St. John—Their Ceremonies—Other Convents of the Order—Their Dress—Ceremony of Clothing and Profession—The Siege of Rhodes—Obligations of the Nuns . . . . . . . . . . . . 21

## ORDER OF MOUNT CARMEL.

Traditions of the Order—The Rule—Dispersion of the Order—Scapular of Mount Carmel—Nuns of the Order—Their Spirit—The Apostolate of Carmel—The Rule—Relaxation of the Order—Its wonderful Reform—St. Teresa—Her Life well known—Her intense Love for God—Her Success in her Undertaking—Her Death—Constitutions of the Order—Spirit of St. Teresa—Qualifications for the Novices—The Night Office—Outline of the Life—Great Care to be shown to the Sick—The Saintly Religious of this Order—Its Foundation in France—Madame Acarie—Her brilliant Gifts—Her great Sanctity—Life of St. Teresa—The Councils at the Chartreux—St. Francis de Sales—Postulants for the Order—Madame Acarie's wise Advice—The Future before her—The Convent of the Order is opened—Madame Acarie's Widowhood—Enters the Order—Her Saintly Life—Her Obedience and Humility—Makes her Profession—Her Illness—Her Last Trials—Her Death—Her Beatification . . . . . . . . . . . . . . 30

## ORDER OF MOUNT CARMEL—*continued*.

Louise de la Vallière—Her Conversion—Determines to be a Carmelite—Her Clothing—Her Life of True Penance—Her Humility and Mortification—Her Forgiveness of Injuries—Her Holy Death—Progress of the Order—Madame Louise de France—The Court of Louis Quinze—Vocation of the Princess Louise—Enters the Convent at St. Denis—Novena of our Lady—Courage of the Royal Postulant—Her Clothing—Splendour of the Ceremony—Marie Antoinette—Profession of Louise—Her Progress in Virtue—Her Advice—Her Self-Denial—Her Love for her Order—Her Death . . . . . . 53

## ORDER OF MOUNT CARMEL—*continued*.

France in 1757—The House of De Soyecourt—*Mademoiselle de Trop*—The Little Camille—Her First Trial—Her First Communion—Her Vocation—Her Trials in the World—Her Entrance into Religion—The *Prise d' habit*—Louis Philippe and Madame de Genlis—Fervour of Sœur Camille—She makes her Vows—Her Advancement in Virtue—Threatenings of Danger—Dispersion of the Nuns—Good Friday, 1793—Camille's Terrible Sufferings—Her Patience and Submission—Her Long Walks—The well-plaited Cap—Death of her Father—Martyrdom of the Carmelites at Compiègne—Close of the Reign of Terror—The First Benediction—House of the *Vache Noir*—Restoration of Property—Convent of the Carmes—Touching Reminiscences—St. Teresa's Picture—Anxieties of Camille—Her Exile—The Père de Clorivière—Breakfast with the Pope—Close of Camille's long Life—Her Peace and Joy—The Carmelite Chronicles—Marie des Anges—Madame d'Autry—Henry III.—A strong *penchant*—Shrine of St. Denis—Sister Louise—The Altar Stone—The Good Angel—The Silver Lamp before the Altar—The Convent at Lanherne—Government of the Order . . . . . . 66

## ORDER OF THE POOR CLARES COLLETINES.

PAGE

St. Francis of Assissi—Rise of his Order—St. Clare—Palm Sunday—Convent of St. Damian—Rule of the *Poor Ladies*—The Seraphic Father—His Farewell to his Children—The Attack on the Convent—St. Clare's Defence—Assissi is Saved—Confirmation of the Rule—St. Clare's Christmas Night—Her Last Blessing—Her Glorious Death—The Spirit of Dispensations—The Urbanistes—St. Collette—Seeks to know her Vocation—Her Hermitage—Reforms the Order of St. Clare—Isabeau de Bourbon—St. Collette's Last Desire—The Rule of the Order—Its Different Chapters—Duties of the Abbess—Testament of St. Clare—Constitutions of St. Collette—The various Regulations—The Elections—The Chapters—Character of the Life of a Poor Clare—Their Daily Rule—Saints of the Order—Blessed Cunégonde—St. Catherine of Bologna—Government of the Order . . . . . . . . . . . . . . . . . 96

## ORDER OF THE PERPETUAL ADORATION OF THE BLESSED SACRAMENT.

Necessity of this Order—The Spirit of Reparation—Catherine de Bar—Her Retreat—Her Profession Ring—War in Lorraine—Catherine becomes a Benedictine—Takes the name of Mecthilde—The War of the Fronde—The Marquise de Beauves—The Idea of the New Order—Anne of Austria—The Priest's Prayer—The Order is founded—The Trials of Mecthilde—Observances of the Order—The Daily Victim—The Watchword of the Order—Their only Abbess—Their Prioress—Their Interior Spirit—Their Ceremonials—Confirmation of the Order—Mademoiselle Louise de Bourbon-Condé—Her Childhood—The Court of Louis XVI.—The Royal Friendship—Charity of Louise—The Père Beauregard—Beginning of Troubles—Louise's Vocation—Writes to her Father—Letter from Louis XVI.—Louise takes the Franciscan Habit—Is driven from her

## CONTENTS.

Convent—Is an Exile—Her Sorrows—Her Retreat—Her Secret Vows—The Order of La Trappe—The *Comte du Nord*—Louise enters a Convent of the Perpetual Adoration—Death of the Duc d'Enghien—Her Affection for him—Her Prayers—Her Spirit of Forgiveness—She goes to England—The Père de la Fontaine—Return of the Bourbons to France—The Novena—The *Temple*—The Cent Jours—The New Convent is opened—Death of the Prince de Condé—Humility of the Princess—Baptism of the Bells—Louise's last illness—Her Holy Counsels—The Chapter of Peace . . . . 124

### ORDER OF THE VISITATION OF THE BLESSED VIRGIN.

Wants of the Age—St. Francis of Sales—Beauty of his Character—St. Jane Frances de Chantal—Foundation of the Order—St. Francis's first idea is overruled—The Spirit of Interior Mortification—The Peculiarity of this Order—Careful Regulations of the Founder—The Three Classes of Sisters—The Different Offices—Care of the Sick—The Infirmarian—The Lay Sisters—Government of the Order—Sanctity of Madame de Chantal—The Last Meeting with St. Francis—The Twofold Relic—Her Last Sorrow—Her Holy Death—Marie Jacqueline Favre—The ball at Chambéry—Jacqueline's Resolve—Her Life of Suffering—Her Calm and Happy End—Anne Coste—The Secret Communion—The Guardian Angels—Anne's work among the Poor—Becomes a Lay Sister—Her Parting with St. Francis—Her Vision of his Death—Margaret Mary Alacoque—The Devotion to the Sacred Heart—The mode of Life of the Visitation Nuns—St. Francis's Exhortation—Renewal of Vows . . . . . . . . . . . . . 158

### ORDER OF THE GOOD SHEPHERD.

Charity of the Middle Ages—New Orders wanted—The Conversion of Sinners—Père Eudes—His Congregation—Founds the Order of the Good Shepherd—Its Confirmation—Death of Père Eudes—The Revolution—The Market Women—The Sisters go out to Glean—The Convent of St. Michel—Its Extent—The Conspirator—The Different "Classes"—The Pope's Brief—The Mother-House at Angers—The Foundation of the Order in England—The Ship's Signal—The Visit to Chelsea—Trials of the Nuns—The First Convent is opened—The Mère Marie de St. Joseph—Increase of the Work—Funeral of the Superioress—The Order at Vienna—Prison Work—The chains of Body and Soul—The Courage and Faith of the Nuns—State of the Prisoners—The Retreat—A Blessed Change—The Prison *régime*—The Fête Dieu—Coming Sorrow—Convent at Tripoli—The East Indies—The Orphan Class—The Christian Prince—The Indian Ladies—Description of the Work of the Good Shepherd Nuns—Their Hardships—Consecrated Penitents—The Magdalenes—Touching Incidents—The Obstinate Sinner—The Haunted Death-bed—The Last Moment—The Five Classes—Dress of the Order . . . . . . . . . . 186

ORDER OF THE SACRED HEART.

The close of the Eighteenth Century—The Père de Tournely and the Père Varin—Madeleine Sophie Barat—Devotion to the Sacred Heart—Foundation of the Order—Its Object—Mode of Education—Love of the Poor—The Rule and Constitutions—Great Progress of the Order—The Noviciate—The Vows—Susanne Geoffroy—Her Destiny Foretold—Her Childish Faith—Wise Advice of her Director—Father Draut—Prediction of the Revolution—Susanne's Courage—The Community of Ladies—La Providence—Susanne enters the Order of the Sacred Heart—Her Noviciate—The House at Niort—The Mère Emilie—Susanne's generous Sacrifice

—General Council of the Order—The Mère Geoffroy goes to Lyons—Her letters—Her Humility—Her Veneration for the Order of St. Ignatius—Her beautiful Death . 210

## CONGREGATION OF ST. CLOTILDE.

Peculiarity of the Rule—Cause of its Foundation—The First Religious—The Pilgrimage to the Calvary—The Père Rauzan—His Views for the New Congregation —His Hesitation—Design of the Order—Courage of the Nuns—Character of their Life—Their Dress—Their Name—Letters from the Père Rauzan—His Advice to the Novice-Mistress, and Superioress—His Death—Education given by the Nuns of St. Clotilde—Its Results 227

## CONGREGATION OF THE SISTERS OF CHARITY OF ST. VINCENT DE PAUL.

Their Name well known—St. Vincent de Paul—Beauty of his Life—His Captivity—His Song in a Strange Land—Founds a Congregation of Men—His various Good Works—His Midnight Walks—His Influence at Court—His marvellous Humility—Confraternity of the Ladies of Charity—Servants of the Poor—The Peasant Girl—The First Sister of Charity—Arrival of others—Simplicity of their Life—The Queen of Poland—Conferences of St. Vincent—Their Beauty—St. Vincent's Prayers—Actual Foundation of the Order—Its Title—Stability of St. Vincent's work—The Keystone—Holy Obedience—The Presence of God—Humility of St. Vincent—Touching instance of this—His Submission to others—Advice on Sickness—Saying of Pope Clement—Example set by Peasants—The Religious Spirit—Destiny of the Company—Love of Contempt—Difficulty of Learning Humility—The First Sisters—Anecdote of St. Vincent—Mademoiselle Legras—Her Early Life—Her Love of God—Is guided by St. Vincent—Governs the Sisters—Her Wise Advice—Her Love of Holy Poverty—Her Obedience—

Her Devotion to the Poor—Her Affection for the Sisters
—Her Deep Humility—Advice to those Travelling—Her
Severe Illness—Her Deep Contrition—Her Death-bed—
Her Last Cross—Her Farewell Blessing—St. Vincent's
Opinion of her—Her Grave—The Close of St. Vincent's
Life—His Confidence for the Future—Mathurine
Guérin—Her First Disappointment—Her Mother's
Love for her—Becomes a Sister of Charity—A Sad
Easter—Triumph of Truth—Mathurine is Superioress-
General—Is miraculously Cured—End of her Life—
Julienne Jouvin—Her Natural Gifts—Her Director—
Her Entrance into the Order—Her Power over others
—Her Sanctity—Her Spiritual Gifts—Her Friendship
with the Queen—Her Longings for Death—Love for
the Will of God—Her Saintly Death—Counsels left by
her—Her Favourite Devotion—Her Opinion of Jan-
senism—Her Love for her Vocation—Her Daily Aspira-
tions—Progress of the Order—The Revolution—The
Mère Deleau—Strange Sights in France—Invita-
tion to Dance—The Assembling of the Order—The
Lineage of St. Vincent—Visit of the Pope—Re-
appearance of the *Cornette*—The Maison Mère—The
Order in America—Eliza Anne Seton—The Journey
to Italy—Mental Conflicts—The Sisterhood of St.
Joseph—Their Hardships—Request to be received as
Sisters of St. Vincent—Letter of Sœur Bizeray—
Refusal of Passports—The Rule—Government of Mother
Seton—Her Sorrows—Her Reflections on them—Her
Last Wish—Affiliation of the Sisters to the Congregation
of Sisters of Charity—Spirit of an Order—The Noviciate
—The Seminary—Form of Government—Number of
Sisters—Graces given to the Order in Modern Times—
Its Foundation in England . . . . . . . . . . . 240

## ORDER OF OUR LADY OF MERCY.

Antiquity of the Name—St. Peter Nolasco—The Fourth
Vow—New Calls for Help—1825—Katherine McAuley

—Her Good Works—Opposition—The Archbishop of Dublin—The Idea of the new Order—Miss McAuley's Noviciate—The Rule—The End the Order had in View —Interior Spirit—Form of Government—Ceremony of receiving the White Veil—Professions—Form of Vows —Character of Katherine McAuley—Her wise Government—Her one Great Desire—Confirmation of the Rule —Close of Mother McAuley's Life—Progress of the Order—Foundations in the Colonies — The Crimean Hospitals . . . . . . . . . . . . . . . . 301

## CONGREGATION OF THE NURSING SISTERS OF OUR LADY OF HELP.

The Usefulness of the Orders of Nursing Sisters—Qualifications required from Postulants—Their Duties at the Sick Bed—Minuteness of their Rule—The Spirit in which they must Act—Ceremony of their Clothing— Form of their Vows—Difficulty of their Calling—Form of Government—Mode of Life in their Convents— Beautiful Provision for the Aged and Infirm Sisters— Exhortations of their Founder—Love for their Vocation —Motives for Encouragement—Service of the Poor— Devotion to Mary—Other Orders of Nursing Sisters— Importance of this work . . . . . . . . . . . . 314

## CONGREGATION OF THE SISTERS OF MARY AND JOSEPH FOR PRISONS.

Prison Work—The Sisters of St. Joseph—Foundation of this Congregation—Its End—Noviciate and Vows— The Rule—Houses of Refuge—Name of the Institute —The Spirit in which the Sisters should act—The Prison of St. Lazare . . . . . . . . . . . . . . . 326

## CONGREGATION OF THE BLIND SISTERS OF ST. PAUL.

PAGE

This Order quite *Unique*—Its Foundation—Two Classes of Sisters—The Blind Asylum—The Sympathy we all feel for the Blind—The Perpetual Cloister—St. Paul's Blindness—New Year's Day—Content of the Sisters . 331

## CONGREGATION OF THE HELPERS OF THE HOLY SOULS.

Devotion to the Souls in Purgatory—The Foundress of this Order—All Souls' Day—The Five Signs—Too much Money—The *Curé d' Ars*—The Order is began—The First Trials—Work of the Sisters—Their Rule—Progress of the Institute—Conclusion . . . . . . . . 335

---

### ERRATA.

Page 52, line 19, for " doctrines " read " devotions."
„ 77, last line, „ "Rodz" „ "Rodez."
„ 171, line 2, „ " Bourgoes " „ "Bourges."

# RELIGIOUS ORDERS.

## INTRODUCTION.

From the very foundation of the Church, religious life took its rise. It has but developed itself as time went on, and adapted itself, as it were, to the wants of each successive century; for all its essentials were to be found in Jerusalem and in the heathen cities, among the "little flock" who were hidden here and there amid the throng of a busy and lawless world. The fervent love of the first Christians led them on, beyond the keeping of the commandments, to the counsels of perfection; and as the community of our Blessed Lord and His Apostles, or the austere life of the Baptist, became the type for men to follow, so did the religious life for women spring from our Blessed Lady and the Magdalene. Standing beneath the Cross of Jesus, the spotless and the penitent, they have left examples for ever after for women to follow.

St. Mary Magdalene, says tradition, retired into Provence, and there lived a life of solitude and penance. Our Blessed Lady had another path to pursue; she had to be the support and help of the infant Church. The rest of her life on earth, from the parting on Mount Olivet, was to be spent in consoling, enlightening, and aiding others. She lived in the house of St. John, and to the eyes of the world seemed, as she had ever done, nothing more than an ordinary Jewish woman; bearing, doubtless, the marks of a more than common sorrow on that meek pale face—which painters have loved to picture as belonging to the Mother of Dolours—and influencing others in a way that awed those who could not understand from whence her power sprang; and reverenced most tenderly by her children in the Church, whose devotion was yet so deep that they spoke only amongst themselves of what she was to them. And after she was gone from her weary exile to her throne on high, the example she had left was diligently followed, and the state of holy virginity was chosen by many. There are traditions of communities at this period, but of course these are very obscure; and the fall of Jerusalem, and the persecutions of the Church, must necessarily have dispersed them.

But in the retirement of their own homes, many a Roman or Syrian maiden and widow consecrated themselves to God, and from henceforth were enclosed in heart and detached in spirit from the world and engrossing family affections. Some names amongst these stand out to us in a halo of light, and the martyr's crown oftentimes surmounts the virgin's veil. But Agnes and Dorothea, Lucy and Cecilia, were only the leaders of a numerous band. For, says one of our greatest modern writers,* " virginity had been honoured and practised in the Church from its origin. Besides the sublime maids who bore it triumphant through the last agonies, there were a multitude who preserved it for many years in the midst of the world. For there were nuns, as there had been ascetics and hermits, before the regular and popular institution of monastic life." And he further adds: "During the first three centuries all Christians retained a certain monastic character; they remained pure in the depths of universal corruption; their life was more or less hidden amid pagan society. They were of that old world as if they had not been. Then came persecutions which shortened the way to heaven; these took the place of penitence and trial. The dungeon of the martyr was as good, says Tertullian, as the cell of a prophet." Later on, the idea of living in solitude and penance, after the example of the Magdalene, began to attract many souls. About the year 300, St. Antony, the "father of monks," commenced his

* The Count de Montalembert.

solitary and austere life, and it was not long before women began to hide themselves in caves and sepulchres, and to practise severe austerity. One of the first of these was St. Syncletica, a nobly born lady of Alexandria, who sold her rich possessions, gave them all to the poor, and herself to prayer and penance. After a time others collected around her, as men had done round St. Antony, and thus a community was formed.

St. Syncletica governed her nuns with great wisdom and prudence. Severe bodily afflictions marked the end of her life; a cancer formed in her mouth, causing intense agony, and necessarily separating her in many ways from the company of her Sisters; and at length, for three months, she was deprived of the power of speaking, seeing, or eating. She endured all with joy, and "was consoled by many visions which she had," till at last she went to behold the unveiled beauty in her eternal rest.

Various other monasteries seem to have existed at this time, and curious traces are left of the ceremonies and customs followed in them. They were always governed by a priest, who was present at the professions; and in early ages the clothing and profession were the same ceremony, and the probation of the postulants was a very short one. The altar was incensed by the Superior saying the psalm *Beati immaculati*; he then read the seventh chapter of the first of Corinthians, and the parable of the ten virgins; the Credo followed; the novice's hair was then cut off, and the following beautiful prayer was said: " Oh, Holy One, resting among the holy! oh, Highest One, who dwellest in the height of eternity! O Lord, who regardest the humble! Thou who provest hearts; who soundest the depths of the soul; who lovest purity, and art the seal of virginity, the Refuge and Fortress of all those who speak to Thee in truth; we pray and beseech Thee, oh Delight of men! that Thou wouldst look with benign countenance on this Thy servant, who kisses the ground before Thee. Bless her, cleanse her, and pour Thy peace on her, and Thy sweetness into her heart. Give her Thy fear, and the grace always to follow Thy word. Awaken her mind, that she may always think of Thee, and that she may conquer all the temptations which can turn her from Thee. Preserve her soul and body pure from stain, and grant that her lamp may never be extinguished. Bless the work of her hands and her daily food; make her sure of the way of eternal life, in which nothing is wanting; and this by the grace and merits of Jesus Christ, Thy only Son, to whom be glory for ever."

St. Machrina, sister to St. Basil, founded a monastery, which she governed with great zeal. The community were distinguished by their love of poverty, and the Abbess gave a striking example of this, for at her death all her personal property consisted of two *cilices,*—a relic of the true cross, and a cross and ring of iron. Nuns of the Order of St. Basil exist to the present day. Some of the monasteries of the Greek Church claim the name of Religious of St. Basil; but as they neither follow his Rule nor his spirit, they cannot be reckoned among his true descendants. Scattered up and down the history of the Church, are records of numerous communities in different places: there is the celebrated one of St. Croix, founded by St. Radegunde: and again, in our own land are records of the old monasteries of Ely and Whitby, associated with the names of St. Hilda, St. Ebba, and St. Etheldreda; but as the object of this work is to speak only of those communities which gradually developed into *Orders,* to dwell further on these traces would be beyond our scope. But before we go more in detail of the religious life, we cannot but observe how different from its birth it was to the idea conceived of it in these busy modern days. The salvation and assistance of others was a leading feature in monastic bodies, but the predominant idea was consecration to God. To give themselves up to God, and to belong solely to Him, in a way beyond that of ordinary Christians, was their aim, their end, and their glory.

## RULE OF ST. AUGUSTINE.

PÈRE HELYOT says,—" As St. Augustine established in Africa the common and regular life for monks and clerks, he has also done the same thing for virgins. For the Church has always had virgins, whom she considered as the most illustrious portion of the flock of Jesus Christ; nevertheless, they have not always lived together in monasteries, and there is scarcely a vestige of a monastery in Africa before St. Augustine." It seems, then, a well-grounded fact that St. Augustine founded monasteries for women, called Canonesses, who were bound to recite the Divine Office and to pray for others. Some of these communities kept enclosure, others did not. To the religious of one of these houses the Saint once wrote of "his joy to see, in the midst of scandals, the pure love which united them together;" and his 210th letter is addressed to the Mother Felicita, who was Superioress of this community. For their benefit he drew up a Rule, which became a model for numerous other communities. The Rule of St. Augustine has been followed by a number of other Orders, who, however, do not consider themselves as Augustinian religious. Many of the modern Orders have adopted it, grafting on to it their own "constitutions," concerning the especial end for which each institute was founded.

The Orders strictly Augustinian are the Barefooted Augustinians, and the Augustinian Recollects, and various Orders of Hospitallers and educational Orders. It is not our intention to enter into their details here. It may be observed that the ancient Orders were never governed by a *generalate;* that is, one general Superior to whom a number of convents in various parts of the world are subject. The reason for this is obvious. The difficulties of travelling, and the hindrances to frequent communication, rendered such government impossible. Each house was independent in itself, and it is therefore far more difficult for a biographer to trace their progress. As, however, the Rule of St. Augustine was a foundation-stone in the progress of religious life, it will be better to give its substance here, and to refer to it as we speak of the various Orders which exist until this day under its teaching. It is divided into ten brief chapters. The first, called The End and Spirit of the Institute, says,—" Above all things, my dearest sisters, love God and then your neighbour, for these are the two commandments principally given to us." Chapter second, On Union and Mutual Charity, enjoins, " In following, then, the things that you are ordered to observe in your monasteries, the first of all is that for which you are assembled, that you dwell in your house with unanimity, and have but one heart and soul in God." The third chapter treats of Poverty:— "All things shall be distributed to each by the Superioress; and those who bring riches shall be contented to give it all into the common stock; and those of high rank must not disdain the poor sisters, and they must not esteem themselves better for having parted with all they had to the monastery than if they enjoyed them in the world, for pride creeps into good works to destroy them; for what good will it be to disperse our possessions to the poor, and make ourselves poor, if the miserable soul becomes more proud or contemptuous than she was in possessing them?" The fourth chapter treats of Prayer:—"Live then," says the Saint, "unanimously and in concord, and together honour God, whose temple ye are. Be assiduous in prayer, at the prescribed time and hour; when occupied in chanting psalms and hymns, let your heart be attentive to that which your voice pronounces." When speaking of the vow of Chastity, in the fifth chapter, the Saint tells the religious—"To subdue the flesh by fasting and abstinence, and only take what health requires. Seek to be more in company with your sisters than alone, and avoid any affectation or softness." When speaking of Humility, he says,—"Let not those who forget their duty seek to conceal it from others, for how can they conceal anything from the eyes of Him who sees from on high, and from Whom nothing is hid? If disputes arise, be prompt to end them, and ask mutual pardon; be careful to repress any feeling of dislike between each other, and demand pardon of your common Lord and Master of all." He bids them wear a uniform dress, which shall be a very plain one; and not to complain about this, for if they do, it shows how much they lack interior sanctity, the clothing of the soul. He forbids the hair being seen under their veils; but the veil at this period, and for long after, was worn by all unmarried women, and sometimes by wives. There is a chapter on Care of the Sick, and St. Austin enjoins "great care to be shown to the infirm and weak; and those who have to serve the sick sisters, to do it without murmuring." In the chapter on Holy Obedience, he bids them "obey your Superioress as a mother, and give her the honour that belongs to her; and still more to the priest who is given you for Superior, and has care of you all." "If anything arises which exceeds the Superioress's power to decide, she ought to ask the priest." "Let not the Superioress esteem herself happy in having the power to rule and command, but as being able to serve the Sisters with charity. She will precede them in honour before men, but before God let her be humbly submissive at their feet, and give example of good manners to all; let her correct the unquiet, console the cowardly, support and embrace the infirm, and be patient towards all; take correction willingly, and improve it with fear; let her desire more to be loved than feared by you, though both are necessary; let her remember that she must render an account to God for you; therefore, in obeying her, have compassion not only on yourselves, but on her who is among you in greater danger because her charge is greater. God give you grace to observe all these things in joy and gladness, loving the spiritual beauty of virtue, and giving forth, by prayer and holy conversation, a good odour in Jesus Christ, not as servants under the yoke of the law, but as free under time of grace." St. Austin ends his Rule, exhorting the Sisters:—" To the end you may see yourself in this Rule as in a mirror, read it once a week, for fear, by forgetfulness, you neglect something; and if you find you have done what is there prescribed to you, give thanks to God, from whom all good proceeds; and if some one perceives herself to have failed in anything, let her repent of the past and take better care for the future, praying God that her fault may be pardoned."

The spirit of the Saint whose heart burnt with love may plainly be discerned in this simple Rule. He does not prescribe a number of outward observances, or of great austerities; he would have his daughters serve God as their strength permitted, but all and each actuated with a most ardent love for God; having, that there was no need to enter into minute details of their daily life. As time went on, however, bringing various wants and an increase of subjects, it was necessary to have more defined rules, which, as statutes or constitutions, were grafted on to the Rule of St. Augustine. The Comte de Montalembert says, speaking of this Rule, "Written in 423, divided into twenty-four articles, and originally destined for these simple African nuns, it was resuscitated under Charlemagne, and became then the fundamental code of an immense branch of the monastic order."

## CANONESSES OF THE HOLY SEPULCHRE.

IF we were to take tradition for our guide, the religious of this Order would claim the first place; and although the line of descent cannot be authenticated, there is nothing which would render it impossible or absurd. They call St. James of Jerusalem their founder, and say, that "near the tomb of Christ the Lord was established a convent of women, in memory and honour of St. Mary Magdalene." The tradition further adds, that the religious spent their time in meditation on the Death and Passion of our Lord; they made the necessary articles for the use of the altar, and "had all things in common." It is certain that at the same time when St. Paula lived at Bethlehem, under the direction of St. Jerome, the high-born Melania "founded a convent at Jerusalem, and collected there fifty virgins. In this house she died; her grand-daughter, also named Melania, built a church and monastery for ninety penitents upon one of the sites where our Lord rested when bearing His Cross." *

The fall of Jerusalem must, of course, have broken up the first community; but as the practice of leading the religious life in their own homes was so common, it is probable this was their lot till they were allowed to assemble again. About the time of St. Helen, writers mention this convent at Jerusalem; and it is further stated that St. Helen herself joined them, and received from Macarius, the thirty-ninth Bishop of Jerusalem, the linen surplice and double red cross worn by the Canonesses of this Order. But when Jerusalem finally fell into the hands of the infidels, all traces of these religious were lost; when their first monasteries were founded, when their rule grew into form, we know not, but this very ignorance proves their antiquity. They were

* Montalembert.

spoken of in Rome, in 1394, as having numerous houses; and Père Helyot says, although they were not known in France till 1620, for a *long time* there had been monasteries in Spain, Germany, and other countries. As soon as traces of them appear, we find that they lived by the Rule of St. Augustine, and their spirit always seems to have been more that of interior mortification than of outward austerity. In 1620, the Comtesse de Chaligny and Princesse de Lorraine founded a monastery of the Order in Charleville, France. The religious who began this house came from Liège. The Comtesse entered the Order, and was professed as Sister Mary of St. Francis, March 25th, 1625. She died in the second year of her profession, leaving a reputation for great sanctity. Her daughter, Princess Louise, became a Franciscan nun, and her eldest son entered the Society of Jesus. At the time of the entrance of the Comtesse de Chaligny, the Order of the Holy Sepulchre was little known; the houses then established were at Aix-la-Chapelle, St. Leonard près de Ruremonde, St. Croix, near Lymbach, and at Cavée; there were two houses in Liège, and one at Visen near that town. But the example of the holy countess drew many subjects to the Order, and the monasteries rapidly increased in number. Houses were founded at Maestricht, Mariambourg, Malmedy, Hasque, Tongre, Vierzon in Berry, Luynes in Touraine; two more at Liège and Paris. The Paris convent was opened in 1635, at Belle Chasse, St. Germain près aux Clercs. The constitutions of the Order were revised and corrected by the Bishop of Tricavio, Apostolic Nuncio in Flanders, and were solemnly approved by Pope Urban VIII. in 1631, as Helyot says, but other writers state in 1642. The Paris house received a very valuable subject in 1651, in Renée de Livennede Verdille, a daughter of one of the most ancient and noble houses in Poitou. Her father and mother died in her childhood, and Renée became sole heiress to their great wealth. Endowed with remarkable beauty and talent, life opened before her in its brightest aspects; but resolutely she turned away from the world, and gave up all things to follow Christ. She took the habit of the Canonesses of the Holy Sepulchre on January 7th, 1651.

"She saw," wrote her religious sisters, "that the success of her noviciate depended on the observance of the Rule, and she studied it well in order to practise it with more intelligence and merit. Nothing appeared to her of little consequence; the smallest practice of religious life was a law to her; and always endeavouring to attain perfection, in all things she gave the preference to that which could inspire her with the spirit of her state." On the 7th of May, 1652, she made her solemn profession, and it is recorded of her, that "what she promised on this great day she kept during her whole life. Never did her fervour weaken; she offered the tree and its fruits together." The government of the convent in Paris had differed from others of the Order; the Prioresses had been elected triennally instead of for life. When, however, the Mère Renée was elected Prioress, her daughters insisted on keeping her in office for life. The convent received young lady pupils, but the Prioress Renée never would admit any of very high rank, saying they brought the spirit of the world into the convent. Many subjects were attracted to the community by her wise government and holy life. The order and beauty of the conventual church were "very near her heart," and she ruled the temporal affairs of the convent with discretion, and completely freed it from some debts that had been contracted. "But," continues her historian, "her application to exterior affairs did not diminish her zeal for spiritual ones. She was animated by a sincere love of God, and she wished Him to be loved by all under her rule. That which was an offence to God was one also to her; and in chapter she spoke in such a touching manner, that we never heard her without being penetrated with respect for the holiness of our profession, and the desire for making progress in it. Her example added weight to her words; she did more than she exhorted us to do; and so exact was her regularity, that at the age of sixty-seven none of the devotions practised in her youth had been relaxed; she heard every mass that was celebrated. She could scarcely believe people to be guilty of faults, and her way of punishing was with deliberation, gentleness, and prudence. She could not endure to see any division among her daughters, who, "being a copy of the first Christians of Jerusalem, ought only to have one heart and one soul;" and often she would throw herself on her knees before one of her religious, asking pardon for another, thus taking the sin of others on herself. Her great *attrait* was prayer, and she loved to communicate very frequently. Her devotion to our Blessed Lady was very deep, and she had a chapel erected in her honour in the interior of the monastery, and thither she would often go to pray. She had a great love of holy poverty; always wore the oldest things she could, and was never to be heard complaining of anything; she often rejoiced at having got rid of her large fortune. She loved the poor, and gave abundant alms to them; and she tried always to do good in the most secret way possible. "All through her life she had a great fear of death, springing from a deep sense of her unworthiness; but as is so often the case with saintly persons, when the awful hour was at hand she was tranquil, submissive, and full of confidence. She left us an example of patience, sweetness, resignation to the will of God, and an ardent desire of possessing Him in glory. When she was dying, she gave us advice which will be for ever graven on our hearts." She had governed her community for fifty-three years when she was called to give up her account; her illness lasted only four days. She was buried in the convent church: "not," said her Sisters, "as an occasion of reminding us of her, because we can never forget her, but that we may preserve her spirit amongst us, and imitate her zeal for the Divine service." The circular letter from which these extracts of the life of the Princess Renée have been taken, ends thus: "We supplicate you, reverend mothers, to have the holy sacrifice of peace offered for her. We hope, also, that charity, which is indifferent to time and place, will always preserve your affection to us, and that you will give us the help of your prayers, so that our new Prioress may animate us to walk in the steps of our last one, and that the resurrection may reunite us in a happy eternity. We are, with profound respect, the Prioress and religious Canonesses of the Order of the Holy Sepulchre.—Paris, April 16th, 1711."

We may observe that the custom of circular letters exists in most religious orders, both in those governed by a Generalate, and also in others in which each foundation is separate. In the former, circular letters generally emanate from the Superiors-General, who send to all the branch houses a brief account of all that has been done in the Order, and a record of the death of any remarkably holy member. In the other cases, these letters emanate from each separate convent, and are more or less frequent, according to circumstance. The Order of the Holy Sepulchre has no Generalate, but each newly-founded monastery is under obedience to the one from whence the religious have been sent, until there are twelve religious professed in it, when it becomes independent. Each convent is governed by a Prioress, who holds the office for life; the other offices are held for five years, and the elections are made in Chapter. Each convent, also, is subject to the Bishop of the diocese, and the election of the Prioress must be confirmed by him. The religious of this Order rise at four, and have half-an-hour's meditation before matins. They are bound to recite the Divine Office, to keep abstinence in Advent and all Wednesdays, and to fast on all Fridays, excepting from Easter to Pentecost; they are bound to keep enclosure, but may undertake the education of girls, both rich and poor. In some of their convents they had a series of chapels representing the holy places, and had a custom of making a procession to these spots on Fridays, ending with the one representing Mount Calvary.

In the time of King Charles the First, when the penal laws were slightly relaxed, and the hopes of the English Catholics for religious freedom were rising, an idea was entertained of the foundation of a convent, the shelter of which was sighed for by many English ladies. With the hope of hereafter founding one in England, two ladies, Miss Hawley and Miss Cary, entered the Convent of the Holy Sepulchre at Tongres, and made their noviciate there. After this they determined to found a convent at Liège, especially for English subjects. After many difficulties this foundation was effected, but the idea of founding a convent in England proved unfeasible; nevertheless, many novices came to them, and the community grew into a large one. In 1794, the political convulsions in France shook Flanders to its centre, and, as we shall see later on in our work, few were the religious communities who were not driven into exile. Such was the fate of the Canonesses of the Holy Sepulchre; they accordingly fled to England in August, 1794. In this country they were enabled to make a foundation, and have here now a large and important community. Besides reciting the Divine Office, the nuns of this Order have much time for prayer; their very name denotes that they are especially called to the great duty of all contemplative Orders, that of watching incessantly by their Lord's Sacred Body with St.

Mary Magdalene, until He shall come again in glory. Their rule forbids their working alone in their cells, but they are to do so together in a common workroom. To this day they preserve the quaint but picturesque costume of the Canonesses; the habit is of black serge, over which they wear a surplice of white linen, without sleeves. On the left side of this is a double red cross, the badge of their Order, denoting that they are bound to bear the Cross outwardly and inwardly; a similar red cross is also placed on the long black cloak which they wear in choir. At the time of the Revolution, the convents of this Order in France and Belgium were swept away; in the latter country, some have regained their footing, and are still in existence.

## CANONESSES OF ST. JOHN OF JERUSALEM.

AMONG the ancient Orders of Canonesses must be reckoned those of St. John of Jerusalem, for it is certain they were founded about the same time as the Knights of St. John, 1048. Hospitals for men and women were erected in Jerusalem, near the Latin Church; the one for men under the invocation of St. John Baptist, and the other under that of

St. Mary Magdalene. When Godfrey de Bouillon entered the Holy City, 1099, the Superioress of the Hospital was a Roman lady named Agnes. Their fate when the city was retaken by Saladin is not known, but it is conjectured that they fled in safety; and the following year a Convent of the Order was founded between Saragossa and Lerida. Their rule was confirmed by Pope Celestin the Third, in 1193; it was, in fact, the Rule of St. Augustine, with certain modifications, and accompanied by *constitutions* of the institute. From the time of their being driven from Jerusalem, it does not seem that hospitals formed part of the work of the religious, but they became a cloistered Order, devoted to prayer. They were completely a part of the Order of the Knights of St. John; and while the Knights were to go forth to defend Christendom, the Sisters were to strengthen their arms by continual prayers. It was a beautiful union of the temporal and spiritual weapons of warfare. Like the Knights, the Sisters were required to be those of noble birth, and all their ceremonies were conducted with great splendour and majesty. Ten priests, living with their Prior, served the convent church. The Divine Office was sung with the greatest care and reverence, and the silence of the night was broken by their assembling in choir to chant their matins.

On feast days their surplices were of the finest

linen, and they held silver sceptres in their hands while singing the Office, striving by these means to typify the resemblance of their employment to that of those who reign in heaven. The Prioress of this Order had a voice at the Provincial Chapters of the Knights of St. John. Various other convents sprang from the one at Saragossa: there was one at Malta, and at one time there were five or six in England; but a dispute arose with Henry the Second, and the various members of these were united in one, called the Hospital of St. John of Jerusalem in London, which existed until the Reformation swept it from the land. At Malta, the rule requiring noble birth in the postulants was dispensed with, but there is no record of the same being done elsewhere.

The ceremonies of this Order were grand and imposing. The clothing and profession seem to have formed but one ceremony; a High Mass was sung, and the religious, wearing the full dress of the Order, assembled in choir. Their robe was red, with a short white surplice, and a long black cloak with a white cross of eight points, denoting the eight beatitudes; their long black veils and *sceptres* completed the attire. After the offertory the habit of the novice was blessed, and then the Priest said to her, as she knelt before him,—

"Sister, what do you ask?"

She answered, "I ask to be received into the company of the Religious Sisters of the Hospitallers of St. John of Jerusalem."

*Priest.* "You ask a most important thing, which is not given to all; but your desire may be granted if you promise to observe all that may be ordered. And first we desire that you be diligent in the service of God and of religion. Will you promise me this?"

*Novice.* "Yes, sir."

*Priest.* "As you promise me this, take this rosary in the name of the Father, Son, and Holy Spirit; with it you will pray for the increase of our holy religion, for the prosperity of my Lord, the most eminent Grand-Master, for all the Knights, Brothers, and other religious of this sacred Order, for victory against Turks and infidels, persecutors of the Church of God. You will offer your soul to God, and your body to the fatigues of life, for the service of our Lord Jesus Christ, and God will give you grace. The purity of this rosary signifies that the good religious ought to be pure and clean from all vices; and principally it signifies chastity, for chastity is always accompanied by other virtues. The first is prudence, by which you remember the past, and govern the present, and provide for the future. The second is justice, with which you will preserve the common property. The third is fortitude, with which you will support the labour of this world, as St. John the Baptist did, under whose name and enlightenment you will ornament and decorate your life, to the end that, as he conquered the world, the flesh, and the devil, fearing not to preach the truth, you in imitation ought to follow the Divine will, with which glorious proof you will witness and testify your courage and magnanimity. The fourth is temperance, with which you will moderate everything, in order that you can be called a perfect religious, according as you wear and are adorned by these virtues, taking them, and holding them always in memory. Arise, my Sister, and sleep not in sin, but be vigilant in the faith of Jesus Christ, of good and praiseworthy reputation, and attentive to good prayers and meditations." Here the Priest gives the novice a lighted candle, saying, "Take this light, and with the grace of the Holy Spirit go and hear the rest of the Mass." The Mass then continued, and at Communion the novice received; after which she again approached the altar, and the Priest said, "Sister, what askest thou?"

*Novice.* "I ask the society and company of the Sisters of the sacred religion of the Hospitallers of St. John of Jerusalem."

*Priest.* "Your request is of great importance, not granted to all, but perhaps it will not be refused you; we confiding that with love and charity you will exercise yourself in the works of mercy, to the service of the Hospital and of your religion, to which the Holy Apostolic See and Christian princes have given very great liberties, privileges, and revenues, in order that the servants of God and of this religion, inflamed with true charity, the source of all virtues, strive doubly to serve the hospitality and army\* for the defence of the Holy Catholic faith against its enemies, in order that, by serving them with affection and fidelity, we may gain the recompense of eternal life, and that, observing the commandments of God, the Church, and our religion, we shall be apparelled and prepared for Paradise. It would take long to tell you all the labours endured by the Sisters of our religion, but in one thing only we sum up all: it is, that you will have to strip yourself of your liberty, giving it and putting it into the hands of her who will be deputed your Superior, who will be a woman like yourself. Are you content?"

*Novice.* "Yes, Father, I am content."

*Priest.* "As you must give up your liberty, we wish to know first if you have it to give; and take care to reply truly to all that is required and demanded of you by us." He then asks if she has taken vows in any other Order, if she has contracted marriage, if she is in debt—all of which would prevent her being received. If the Novice replied in the negative,

\* The knights.

the Priest continued: "Take care, my Sister; for if at any time we find you have deceived us, your habit will be taken from you with great disgrace, and you will be driven from our company. However, if it be as you say, we will receive you benignly; but according to our statutes we promise you only bread and water, and humble clothing."

Then the religious chanted the anthem, "*Veni Sponsa Christi,*"* and a procession was made through the cloisters, in which the Novice walked, holding a palm in her hand, by the Prioress's side. At its close, the Novice laid aside the rich dress in which she was attired, and her jewels. She stood, saying twice, "Vanity of vanities;" and then a third time, raising her voice, "Vanity of vanities, all is vanity;" she threw the jewels from her, her hair was cut off, and the habit of the Order was given her, and the Novice then pronounced her vows, having her hands placed on the crucifix in the canon of the Mass, in the Missal: "I, ——, promise and vow to Almighty God, and to His immaculate Mother, the Virgin Mary, and to St. John Baptist our Patron, to observe perpetually obedience to some religious of this Order, who will be by religion given to me as Superior; to live

---

* "Come, spouse of Christ, receive the crown that the Lord hath prepared for thee."

without property, and to be chaste, according to the rule of the said religion."

The Priest then said, "At this moment I know you to be truly received into the number of our religious Sisters."

She answered, "I esteem and repute myself such."

*Priest.* "From henceforth we make you and your family participants in all the indulgences and graces conceded to our religion by the Holy Apostolic See; and for your first obedience I command you to carry this Missal to the altar, and then bring it back to me." Having done this, the Priest continued: "We will further that you be attentive to prayer, and therefore you will say each day, according to the law of Holy Church, and usage and custom of this convent, the great office and an hundred and fifty *Pater nosters,* or the little office of our Lady, or of the dead, for each sister or brother who dies." Then showing her the mantle of the Order, he said, "This is your proper dress, it is the form of your penitence; this will represent to you the very hard life of our patron, St. John Baptist; this will represent his habit, which was of the skins of beasts, signifying that we ought to leave sin, and, without opposition, follow virtue." Then showing her the sleeves of the mantle, he said, "These are arms which restrain and bind you, signifying that you will be restrained and bound by true obedience to your Superior, and the observance of the works of hospitality and others, as has been said to you." Then showing her the cross of the mantle, he said, "It is the sign and the habit of the true Cross, which I command you to carry continually on your habits all your life. This white cross signifies that all our works ought to be pure, clean, and white. The eight points signify the eight beatitudes, which are promised to us if we carry this sign in our hearts with ardour and fervour; and in token we put this cross on the left side, in order that you may have it always on your heart, and with it you ought to be buried." Then showing her the ornamented girdle, "This cord represents that often we ought to remember the very bitter death and passion of our Saviour Jesus Christ. This which binds the mantle signifies the cords with which Jesus Christ was bound. Here are the scourges, here is the pillar, here is the sponge, and here is the cross, on which, for love of you, he took His passion and His death." Then the Priest puts the cord round her neck, "Take, then, my Sister, the yoke of Jesus Christ our Lord, which is most light and sweet, and which will conduct you to eternal life in the world without end. Amen." And putting the black veil on her head, he said, "Receive, my Sister, the holy veil of virginity, which will lead you to eternal life, world without end. Amen."

The nun, after having received the priest's blessing, and some other prayers being said, went to embrace her religious sisters. Before eating that day, she was obliged to serve the others in the refectory with bread, water, and salt.

After the siege of Rhodes, the nuns changed their red habit for black, in sign of mourning for the misfortunes of their Order. This Order took rise in France in very early times; then the religious were not cloistered there, but served hospitals. Later on, however, they lived as did the nuns at Malta, it being decided that " they participated in the charity practised by the Knights in their hospitals." The nuns were bound to fast every Friday and on many vigils, to abstain the whole of Lent and Advent, and not to receive visitors in those times. The Order was existing in France until the Revolution, but its last traces perished in that wreck, whether ever to rise again from its ashes with new vigour remains yet to be seen.

## THE ORDER OF OUR LADY OF MOUNT CARMEL.

If we go back into the old traditions of the Order of Mount Carmel, we are led to far distant ages.

for the date of its foundation, even to the time when the prophet Elias dwelt on Mount Carmel with the "sons of the prophets." The first rule, however, which is entirely authenticated is that given to Brocarl and his hermits by Albert, Patriarch of Jerusalem. It would seem that the hermits living on the mountain had voluntarily put themselves under the guidance of Brocarl, and he entreated the Patriarch to give him a rule whereby he might govern his religious. His request was granted, and the rule was given; some say in 1171, others in 1204. It was approved by Pope Honorius the Third in 1224. Not long after this, about the year 1229, the Order withdrew from Syria, being no longer able to preserve their monastery from the attacks of the Saracens. The religious were divided by their General, Alain, into different bodies; one going to found a monastery near Messina, another to England, and another to Provence. The first General Chapter of the Order after its dispersion was held in England, and the Blessed Simon Stock was elected General. This chapter took place in 1245. There is a tradition of the Order, that when the monks were deliberating whether they should quit Syria, our Blessed Lady appeared to them and bade them depart. This would seem very probable, on account of the great favour bestowed on the Order by its Lady and

Patroness, who appeared in July, 1251, to St. Simon Stock, and gave him a scapular, or little habit, bidding him have it worn by his community in her honour, and therefore a scapular of the same brown stuff as the habit was ever after worn by the monks. Later on, the confraternity of our Lady of Mount Carmel was formed, in which everybody could be admitted to the privilege of wearing the brown scapular, (made, of course, of very small dimensions,) and thus being put under the special protection of Mary. Of all the various confraternities which have arisen in the Church, none have spread so widely as this ancient one, and the title of our Lady of Mount Carmel is cherished by every Catholic heart.

The nuns of the Order were founded about 1452, by the Blessed Jean Soreth, then General of the Order. Their rule was the same as the monks, with certain adaptations to enable women to follow it. The rule now followed by the Carmelites is one and the same with that given by the Patriarch Albert. It is grand in its perfect simplicity. Indeed, simplicity is the very element of the Carmelite life, which may be briefly comprised in one word. Solitude and zeal for souls, to retire from the company of others, and to burn for the salvation of the world, are the especial calling of the Carmelite nuns. They live together in community, it is true, in mutual charity, and united in prayer; but they should be solitary in spirit, and seeking more and more continually to enter into close union with their hidden Lord; and yet, at the same time, they are also called to the "Apostolate of Carmel,"—they are to be "Apostles seeking souls, even as in the ocean bed is sought the hidden pearl." *

The Rule of Mount Carmel had originally only sixteen articles, all of which are exceedingly brief. The first treats of the election of the Prior,† and the obedience due to him. The second, of the cells, and that they should be separated one from another. The third forbids any change of cell without permission. The fourth prescribes the situation of the Prior's cell. (We may remark that these two latter articles would apply more particularly to the time when the Monks lived on Mount Carmel, each in his own cell or hut.) The fifth article orders them to dwell in their cells, and to give themselves day and night to prayer. The sixth speaks of the canonical hours which are to be recited together by all except the lay brothers; and the prayers which these latter shall say instead of the Office are also specified. The seventh forbids

---

* Père de Ravignan.

† The *Titles* in the *Rule* have never been altered; thus, it must be understood, Prioress for Prior, sisters for brethren, &c.

the brethren to possess any personal property. The eighth orders an oratory to stand in the midst of the cells, in which Mass shall be said, and all the community shall be present. The ninth speaks of the chapters and the penances. The tenth of the fasts, which shall last from Holy Cross Day to Easter, excepting on Sundays. The eleventh prescribes perpetual abstinence. The twelfth bids them clothe themselves with spiritual armour against the attacks of the enemy. The thirteenth commands them to labour with their hands. The fourteenth imposes on them strict silence from vespers to terce. The fifteenth bids the Prior to be humble. And the sixteenth, and last, bids the religious to be careful to treat their superior with becoming reverence. This Rule, given by the Patriarch Albert, was, when laid before the Pope, enlarged by him into twenty-eight chapters, but no alteration was made in its substance. The daughters of Mount Carmel have another title, which is only less dear to them than that which marks them as the chosen children of Mary,—they are also called the daughters of St. Teresa.

For, as time progressed from the period of which we have been speaking, the first fervour of the children of Carmel grew cold, the fine gold was dim, the love of unnecessary dispensations crept in, and then came all its attendant evils. Relaxed religious! the very bye-word that the foes of the Church love to bring up against her, and yet in one sense, if we may say so, her very glory. For where, save in her pale, are miracles seen like unto her reforms?—reforms which bind together, and gather in, and strengthen the weak, and raise up the fallen; reforms which kindle up fire out of what looks like heaps of ashes: so in this instance, the mighty prayer had gone up from the Mother's heart to save the Order which bore her name and sign. And the "still small voice" came into Spain, and spoke to the heart of one destined to be His instrument. Was it a holy Priest or zealous Bishop? No; it was a young and beautiful Spanish girl, with so delicate a constitution, that on her entrance into religion she would not choose the Order of St. Augustine, as being too severe, but entered the then *mitigated* Order of Mount Carmel. It is not our intention to trace the history of St. Teresa, for her biography is well known to all. All over the Catholic world has her fame spread; her picture brings her familiarly before our eyes, and her sweet name is a household word. We know her well, with the burning soul speaking in those large, dark Spanish eyes; we see the rude Carmelite habit, which yet cannot conceal the majesty of her form, worn though it be with penance and sickness,—that sickness which she loved so well; saying, that it was sent to her because she should not have had courage to seek so much suffering for herself. We see her hand holding the pen with which she traced those wonderful works that have raised her to be considered a teacher in the Church. We see her smile full of raptured love, and we can almost hear her cry, in low, impassioned tones, as she speaks to her Beloved,—" Others may serve Thee better, that I do not deny; but that others should love Thee more, that I will never suffer."

To such a soul was committed the reform of Mount Carmel, and we cannot wonder that it was eventually accomplished. Long indeed and weary was the task! The enemy did his worst against the Teresa whom he so hated, but, weak woman as she was, she came off victorious. In vain did he raise storms against her outwardly; her courage and perseverance survived them. In vain did he strive to darken her spirit; her deep love could know no change. In vain did he shut the hearts of men, so that she, on one occasion, found herself in the town, where she had come to found a monastery of the reform, possessing only a few ducats in her pocket with which to commence the work. "Teresa and these ducats are nothing," said she; "but God, Teresa, and these ducats are more than enough." What wonder, then, before her death she saw seventeen convents of women, and fifteen of men, adopting her reform. Did any thought of pride or of human exultation mingle with her retrospect? "Let us carry your body back with us to Avila," prayed her weeping religious. "Will they refuse me here a little earth?" answered she, who almost then could hear the echo of *that* praise, in which the praise of earth is lost. Thus was the Order of Mount Carmel restored to its original vigour, and after St. Teresa's death it rapidly spread into all parts of the world.

If we study the constitutions of the reform, we find the spirit of St. Teresa breathing throughout. Hers was essentially a "spirit of liberty," and we find it to be so in the convents of Carmel.

"The religious are not to be too much pressed to open their hearts to their Superior, it must be done willingly;" and she is bade to govern by love.

The great qualification in the novices is, that they must be "people of prayer, who seek perfection, and despise the world." They must be in good health, and if choir nuns, must be able to say the Office. Holy poverty is to be strictly observed. St. Teresa preferred the houses which had no fixed income or endowment; she wished "poverty to spread an odour." She would not have the nuns attach themselves even to their poor cells or their few books, and their bed was to be of straw. It is rather a peculiarity that in the Order of Mount

Carmel the nuns do not rise at night to say Matins; they are said at nine P.M. St. Teresa had two reasons for this: the first was, that she considered fewer people were praying at that hour, from the reason, that the numerous communities which rise at midnight retire to rest at eight or nine, and secondly, her wish of having but a small number of religious in each convent would prevent its being possible to have the night Office said by all. St. Teresa ruled that in each house there should only be twenty nuns, including three lay sisters. This number is only exceeded in convents from whence it is intended to make a new foundation. The Carmelites rise at five in summer and six in winter; Mass is said at eight; they fast until twelve, when they dine; an hour's recreation follows this meal, another hour of recreation follows supper, Matins are said at nine, and they go to bed at eleven. Frequent meditation, the Divine Office, other religious exercises, and the necessary work of the house, or needlework, fill up the day. They are forbidden to work "at curious and delicate things, which occupy the thoughts, and prevent their resting in God;" "they must not work with gold or silver;" "they must not work all together, for fear silence should be broken;" their especial love shall be for solitude; and that they may in some sort continue the hermit life first begun on Mount Carmel, hermitages are built in the garden, to which they may for a time, and with permission, retire, and they are to endeavour by this solitude to "go forwards." "They are never to excuse themselves when blamed unjustly; their penances are to be offered for the increase of the faith, the well-being of sovereign princes, and of benefactors; for the holy souls, for captives, and for those who are living in mortal sin."

The Prioress is to have nothing better than the others, and never to be called by any high-sounding title. Great care and tenderness are to be shown to the sick; "they are to sleep in linen, and have good beds." On the other hand, the patients are to "obey the Infirmarian, to show patience, and not to be eager about a speedy cure." "They must not be unhappy when they lack anything, remembering that true poverty consists in feeling want in the time of great necessity;" and when those who are in health have need of anything, they "shall ask our Lord first, because our nature often demands more than we really want, and sometimes the Devil has a hand in it, and tries to make us fear penance and fasting; but if the necessity be really urgent, it is then to be laid before the Prioress."

Such is a brief outline of these beautiful directions. They were laid before the Holy See for approval, and were solemnly confirmed by Pope Pius the Fourth, on the 11th of July, 1562.

Since the death of St. Teresa, this Order, which has been called by no mean authority "the grandest Order in the Church,"* has been fruitful in saintly religious; and to speak of the way in which their lives were passed is the best commentary that can be given of the Rule, and the best proof of the work the nuns of Mount Carmel are called upon to do in the Church.

Soon after the death of St. Teresa, the idea of founding a convent of her reform in France was raised, and the project became dear to the hearts of two persons of eminent piety, Monsieur de Bretigny and the Maréchale de Joyeuse; but the latter did not live to see it carried into execution, and its accomplishment fell into the hands of one destined to be not only the foundress of the Order in France, but one of its greatest glories. We must speak awhile then of the preceding life of Barbe Avrillot, better known by her married name of Madame Acarie. Her youthful desire of entering religion had been crossed, and she had been taught to serve God under the burden of domestic cares, and amid the glare of the world. Every gift that could make life precious to her was hers. Even by the fastidious taste of Paris she was called "*La belle Acarie.*" Her wit and talent were of no mean order, she was nobly born, and

* Father Faber.

had wealth at her command, husband and children to claim her love, yet amid all this God was the absolute master of her soul. In the midst of Paris luxury she led a life of severe austerity. Little did those dream who met the young and beautiful Madame Acarie in society, that on returning from the gay assembly she might be seen at the feet of her waiting maid, accusing herself of faults against the rule of life they had imposed on themselves, for both the high-born lady and her maid had determined to attain together the way of perfection, and a holy friendship existed between them.

Madame Acarie had no love of singularity; her great effort was to conceal her life of devotion from the sight of others. She obeyed her husband with exactness, she dressed in the fashion to please him, but not without many secret sighs. "Alas!" said she one day to her mother-in-law, "is it not possible to find a dress that can be put on all at once without all these fastenings and ornaments?" "Not yet," answered the lady, in a tone of unconscious prophecy; "that will be your lot some day." We must not pause to dwell on the virtues that adorned Madame Acarie as wife, mother, and friend. Her husband used to say, laughingly, "They tell me my wife will be a saint some day; if so, there will be mention made of me in the process of her canonization as having contributed to it by trying her patience." For indeed she seemed to have no other wish than his. Her children were trained up with more than a mother's love and care; her servants were treated more like children; her friends never found her cold or changeful, the poor knew that by day and night she was ready to be at their service, and she loved best to be with the sick and dying. But her spiritual works of mercy were the most remarkable, for great supernatural gifts had been bestowed on her. She possessed the spirit of prayer in a high degree, and not only did God vouchsafe to her the gift of frequent ecstasy, but He also gave to her that great and mysterious favour accorded to so few, the Stigmata of the precious wounds of our Lord Jesus Christ; thus showing plainly how in the marriage state, and amidst a gay and worldly capital, it was possible to attain as close an union with Him as in the cloister.

Such was the life Madame Acarie was leading in Paris, when a great sensation was made among religious people by the appearance of the life of St. Teresa, just translated into French by Monsieur de Bretigny from the Spanish of the Jesuit Father Ribera. For eighteen years had Monsieur de Bretigny been praying to see the Order of Mount Carmel brought into France, but as yet the task seemed hopeless. Madame Acarie read the life of St. Teresa and it made no impression on her, which surprised her friends greatly, knowing how soon any spiritual book would raise her above herself; but a few days afterwards, being rapt in prayer, St. Teresa herself appeared to her, wearing the Carmelite habit, and bade her found the reform of Mount Carmel in France. Madame Acarie submitted this vision to the decision of her spiritual advisers; and, in consequence, most interesting meetings took place in the priory of the Chartreux at Paris. At them were assembled the Cardinal de Berulle and Monsieur du Val, Monsieur Gallemand and Monsieur de Bretigny, and one or two others, all eminent for their love of, and union with, God; and when the little band were discouraged by the overwhelming obstacles which stood in their way, St. Francis de Sales was called upon to give his counsel. "After having examined this affair with attention," wrote he to the Pope, "it seems to me without doubt that God has inspired this design, and that it will contribute to His glory and the salvation of a great number of persons." At last it was determined that the design should be realized; the Holy Father had granted the bull of authorization, and the old priory of Nôtre Dame des Champs, in the outskirts of Paris, was to be put in order for the community. Various postulants had already offered themselves;

and in order that time should not be lost, a congregation of these ladies was formed, to serve as a preparative for the austere life they were about to choose. It was called the Congregation of St. Géneviève, because their house was situated near the church of that name. They were chiefly under the direction of Madame Acarie. She was always consulted in the choice of new subjects, and some of her counsels on this point show well of what spirit she was.

Two persons once presented themselves: one happy and tranquil, showing a great desire for the religious state; the other weak in virtue, and tormented by spiritual suffering. "The first," said Madame Acarie, "will advance in virtue, but she will not make progress in the interior life; she has reached the point where God wills her to remain. But it is not so with the other; she will advance by means of many falls, from which she will rise with profit to her soul. It is thus that God fashions and *grounds* souls, making them advance by the faults which they commit." Another time a lady with a large fortune came to offer to assist in building the new convent, if she were received as a nun. Madame Acarie refused her. "If a woman were to bring all the riches of the world into religion, I would not receive her if she were not called; and if another were quite destitute, I would move heaven and earth to make her a religious, if she had the vocation." At another time she said, "I am not uneasy about the money to build the material building, I am only anxious for the living stones which are necessary to build the spiritual edifice."

"If I knew a soul worthy to be of this building, I would give all the gold in the world to buy her; and I would give as much gold to exclude one who was not fit." The convent of the Carmelites was nearly finished, and to complete it properly more money was wanted, but there was none. The generous benefactors had given already beyond their means. Madame Acarie was calm; she relied on Divine Providence. "His purse is large and well filled," she said; "all the treasures of the earth are contained in it." About this time she made a pilgrimage to the Church of St. Nicholas, near Nancy, and was praying there, when St. Teresa appeared to her again, and told her she should be called one day to the Order of Carmel as a lay sister. The first part of the announcement filled her with joy, but not the second. It was not, indeed, that she shrank from the lower rank or the harder labour of a lay sister, but not to join in the Divine Office, this, to her who loved so well that holy exercise, was the sacrifice. For a *few moments* she struggled, but submission with her was not a long or difficult matter, and as she rose from her knees she made a vow only to enter the Carmelite Order as a lay sister. At length the many difficulties were conquered, and the convent finished. Six Spanish nuns, trained under St. Teresa herself, entered Paris and took possession of their new house; seven novices from the little Congregation of St. Géneviève were in a few weeks admitted among them. One obstacle to the solid foundation of this new community appeared in the fact, that the Spanish nuns could not speak French, or the French Spanish; but loving God as they did, this was not a real hindrance. The nuns watched the "air, and the steps, and the actions of each," and formed a judgment by these signs as to their advancement in the spiritual life, and the novices soon learnt enough of the foreign language to speak to their Prioress. Such was the rapid progress made by the novices in the way of perfection, that the Spanish nuns, writing to their General, said of them, "They are not women, but angels, whom we have to direct." Fervour and charity formed such an union between the mothers and daughters, that "one scarcely perceived the difference of character between the two nations." Other foundations rapidly spread, and the reform of Mount Carmel was firmly founded in France. Nor did Madame Acarie's good works end here. Finding that there were a certain number of the ladies of the Congregation of St. Géneviève who desired to enter religion, yet were not called to the life of Carmel, she engaged Ursuline nuns to come to Paris and found a house of their Order, where these ladies might be received.

The sudden death of her husband set her free from domestic cares. Of her six children, her sons were settled in life, her three daughters had all become Carmelite nuns; it only remained for her to follow their example; and she, the foundress of the Order in France, now asked admission into the poorest convent of the Order as a lay sister. The superiors represented to her that as the state of her health would prevent her from working hard, it would be better to give up this desire. She replied that she felt she must make the request. "Yes," answered they; "it is true, you must make it; but it is not necessary for us to comply." "If you refuse this grace," she answered, "I will go to the end of the world to solicit it." Not only was the health of Madame Acarie very feeble, but in a fall from horseback some years before she had broken her leg, had since been lame, and subject to violent attacks of pain.

At length, however, she was received into the convent at Amiens. It was a very poor one, and its distance from Paris would prevent the number of visitors from coming who were likely to follow

Madame Acarie into her retreat. The Prioress of the monastery at Amiens was one of her former pupils at St. Géneviève—nevertheless, when Madame Acarie entered the convent, she threw herself at her feet, entreating her most humbly to help and guide her, and then she hastened at once to her duties in the kitchen. Her joy at finding herself at last a religious in name was extreme, but she had long been a true nun in spirit and in practice. She received the habit on the Feast of the Annunciation, 1614, taking the name of Mary of the Incarnation. She was then forty-eight years of age. The ceremony took place very early in the morning, for it was not desirable that a multitude should be admitted to comment on the supernatural favours it was likely the novice would receive; and, indeed, during the whole of Mass she was in ecstasy. "Her eyes were closed," said one of her sisters, "and her face shone with surpassing beauty." Perfect in truth was she in her noviciate. As faithful as she had been to her duties in the world, so was she in religion; industrious in her work, constant in her obedience, her charity, her humility. It must have been a lovely sight to see her doing all the work she could manage while sitting down, for she was unable to stand. She begged her sisters to bring her everything she could do in that position, and she prepared the vegetables for dinner, and washed up the dishes; she who might have guided many souls, wrought many conversions, turned many of the great and noble to good deeds; but if any thought thus about her, they were answered by the silent witness of the picture before which Marie de l'Incarnation loved to sit when occupied in labour—the Holy Family in the House at Nazareth. "Behold," said she one day, "with what ardour the infant Jesus labours; with what humility He occupies Himself with things unworthy of Him! After such an example can we be idle, or complain of the lowliness of our occupations?" And she who was so accustomed to teach and to govern, was no less skilful in learning how to obey. She obeyed her former pupil, the Prioress, with the greatest exactitude. One day she asked leave to go to Communion, though it was a day usual to do so. The Prioress told her to do as she wished. She did not go, and said afterwards, "I wish not to do my own will, but that of our Lord, whose place you hold towards me." And no less obedient was she to the other Superiors, and to the rule, calling the bell that marked the exercises "the signal of the Great King." Her love for poverty was intense. She had loved this virtue in the midst of her luxurious home, she loved it still more in the life of Carmel; and when her companions tried to check her austere self-denial, she replied, that "the poor did these things; must she not imitate them?" And so deep was her humility, that her greatest joy was in being reproved. One day she was blaming herself for her pride, when a sister reminded her how many proofs of humility she had given; how, though a lady of high birth, she had become a lay sister, and yet still she thought herself unworthy. She replied, "Humility does not consist in these things, but in the true knowledge of oneself."

And when the time drew near for her profession, she shrank back in fear. She was unworthy of the grace, she said. "What then," said her friend, Monsieur de Marrilac; "do you wish to leave the cloister?" "Oh no," she replied; "but I will ask the superiors to allow me out of compassion to remain in some little corner, but not to make any engagement with me, so that they can send me away when they think proper; for it is not reasonable that so useless a servant should take the place of a useful one." But our Lord caused her to accept the decision of her Superiors on this point, and she made her profession on the 8th of April, 1615, in the following words:—" I, Sister Mary, of the Incarnation, make my profession, and promise obedience, chastity, and poverty to God our Lord, to the most blessed Virgin Mary, and to our Reverend Fathers Superiors, now established by the bull of the late Pope Clement VIII., and to their successors, according to the primitive rule of Mount Carmel, which is without mitigation; and this until death."

One of the most touching instances of the perfect submission of Marie de l'Incarnation was seen in the obedience she paid to her own daughter, who happened to be the Sub-Prioress of the convent at Amiens. "She obeyed her in all things," said one of the religious, "with the simplicity of a child." Long and severe were the bodily sufferings of this holy Carmelite. At one time she was so ill that she received the last Sacraments. When the priest came to her with the Viaticum, he asked if she believed Jesus Christ really present in the Host. "Oh yes, I believe it, I believe it," she answered. "Come, my Lord, come;" and she was lost in ecstasy. And when she received the holy oils she said, "These are the jewels with which I attire myself before I appear before my Celestial Spouse." The crucifix she was holding being a large one, the Prioress wished to give her a smaller one; "Not a little cross, my mother!" she said. "What! to die without suffering! I would suffer, Lord, till the day of judgment, if it were Thy will; our holy mother said, in her last moments, it was good to die a child of the Church; and I say, also, that it is good to die a daughter of the Holy Virgin—it is good to die a Carmelite."

From this illness she recovered; and at the next election of a Prioress, the community with one voice elected Marie de l'Incarnation. But nothing could induce her to accept such an elevation; and the Superior, Monsieur du Val, would not insist on her doing so. Afterwards, in hopes of benefiting her health, she was removed to the Convent of Pontoise, where she continued to practise the same angelic virtues, growing daily brighter as she approached nearer to heaven. One trial yet remained to purify this saintly soul, who had learnt to love suffering and hunger for blame and contempt. That her loved friend and director, Monseigneur de Berulle, should not only differ from her on some important points, but that this difference should cause a bitter estrangement between them, was, indeed, "not a little cross;" yet so it was. It seems that the Cardinal de Berulle wished to introduce certain doctrines into the Carmelite Order which were judged incompatible with the rule: the other Superiors of the Order opposed him, and Marie de l'Incarnation was of their opinion. The last interview, therefore, between Sœur Marie and he who had guided her for so many years, was spent in hearing severe reproofs from his lips; and then, the end came. Many and great were her sufferings; great also was her patience. One day she *asked leave to complain*, and, when granted, her complaint was uttered in these words: "*I will bless the Lord at all times; His praise shall ever be in my mouth. May the Divine Will be accomplished in me.*" She spoke but little, fearing to lose the presence of God. On the afternoon of Easter Wednesday, the 8th of April, the Prioress, bending over her, asked her with what she was occupied. "With God, my mother," she whispered.

They were her last words on earth: in them was comprised her life's history. After her death, her body was so beautiful that crowds came to look at it; she had the appearance of a young girl, although she was aged fifty-two. Many from the moment of her death began privately to invoke her. A long interval, of course, elapsed before the Church would sanction this reverence. More than a century passed after her death before she was raised on the altars of the Church. But at length her name was echoed within the walls of St. Peter; and Carmel reckoned in its ancestry a new and glorious Saint.

### 2.

To the walls of Carmel, in 1674, came a trembling suppliant for admission; and in their great charity the nuns, whose own lives had been spotless before men, did not disdain this poor outcast, who came to do penance for "many sins." The beautiful and unfortunate Louise de la Vallière at last could no longer resist the pleadings of her conscience. Suffering, contempt, and neglect had not availed to break the chains in which the devil held her. But the Good Shepherd sent one of His servants to call back the lost one; and, under the direction of *Bossuet*, she left the Court and entered on the austere life of Carmel. Her beauty and fascination were still very great; and could she have stifled the voice of conscience, she might have retained the rank which, in that corrupt circle, was not considered a disgrace, but which brought her admiration and attention. "Her glance had an inexplicable charm," said the Duchess of Orleans; and in speaking of her, La Fontaine's words were often quoted, "*Et la grâce plus belle que la beauté.* It seemed, to those who knew her delicate frame, a madness to enter such an austere order as Mount Carmel; but when Madame de Maintenon represented this to her, she replied, "When I shall suffer at the Carmelites, I shall remember what they" (meaning her enemies), "have made me suffer here." She chose the Third Sunday after Pentecost as the day for taking the habit, because the Gospel for that day is the parable of the lost sheep. The preacher took his text from it, and spoke in most touching language of the mercy of God to sinners. The outer chapel was crowded with Louise's former worldly friends, whose curiosity brought them to the sight of one of their former companions taking as a reality those solemn warnings of the Church which day by day fell unheeded on *their* ears, and it is said the touching spectacle moved many of them to tears; but, alas! it was but a transient emotion. The life of Sœur Louise de la Miséricorde became a most edifying one; she showed in everything the humility and fervour of a true penitent. On entering the Convent she said to the Prioress, "I have made a very bad use of my will, but I come to give it up into your hands, and never to take it again." Continually was she to be found weeping over her sins at the feet of Jesus Christ. She gladly accepted humiliation and contempt, and begged to be professed as a lay sister; the superiors would not permit this, but they allowed her to assist the lay sisters in their work, and to practise many severe penances, for which Louise was continually asking leave. So occupied was she with the desire of doing penance, that when one of her sisters told her she ought to have asked permission before undertaking one of abstaining for a long time from drinking, in honour of the thirst of Jesus Christ on the Cross, she answered, "I did it without thinking. I was occupied only with the desire of satisfying the justice of God." Her deep humility when she approached the altar to receive Holy Communion was an edification to the whole community. She was desired to write down some of her meditations on the mercy of God; and so useful for others were they considered to be, that a small volume of these was published after her death. One of Louise's greatest enemies, (Madame de Montespan,) who had treated her with scorn and cruelty, fell into disgrace at Court, and was forsaken by all her worldly friends; but in the convent parlour of the Carmelites she met with a different reception from one she had so deeply injured. Kind and loving words flowed from the lips of Louise, who had learnt truly how to forgive, and earnestly did she endeavour to lead Madame de Montespan to seek the rest and consolation she had found at the foot of the Cross.

Towards the close of her life, Louise suffered acute bodily agonies, and she bore them patiently and joyfully. When her death agony came on, she said, "To die in sharp pain is most suitable to a sinner such as I am." And with humble trust in the mercy of her forgiving Lord, she died, June 6th, 1710, and went, we may firmly believe, to have her portion with Blessed Magdalene and the glorious band of penitents who have won their crowns. Louise was sixty-five years of age when she died, thirty-six of which she had passed in religion.

After the death of Madame Acarie, the Order of Carmel in France continued to flourish, not by growing rich and powerful, but by its constant fidelity to the Holy Rule, and by maintaining in its-vigour the spirit of St. Teresa. And such was the sweet odour of the holy lives of the Carmelites, that it seemed to a Princess a better and more preferable life than that of Court luxury and adulation, and, in 1770, Madame Louise de France entered the walls of Carmel.

Truly, when we turn our eyes upon the Court of Louis Quinze, it is the very last place in which a religious vocation might be supposed to grow. Vice seemed positively to have run wild; and we feel as we read, that it must have been a far greater trial to faith to have lived in those days in Paris, than in the very worst of the Revolutionary fury. But never does God leave Himself without a witness, a living proof that His grace is sufficient for all things, for all temptations, in all circumstances; and it is like a green spot in a parching desert, to turn our eyes in the sad history to Marie Lechintsa and her daughters. In the midst of that corrupt Court, the Queen of France lived a saintly life, and seems to have had an influence over her children which resulted in their giving their hearts to God. Of the four Princesses, the gayest and the most lively was Louise. She was formed in every way to enjoy her high position, and, in her childhood, many instances of a naturally domineering spirit and haughty bearing manifested themselves; but the careful education given to her by the Benedictine nuns of Fontevrault, and the holy example of her mother, corrected these evils, and from her early youth her heart could not find rest in the world. She had for many years desired to enter a Carmelite Convent before she was allowed to do so. Her director and the Archbishop of Paris wished to take time to watch over a vocation so rare in one of her rank; but after the death of the Queen, they gave her leave to seek the King's consent. Well did Madame Louise use these years of delay. She procured the Carmelite Rule, and studied it constantly. Secretly she accustomed herself to practise rude penances. Beneath the royal purple, fine-woven linen was no longer worn, but coarse woollen garments took its place. Prayer became her delight, hours were spent in it, and thus she prepared herself for her longed-for future. When the King's consent to her entrance into religion was obtained, the great desire of the Princess was to enter one of the poorest houses of the Carmelites; and having heard that the Convent at St. Denis, near Paris, answered this description, she fixed upon that House for her future abode. It was a singular fact that the Convent of St. Denis had been reduced to such a state of poverty that it was feared the House would be suppressed. To avert this calamity, the nuns began a Novena to our Lady, begging her to send them a postulant with a true vocation, and who could bring money to save the House. During that Novena the King consented to the wish of Madame Louise, and the Carmelites saw entering within their doors one who could bring with her sufficient riches to re-establish their house and clear it from debt. For no more did Louise bring. Our Lady granted their petition wholly. She sent them a rich Princess, but with a true vocation. There were no luxuries, no dispensations introduced into that community. The poor Carmelites themselves, stunned almost at the event which made Europe ring, that a Daughter of France had come to adopt their rude life, and fearing to make the transition from splendid Versailles to Carmel too abrupt, tried to soften the rigours of the Rule for the Princess. But she would not suffer it. Bravely did she set to work to conquer her natural repugnances. She was washing the dishes and cleaning the candlesticks; and there is a story told of her, that, while a postulant, having no other dress to wear than a rose-coloured silk gown, she was found cleaning, in her ignorance, the outside of a kettle, till her gown was equally as black. Delicate food and wine were sometimes sent from Court; she would never take them except when sharing equally with the community. Accustomed at Court to wear high-heeled shoes, the flat slippers of the Carmelites were a real torture to her; she was advised to give up trying them. "But I must, sooner or later, put them on again," said she; "therefore I prefer conquering the difficulty from the beginning." In short, the greatest mortification they could give her was to remind her of what she had been in the world, or treat her with any distinction beyond her sisters. The title she disliked to hear was that of Madame Louise; the one she loved, was Sister Teresa of Saint Austin.

It was a grand day when Madame Louise took the habit of the Carmelites. The Nuncio came to represent the Holy Father, and give the habit to the royal postulant. Almost the whole body of the French episcopate were present, as well as the Royal family and a crowd of distinguished persons. The poor humble chapel of the Carmelites, a year ago so forgotten and neglected, was now richly hung and adorned, and filled with the great ones of the Court. The Princess herself was arrayed in all her royal splendour. Calmly did she answer the solemn questions of the ritual, and, receiving the veil and habit, withdrew from the chapel, to lay aside the rich garments of her birth. The mantle of St. Teresa herself, which was preserved at one of the Carmelite Convents, was brought to St. Denis for the occasion; and soon was Madame Louise to be seen lying prostrate on the ground, covered by this mantle, according to the custom of the Order. It is related that most of the assembly were in tears, and the young Dauphiness was deeply affected. Wonderful, doubtless, did it seem to her, to whom the world bore so bright an aspect, that any one could renounce it all for solitude, fasting, and the grille; but in after days, in the Temple and in the Conciergerie, might not the thoughts of Marie Antoinette have travelled back to that day, to long that *her* life had been closed in the peace of a convent home?

When Madame Louise went to her convent, the world said she would never stay to be clothed. When Madame Louise was clothed, the world said she would never be professed. The day came, however, and all the bells in Paris rang out as if for a royal nuptial. Workmen left their work undone; artisans went out of their shops; crowds of people gathered together in the midst of the streets. The one topic of the day was that Louise de France had bound herself by irrevocable vows to the life of Carmel. But, said the world, she will be dispensed from strict observance; a great difference will be made for her. The world was wrong, as the world not unfrequently is when it speaks of Religious. The most austere, the most fervent of the nuns were edified by the Princess's rapid advance in virtue. It was considered so eminent that she was soon made Mistress of Novices.

In this employment she showed well how truly she was imbued with the spirit of St. Teresa. She taught, not so much by word, as by example. Naturally impetuous and fiery, she had obtained perfect command over herself, and nothing seemed able to disturb her patience. She used to say, "The yoke of a Carmelite is either very light or very heavy, according as she carries it with courage, or drags it along with cowardice." "A true Religious seeks her greatness in littleness; she always keeps before her mind the thought that our Divine Master threatens to shut the gates of heaven against us if we do not become like little children; that is to say, if we have not their docility, candour, and all their simplicity."

"You feel," said she in one of her instructions to the novices, "a repugnance for some particular observance: never recur to any means, however lawful, of obtaining a dispensation from it. You do not like much the company of some of your sisters: redouble your attentions and affability to them in their presence, and your charity when absent, without letting anybody penetrate your motives. They contradict your opinions, and with a single word you might gain an easy triumph: abstain from that word. They relate a piece of news which cannot contribute to your edification, though it may satisfy your curiosity: decline the information, but do it without affectation. They rehearse in your presence some historical facts with which you are perfectly acquainted, and which are much disfigured; you have it in your power to represent them as they are: do not allow yourself that satisfaction." And she concludes, "All this must be hid, and known only to Him who is to give you your reward."

On another occasion she said, "When you have made real progress in an interior life, if by chance they accuse you, either through mistake or otherwise, of a fault which you have not really committed, you will humble yourself in silence, praying at the same time for the person who is mistaken. If you had solid reasons to think that scandal would be taken from permitting yourself to be judged guilty, it might be then lawful, and sometimes it might be a duty in you, to represent that you are not really so. But if, after the *Yes* or *No* of a Christian, there appears no disposition to believe you, you should not insist. It is then a precious moment for you to make to God the sacrifice of your self-love, saying to Him in the secret your heart, '*It is very right, O Lord, that having so often sought to exculpate myself when I was truly in the wrong, I suffer now for Thy sake to be accused of a fault which I have not actually committed.*' We begin to be guilty, when we endeavour with too much obstinacy to prove that we are not."

Not only did Madame Louise speak wisely to her novices, but she won their hearts by her constant deeds of love. When sick, she nursed them; when sorrowful, she consoled them; when depressed, she encouraged them. She seemed entirely to forget herself. She would give up her rare leisure moments; she would interrupt her sleep for the service of others without a moment's delay. And as years passed on, and she was elected Prioress, her conduct was the same. She governed with the same sweetness and humility. She shrank from authority, and was never better pleased than when her three years of government ended, and she went out of office. She was often told that she fatigued herself too much. "Do not all the hours and moments of a Superioress belong to her community?" she answered. "The person who holds the first place must never forget that she no longer belongs to herself, but to others; that she owes them the sacrifice of her time, repose, health, and, if necessary, life itself."

After her death it was found out that every day she shortened the brief repose of a Carmelite nun by getting up before the others in order to dress a lay sister who suffered from rheumatism. She still took her share in the lowest offices; still was she seen sweeping the stairs and serving in the kitchen. As years passed on, her love for her holy vocation appeared to increase. "Every time," said she, "that my sisters (the princesses) leave me to return to Versailles, I feel myself urged to bless Divine Providence for being no longer under the necessity of following them."

Once, when the Queen (Marie Antoinette) was making a progress in royal state, she wrote to a friend,—" What I well know is, that all the clothes which a Carmelite wears are not so troublesome as what I have worn on such occasions, and all that was lost for Heaven, but even the dust of our convent may one day become shining stars for me."

So passed her life, daily increasing in sanctity, in devotion, in love to God. Her last illness came on, and she displayed the same spirit as in health crushing self and enduring suffering. When she became too weak to descend to the chapel, it was proposed to erect an altar in the infirmary,—a privilege which those of royal birth may claim. "No," she replied; "living or dying, I will be a simple Carmelite." Nothing but prayers and holy words flowed from her lips. Keeping the Rule to the very last, she would not break the strict silence which is prescribed for the night, nor let linen be laid on her straw bed and woollen sheets. She asked pardon of all for her faults against them. She gently rebuked the nuns, too much overcome by their grief in losing her. "God alone, dear sisters! God alone!" "Oh!" she exclaimed, "I never could have thought it was so sweet to die!" Her whole soul seemed to pass into longing for her Viaticum, and *It* received, she was in peace. Her last words were, "Come, let us arise, and make haste to go to Heaven;" and death came for her sweet and tranquil as sleep. On December 23rd, 1787, she went to wear a crown never to be laid aside.

### 3.

The wildest imagination, and the most far-sighted politician, could never have foreseen France's future when they looked upon her in 1757. If any one had entered the gay *salons* of St. Germains to speak of the downfall of the Bourbons and the rule of the people, how insane would his words have sounded! Luxury and careless living abounded in France, and especially in the capital. Life was trifled away by the rich, the court was corrupt, and unbelief and immorality were rife. In such days as these, on one 25th of June, some of the numerous kinsfolk of the house of Soyecourt were gathered in their hotel to await the birth of an hoped for heir. Already had two daughters been born to the noble line, and now a son was anxiously expected, and a general blank fell on them all when the birth of a third girl was announced. "What shall we call her?" said somebody to one of her aunts. "Call her?" was the answer; "call her *Mademoiselle de Trop.*" "Poor little one!" answered the inquirer, "she will perhaps be the honour and consolation of her family;" and as the little Camille grew in years, her beauty and grace, her wit and winning ways, made her soon very dear to her parents' hearts. Camille's parents were less infected with the worldly spirit of the age than many others, and thus she had the blessing of a Christian education. "At seven years old," she relates, many years afterwards, "my governess prepared me for the Sacrament of Penance; and having caused me to make a serious examination of my pride, my obstinacy, and my vanity, she took me to St. Sulpice, to the Chapel of the Five Wounds, where I confessed to a Capuchin Father." Too early, indeed, would the world have withered this fair blossom had not her parents, in compliance with the custom of the day, placed her, at eight years old, as a pupil in a Convent of the Visitation.

It was Camille's first trial. The parting with her mother was very bitter to her, and scarcely less dreadful was the putting on of the uniform dress worn by the pupils, and having her long curls cut off, and her head hidden in a close cap. This was hard to bear, for the little one loved dress very much; but these first clouds passed away, and Camille grew contented and happy in her school. In the Convent she received Confirmation when she was eleven years old. At this early age a change came upon Camille, or rather, it was that her baptismal grace "grew into colour and distinctness there." * From the moment of her Confirmation the Holy Spirit called her to a close union with her Lord, and she answered that she was ready. From that day her *heart* was hidden in the cloister. But her path thither was to be long and dreary. Quickly passed away her happy childhood. Earnestly did she long for and joyfully hail the day of her First Communion. From that day she made rapid progress in grace; her love for prayer and solitude daily increased, and more and more ardently did she long to retire to a convent. Her design was as yet unknown to her parents, and they therefore proposed a suitable marriage to her. Her heart quivered at the task of telling these beloved parents that which would cost them so much pain. She did it, however, and received their answer, that never would they give their consent. "Then," she replied, "that she would wait until she was twenty-five years of age" (the French majority); and with the calm resolution which was her characteristic, she entered upon this painful trial.

* Faber.

Many were the obstacles that arose. When she was scarcely eighteen, a place in the household of the wife of the Comte d'Artois (afterwards Charles the Tenth) was offered for her to her father. Camille knew well the entanglements and difficulties this would bring on her. She could do nothing but pray, and with that weapon conquered. Her parents refused the offer. Years went on; again a brilliant alliance was proposed for Camille, and it met with a firm refusal. Up to this time she had been allowed by her parents to live a comparatively retired life, often spending days together in a Benedictine convent, within whose walls she was able to hire rooms. But at this period their tactics changed, and they insisted that from henceforth she should appear in the world, and they plunged her at once into a round of dissipation. It was a fiery trial. No woman was ever more formed to shine in society than Camille, and it is seldom we dislike that in which we excel; and though the desire of quitting the world never left her, yet its seductions and its vanities obtained a momentary power over her heart. "I liked that what I wore should be in good taste," she confessed afterwards, "and I was not indifferent to flattery, but in the midst of all this frivolity the sound of the convent clock would strike on my ear, and turning my eyes to Heaven, I conjured the Lord to have pity on me;" and thus turning from the dangers that surrounded her, she was more constant than ever in her prayers, meditations, and frequentation of the sacraments. "Alas!" said she one day, "how I envy the liberty of those good women who can go alone to church when they like!" For grievous indeed to her was the yoke of the stern etiquette which did not permit her to go even to confession without lacqueys and coachmen, so that the "confession of Mademoiselle" was the constant joke among the domestics.

At length the weary years of waiting were drawing to a close, and Camille began to make serious preparations for her entrance into religion. Her leaning had always been to the Benedictine convent, in which she had so constantly resided, and where she was known and loved. One thing alone troubled her in thinking of this Order, and while conversing with her Confessor on the subject she expressed it. The duty of entertaining "*dames pensionnaires*" obliged the religious to hear much of what went on in the world. "You would not find this drawback with the Carmelites," replied the priest. A light, as if from Heaven, burst on Camille at these words. "I implore you, my father," she answered, "to go and propose me to them." Soon afterwards Camille went herself to the Carmelite convent in the Rue de Grenelle, where she was strictly interrogated by the Prioress upon the marks of her vocation. The important answers were satisfactory. Towards the close of the interview, the Prioress said, "Mademoiselle, do you like fish?" "Madame, I hate it!" was the answer. "And eggs?" she continued. "I detest them," replied Camille. "I eat *maigre* every Friday, and generally have the *migraine* on Saturday." "How, then, can you be a Carmelite?" rejoined the nun. "I will do penance," answered Camille, brightly; "that is all that I desire."

On the 2nd of February Camille entered the convent. Long and agonizing was the parting with her parents, prolonged even after her entrance, for they would come to see her in the parlour, and there pour forth their bitter grief. It is easy to see how good and endearing Camille had been in her home to cause such violent sorrow from parents accustomed to see women choose the religious life. But Camille was so far safe at last, and now the hardships and the austerities of the Carmelite life were to do battle with her ardent spirit. The first night of her entrance, the nuns, wishing gradually to accustom her to hard living, gave her an infirmary mattress instead of the straw bed prescribed by the Rule. Years afterwards, Camille acknowledged that the mattress seemed to her so hard she thought the straw could not have been worse. Her delicate health presented a serious obstacle to her perseverance in the austere life she had chosen; but her undaunted spirit, and the grace of her vocation, to which she was faithful, triumphed over all; abstinence, fast, and penance had no power to affright her, and the time of her postulancy would not have been delayed even so long as six months, had it not been at the earnest entreaties of her parents.

The 24th July, 1784, it was a *prise d'habit* in the Carmelite convent,—a ceremony which generally excited little attention in the gay, careless world of Paris, but on this day the chapel was crowded with the *élite* of French society.

There came to the chapel that day no less a person than the celebrated Madame de Genlis, bringing with her two pupils, the children of the Duke of Orleans; and if a prophet had pointed to the young prince, now so far removed from the throne, and declared he should both wear and abdicate the crown of France during the lifetime of her who was making her adieus to the world, who would not have laughed him to scorn? Yet so it was, and in after years *Louis Philippe* was wont to ask news of Camille de Soyecourt, at whose *prise d'habit* he had assisted. The noble bride was gorgeously arrayed in a heavy Court dress, and kneeling before the altar she made her humble request to become "an abject in the house of the Lord." Her witnesses were the President Molé and the Marquis de Feriquières, her uncle, who had wished to make her his heiress, and was grieved that she had chosen a "better inheritance." The Archbishop of Paris gave the habit; the Jesuit father *Le Quay* preached the sermon; and at last the convent doors were thrown open, and, according to the beautiful and touching ceremonial of the Order of Carmel, the Sister Camille of the Infant Jesus bade adieu to her friends, and throwing herself at the foot of the crucifix was left in her cloister, as she deemed, for ever. She little thought how soon, or under what circumstances, the convent gates would open wide. The year of novitiate fled quickly by; it was no difficult task for her superiors to lead her on to perfection; rather, they had to moderate her fervour. "Remember," writes her director, Monsieur de la Blandinière, "that the motto of your seraphic mother, 'to suffer or to die,' was not uttered when she was a novice." "I fear for your health," again he wrote; "take care of it, for if it be injured I see the carriage of Monsieur *votre père* at the door to carry you off and *decarmiliser* you." He did not, however, spare her interior mortification; for we find him warning her gravely against indulging her strong affection for her Prioress. "Be generous," he says; "remember that God calls you to perfection, and that too lively affections are an obstacle to it." He told her also of a case which he had known of a young religious, who had indulged so strong an affection for her Superior, that when the latter was sent for for a new foundation, the heart of Sister Thérèse was almost broken, and she went to throw herself at the feet of the Lord, and pour forth her sorrow; and a voice answered her, and said, "Is it *I*, then, who have quitted thee?" "Shall *I* not suffice for thee?" "Have *I* ever failed thee?" These words sank into the heart of Camille, and, by detaching her more from creatures, prepared her for that awful trial which Almighty God had destined for her. The day for her profession drew near, and her mother, unable to believe that her beloved child could really prefer a life that seemed to her so frightful, to all the enjoyments of life, besought the Archbishop to have a second examination made of the reality of her vocation; the first, according to the laws of the Church, having already taken place. Accordingly, the Bishop of Senez went to see Camille, after having first seen her parents and heard all their doubts and fears. "Monseigneur," said Camille, "my parents persuade themselves that I am entering a tomb; they are ignorant that calm of soul and peace of heart are the best auxiliaries of a long life, and the sweetest counterbalance to the austerities of the cloister. Undeceive them, Monseigneur, I beseech you; persuade them to make the sacrifice generously to God. If you can soften their trouble by your consoling words, you will double my happiness." After this it was no longer possible to refuse Camille permission to make her profession.

In the Carmelite Order the vows are made in Chapter, and the public ceremony of receiving the black veil takes place soon after. On the 31st of July, 1785, Camille bound herself by irrevocable vows to Him Whom from eleven years of age she had chosen as her Spouse. "Accept, dear sister," said one of her companions to her that day; "accept these three pins to fasten your black veil with; they will remind you of the three nails with which you desire to nail yourself to the cross of your Spouse,—I mean your three vows." And the delicately nurtured daughter of De Soyecourt gratefully accepted the simple offering. Her public profession took place in August; and among many deeply touched at the ceremony, two persons, who had been long absent from the sacraments, resolved at once to reconcile themselves with God, and for that purpose chose the confessor of Camille.

The years fled quickly—the years that the world deems must be so monotonous to religious; but they are not, for their feet are ever hastening onwards towards a desired object; and thus the highborn lady was learning abnegation. We find her washing the altar linen when the cold was so great that sometimes the water on her fingers would freeze. It was the custom to raise the linen in baskets by a pulley to the garrets where it was laid out to dry. Camille's delicate arms had to assist in this hard labour, and though she lacked strength, her good-will and ardour were so great, that no one could surpass her in activity and perseverance. It might have seemed as if such occupations were penances severe enough for any one. But her love was not satisfied; she was continually imploring leave for penances beyond what are required in the Rule, and yet she was always contented when her requests were refused, for in holy obedience she found her true rest. She was appointed to the office of mending the clothes of the community; she took great delight in this occupation, the reason being, as was discovered afterwards, that she had heard it was given to the most incapable of the religious. But these happy years were drawing to a close. Not calmly passing from her convent life to the presence of her Lord was to be Camille's lot, at least, not awhile; to suffer, to witness, to confess His name in scenes of horror, such as we can now hardly realize—this was to be her portion.

The first roll of the distant thunder was heard in France; already were religious houses being despoiled and suppressed, and the Carmelites could not be long behind. "Your patron is that of the

agonizing," wrote Monsieur de la Blandinière to
Camille on the Feast of St. Camillus, July, 1792;
"invoke him with much devotion, for all around us
is in agony." At length came the time when the
religious lay down in their beds ready dressed, in fear
of any sudden awaking, for cries and menaces outside
the doors, and the news that reached them, told them
their hour was at hand, and on Holy Cross Day,
1792, it came. The Commissioners entered the
house, broke the reliquaries and other vessels in gold
or silver, casting aside the relics themselves in contempt, to the joy of the religious, who gathered them
up and took care of them; and the spoliation finished,
the mob were let in, and the nuns bade to depart.
The Prioress, who had long foreseen the blow, had
prepared secular dresses for her community, and had
also sought out secret abodes for them in parties
of six and seven. Then, laying aside the habit so
dear to them, the nuns separated; few indeed of
them were ever to meet again in life. Their places of
concealment were soon discovered. Some few escaped
to foreign countries, and entered other convents of
their Order, most languished in prison, and some
there ended their lives. We are told a touching
incident respecting seven, who were imprisoned for
eighteen months in Saint Pélagie, then known as
the *vestibule of death*. A priest, afterwards Bishop
of Rodz, came every week to the prison, disguised

as a wine merchant, carrying on his head a pannier of bottles; and having thus obtained entrance, he put down his basket, and heard the confessions of the nuns. Monsieur and Madame de Soyecourt would fain have had Camille return home to them, little thinking, even yet, how soon they would be unable to afford a refuge to their child; but Camille, who had been appointed by the Prioress, Superior of the little band of seven, among whom she was, would not quit her charge. These seven remained for some time concealed in a house in the Rue Mouffetard, and from time to time a disguised priest crept thither to say mass and give communion, so that the Blessed Sacrament dwelt with them, and the nuns were in peace and joy.

A spy was at hand; information was given, and on Good Friday, 1793, thirty armed men came to drag out these innocent women from their refuge. Camille was the first to perceive their entry. Her instant thought was for her Lord; reverently taking the Ciborium, she hid it in her bosom, and thus calmly awaited her fate. "My God," whispered she often; "my God, protect Thyself!" Well was it He was hidden on that loving heart, for the ruffians, in their strict search about the rooms, coming upon a kind of altar or tomb, cried out, "*Here is God!*" and inspected it narrowly, hoping to find a gold or silver Ciborium. At length they withdrew, and then the religious, who had never broken their fast, although it was now evening, reverently received the Sacred Hosts—for many a long day it was to be their last communion. On Easter Monday, Camille and her companions were also sentenced to imprisonment in Saint Pélagie, which until this time had been the prison for women of immoral life, and thus they followed closely in the steps of Him who was "reckoned among the malefactors." Their souls were filled with joy; vile words were uttered in their hearing, but they prayed for those who spoke them. Allowed to have one sleeping-room to themselves, they said their Office, and endeavoured to observe their holy Rule.

After four months' detention they were released, and again dispersed. Camille, with one other, took refuge in her father's house, which was still untouched. Overjoyed indeed were Monsieur and Madame de Soyecourt to have their beloved child once more with them. The two religious kept their Rule as far as possible, and only went out to seek for a mass said by a priest still true to the Church, for the masses said in public were only those of the excommunicated priests. But Camille pined for a convent's blessed shade again, and formed a design of begging her way to Rome on foot, and there entering a Carmelite convent. She was, however, forbidden to put this in execution, and not long after, the arrest of her father and mother again left her homeless. She fled from their house with six francs, her only possession.

She was at last alone, in terror for her life, and starving. One day she crept trembling into the street to buy a little milk from a passing vendor, and the man, recognising the unconscious grace of that form and step which had once graced the court of the Bourbons, exclaimed, "How, *citoyne*, they have then forgotten to *shorten* thee!" Camille fled in terror, without waiting for the milk, and then offered this fresh suffering to God. Another time the betrayal of her noble birth did her a good turn; for an old apple woman, of whom she was buying, exclaimed, "Take them, *ma mignonne*, put them in your pocket, and keep your money." In her extreme poverty, and ignorance of cooking, she tried to make the water in which she boiled fish serve for soup! and when the servants of her father's house gave her some eggs, she did not know how to boil them. Once, when these same servants had filled a little basket for her with provisions, Camille went on her way back to her abode to visit some of her fellow-religious, who were living together in poverty and concealment. Not wishing to sadden them, she would not tell them how badly off she was; and they, deeming she was well supplied from her father's house, thought the little basket was a present, and thanked her warmly for it, and Camille went quietly away, leaving them in their mistake.

Soon after, Madame de Soyecourt died in prison, and Camille was sent for by the officials to put seals on the property. The message reached her through her Prioress, who alone knew her hiding-place. Camille, fearing it was a *ruse* to take her to prison, was unwilling to go. The Prioress, however, thought otherwise. "Well then, my mother," replied Camille, "I will go according to your order; and if I die, it will not be only because I am of noble birth, but in obedience." She was, however, left at large, and from henceforth had less fear of arrest, so that she went to the prison of the Carmes, to endeavour to see her father. This was refused her. She did, however, contrive to correspond with him, and she found his letters full of sanguine hopes of speedy release, and of plans of flying with her for a time from this land of terror and death. The decree exiling all persons of noble birth from Paris obliged Camille to remove from the city. She accordingly went to Moulinaux, about three leagues from Paris, and once a week she walked this immense distance, and back again, in order to go to confession, and then midway on the road she stopped to change her dress, and entered Paris attired in white, with the republican cockade in her cap, carrying as a parcel her other clothes. And in the midst of this life of

G

constant terror, privation, and suffering, Camille never forgot she was a daughter of Carmel. She persevered in fast and abstinence, in saying Office, even when overwhelmed with fatigue, till her health so completely gave way, that her confessor ordered her to desist from some of her austerities. Nor was her sweet humility conquered, for though she wore the peasant costume, which seemed rude to her who had once "loved to dress in good taste" in the fastidious *salons* of St. Germains, her natural grace so adorned what she wore, that an acquaintance deemed her vain, and reproved her for having a cap better plaited than other people. Camille began to explain, but the censor persisted, and with a childlike submission she went to put on another cap.

On the 23rd of July, 1794, Monsieur de Soyecourt was told to leave the prison; he took a little packet in his hand, and joyfully obeyed the summons. "You need not take anything with you," said the jailer, and in those words he learnt his fate. He returned for a few minutes to throw himself at the feet of an imprisoned priest, and then, strengthened by absolution, went to his death.

Three days afterwards, his married daughter, the Comtesse d'Hinnisdal, died in prison. Camille was also compelled to leave her asylum, and she knew not where to go; she sought her Prioress, but found her in such distress, that she could not assist her, and Camille was therefore without shelter or food. A republican, however, took pity on her, and gave her an empty house to live in. A former lay sister of her convent found her out, and came to live with her, both supporting themselves by the little work they could get to do: it was no more than a bare existence. In this empty house, however, one consolation was afforded them, and in it all sorrows were swallowed up. They could fit up a room as a chapel, poor and rude enough, and thither now and then would come a fugitive priest to say his Mass.

Their fervour, together with that of all the Carmelites, was strengthened by the good confession witnessed for the faith by the nuns of their Order at Compiègne. The whole of this community were guillotined at the *Barrière du Trône*, and died with triumphant joy.

An end at length was coming; the name of Camille de Soyecourt was entered as one of those to be put to death in August, when a sudden blow was struck—Robespierre was dead,—and France began to breathe.

In October, 1794, Camille was allowed to return to Paris, and took a lodging in the Rue des Postes, where also she had a little chapel, and Mass was said secretly. Not long after, it was found feasible to re-open some of the churches in Paris; and as the chapel of the Collége du Saint Esprit had never been profaned, it was the first to open its doors.

A number of the faithful, headed by Camille, set themselves to clean and ornament the long deserted temple. Then the Blessed Sacrament was taken from the little chapel in Camille's house to the church, and there exposed for adoration; after which Benediction was given to an immense crowd, prostrate in worship. Two years had passed (and what years!) since the chant of the *Tantum ergo* had been heard in Paris, and tears choked the voices of those who were spared once more to raise the strain. Never did Camille forget that day. It was her first taste of joy after so many sorrows, and the joy was so intense, it seemed as if it were too much to bear; and in all her after life she could never recal the event without re-tasting, as it were, for a moment, the consolation which then made her heart overflow. Very gradually was the work of restoration accomplished; one by one prisoners were released, and one by one the faithful priests and others came out of their hiding-places. As to Camille, she rested not day nor night till she could once more enjoy the semblance at least of a Carmelite convent; and at Easter, 1795, she took a house known by the name of the *Vache Noir*, in the Rue St. Jacques. She added a chapel to this house, and it was much frequented, for the parish church of St. Jacques was held by a constitutional priest. The first child baptized in this chapel received the name of Camille. Many pious priests came to say their Mass, and such was the crowd of people who thronged to assist, that even the staircase was filled by them.

In the house of the *Vache Noir*, the Order of Carmel, in Paris, first re-established itself. The Prioress was living, and came to join Camille, together with a few of the still surviving religious. Far off, however, yet seemed their cloister and their loved Rule in its strict observance. They had to go about and nurse the sick, and attend upon the distressed. Camille was called upon to soothe the last moments of Monsieur de la Blandinière, her former director, and one of the holiest priests of his time; and as she tended him in his helplessness with dutiful care, he said gaily to her, " Madame, you have been my novice; now I am yours." In her presence he breathed his last.

The restoration of property to the nobles who had been despoiled was now beginning to be made, and Camille was urged to make good her claim, as almost sole heiress to her father's wealth. This, however, she shrank from doing, fearing it would be contrary to her vow of poverty. The matter being carried to Rome, the Holy Father issued a brief, authorizing her to take possession of her property, to be applied only to the use of others. With this newly-restored fortune Camille purchased the ancient monastery of the Carmes, so called from its having originally been occupied by monks of the Order of Mount Carmel; but which, since their dispersion, had been the scene of that most bloody episode in the Reign of Terror, the massacre of the priests and bishops, and since then turned into a prison, within whose walls the Comte de Soyecourt had been confined.

And now Camille set herself with all her vigour to re-establish her lovèd Order in France. The task would be long and arduous, but her spirit rose before difficulties, and she was not afraid. In August, 1797, the first Mass was said in the Carmes by the curé of Saint Sulpice, who was kept out of his own church by a constitutional priest. At this Mass were present twelve out of the thirty-one religious driven from their peaceful convent five years previously. The church of the Carmes being the first church belonging to a religious order opened in Paris, an immense crowd came to its benediction, (for all the profaned churches were solemnly re-blessed at their opening,) and among that crowd scarcely an eye was dry, for each heart was filled with the remembrance of those holy men who within these walls had shed their blood; they recalled how, praying at the foot of the altars, they had been offered life and liberty if only they would take the schismatical oath, and how one and all having refused, they won their martyrs' crown.

For some time, while St. Sulpice remained closed to the faithful, the church of the Carmes was much frequented. The confessionals were thronged, and crowds hung on the words of the different preachers who there gave discourses. In these humble walls began those celebrated conferences of Monseigneur de Frayssinous, then a simple priest, which he afterwards gave at Nôtre Dame, and which were continued after his departure by the Pères Lacordaire and De Ravignan. Full of solemn and touching associations did the nuns find their new abode. A tree in their avenue marked the spot on which died the Archbishop of Arles. Within the garden they found a Breviary, pierced through with a ball, and stained with blood; and above all was the heart of Camille moved when she entered the cell in which her father had been imprisoned. She fixed upon it at once as her own cell. The year following the acquisition of the Carmes, the aged Prioress died. It was impossible in the still perilous state of affairs to make a new election, and the convent was governed for some years by the Sub-Prioress. At length an election was held, and Camille was appointed Prioress.

The First Consul ruled France. Peace seemed coming back. Saint Sulpice received again her lawful pastors, and the church of the Carmes was occupied only by the religious. In October, 1803, Camille desired to celebrate with becoming pomp the fête of St. Teresa. To her joy, she heard there was for sale a picture of the Saint in ecstasy, which had formerly been the altar-piece in the convent of the Rue de Grenelle. She hastened to purchase it, and place it over the altar in the Carmes, and looking fondly at it, she exclaimed, " My good mother, they had sold you; I have redeemed you; here you are replaced. '*Laudate Dominum omnes gentes.*'"

The wish dearest to Camille's heart was to collect together the dispersed Carmelite nuns of France, whether belonging to her own convent or not; and she joyfully welcomed those who came one by one, hardly believing the reality of the good news, to reenter the doors of Carmel. Some of the religious of her former community who had fled into Flanders, and there taken refuge in Flemish convents of the Order, came back to their native land. To one especially the change was grateful, for in her foreign convent she had been unable to speak Flemish, or to find a confessor who could speak French, and had therefore been obliged to make her confessions through an interpreter! Still the nuns dared not resume their habit; and though, in 1806, they ventured to receive novices, yet after the reception of the habit it was not worn publicly. Many and heavy were the cares that pressed on Camille de Soyecourt. Not only had she gradually and cautiously to re-establish her Order, but to guide the distribution of her large fortune, of which she truly deemed herself but the steward. By her means starving priests were found out, rescued from some miserable occupation or other, and re-took their place in the sanctuary; poor neglected churches were re-furnished, and many a foundation for schools or other pious works were raised from their ruins by the Mère Camille.

Her troubles were not yet terminated, although she was no longer young. She was again to witness for her Lord. She assisted by money, and in other ways, the Holy Father, Pius the Seventh, at the time of his persecution by Napoleon, and thus fell under the displeasure of the Emperor, who had her arrested and imprisoned, and, after some time, she was sentenced to exile from Paris. Taking with her one companion, the Prioress calmly prepared for her departure; but still her heart was torn. " Alas, Father," said she to the saintly Père de Clorivière, "I go into exile, not knowing when it will be over." " My daughter," replied he, " when the Angel bade St. Joseph fly into Egypt, he did not ask when it would end." No further murmur passed the lips of the exile. At *Guise*, the place of her banishment, she found friends anxious to soften her fate. Even the officials were won by her gracious and sweet manner, and they permitted her to lodge in the Hospital of the Sisters of Charity. Here, as everywhere else, Camille found means of doing good to others, and her charity was so abundant that Sister Vincent, the Superior, had sometimes to check her bounty. At length, after two years of exile, the intercession of her friends availed, and she was permitted to rejoin her children in Paris. The Holy Father was now, Napoleon deemed, too completely in his power for intrigues to do any harm. Camille was allowed to go to Fontainebleau to see the exiled Pontiff, and hear his Mass. " Come again to-morrow," said the Holy Father to her afterwards, " and I will give you Communion myself." Nor was this all; he made her take breakfast, and presenting her himself with one of the dishes, said, " I wish you to be able to say you have been served by the hands of a Pope."

When happier days dawned on the Vicar of Christ, and he, with the Sacred College, were once more in Rome, he sent to invite Camille, whom he called the " Mother of the afflicted," to establish herself at Rome. Succeeding Popes honoured Camille with marks of their favour; the last being a letter from our present Holy Father, Pius the Ninth

—for down to our own days was the life of this holy religious prolonged. She lived to restore the strict enclosure in her monastery, to resume the loved habit of Carmel. She restored the Rule in its most rigid observance, and before her death she had the joy of knowing that sixty monasteries of the Order were re-established in France; and feeling that her stewardship was now over, she resigned whatever was left of her large property into the hands of her nephew, wishing, in her old age, to share once more the poverty which she had chosen in youth. Long bodily sufferings were her last trials on earth, borne always not only with patience, but with joy. She used to lie in her bed and *sing*, adding gaily, "My voice is not as good as it was, but it will be so *to-morrow*,"—that sweet to-morrow which she was approaching. "It remains then only for me, my children, to say my Nunc Dimittis;" and very soon after she calmly ended her long life of an hundred and five years, on the 8th of May, 1849.

Scattered up and down in the Carmelite Chronicles are numerous mentions of saintly lives and heroic deeds wrought in the obscurity of the convent. Great praise is often given to the active orders, whose works of mercy are visible; while little falls on those who have advanced in the path of self-conquest, and the acquirement of those interior virtues, without which exterior works are of little avail in the eyes of God. Thus we read of Marie des Anges, mother of the Cardinal de Berulle. Up to fifty-five years of age she had been her own mistress, and surrounded with every luxury. She became a Carmelite, and kept the Rule with fervour, and was distinguished by her hatred of praise. She never would converse with her son, who was Superior of the monastery, without necessity; and though he often came to the house, years passed without her asking to see him. She lived in religion twenty-two years, never asking for a dispensation, and even in her last illness refusing any alleviation. Her last conscious words were, " Stay with me, Lord, for the day is far spent;" and when she could speak no longer, she stammered the name of Jesus, and passed into His unveiled presence. After her death, her face, which had been so disfigured by age and sickness, became quite beautiful. Many persons wished to touch her body, but the Cardinal de Berulle would not allow it.

Another of the Cardinal's relations entered the Order, the beautiful Madame d'Autry. In her youth she attracted the notice of King Henry the Third, who, seeing her in church one day without a book, sent her a copy of the *Hours*, ornamented with precious stones. Madame d'Autry quietly refused the gift. The King, not repulsed, came soon afterwards to pay her a visit. Madame d'Autry entered the room with her hands full of roots, saying, "I am not fit to appear before your Majesty, suffer me to wash my hands." She then withdrew, but did not return; and Henry was wise enough to take the hint, and never paid her another visit.

At twenty-nine she became a widow, and though she wished to be a religious, her duties to her children detained her in the world till the age of forty-six. Although pious and charitable, she was of a haughty and domineering nature, with a particular *penchant* for setting other people to rights. Many people warned the Carmelites not to receive her; they, however, resolved to give her a trial, and see if her vocation really came from God, and the event proved they were right. During her noviciate, it was only once observed that she brought forward her own opinion, and at length she became as remarkable for humility as she had formerly been for pride. When she was dying, she begged the Prioress not to let her go to sleep, as she was so close upon seeing God. But the Prioress answered that she might do so. "Well then, my mother," said she, "I will sleep in obedience for Jesus Christ, who obeyed unto death." She had been forty-two years in religion, and of her death it is recorded, "she had no agony."

Under the chapel of the Convent of St. Denis

was a cave, which, tradition said, had been a place of refuge for St. Denis in the persecutions. It was an extensive place, with side chapels and numerous altars. One of the nuns, Sister Louise of Jesus and Mary, had a great talent for painting, and she undertook the task of painting the whole in a way to imitate mosaic. She accomplished her task, and her work had a surprising variety and beauty. Many months she passed in this employment, spending her time in this cold dark place, for she had no assistants in her work. When she had to paint a very high part of the cave, she would do it, holding her lamp in one hand and her tools in the other. But in this arduous employment she found means to sanctify herself, and on one occasion we hear of a miracle being worked in her favour. There was an immense stone at the end of the garden, which Sister Louise thought would do beautifully as the step for the altar of St. Denis. She asked one of the lay sisters to help her carry it down. This sister, not knowing how large the stone was, and that four men could hardly have moved it, consented to come; but saying she was very busy at the moment, asked Sister Louise to wait till the afternoon. At the appointed hour the lay sister went to the spot, but the stone was gone, and going to Sister Louise to learn how she had managed, she was told, " I asked my good angel to help me, and then

I put it in my scapular, and took it down without any trouble."

Still do the daughters of St. Teresa pursue their heavenly vocation. When persecution overspread the land, and men worshipped in fear, not even daring to let the light of the sanctuary burn before the Most Holy, one spot is recorded, hidden far away in one of the loveliest of England's green valleys, where the storms without did not penetrate, and where still the silver lamp gave its trembling ray before Jesus, in His Sacrament.

A century passed away, and fleeing from the misery of revolution in the Low Countries came to England a community of Carmelite nuns. To them this quaint old dwelling-place of the Cornish branch of the Arundells was assigned, and ever since within those walls prayer and penance have been unceasingly offered up to avert the judgments of God.

"From many a hidden dell,
From many a rural nook unthought of there,
Rises for that proud world the saints' prevailing prayer." *

And still the same silver lamp burns before the Tabernacle, and now and then a passing pilgrim tarries to pray in the time-worn chapel at Lanherne. Another convent of Carmelites exists at Darlington. There are numerous communities of the Order

* Keble.

in France, and various ones in other parts of the Continent.

The Order of Mount Carmel has no Superioress-General, or General Noviciate; each house is independent in itself, and subject to the Bishops of the respective dioceses. The postulantcy is from three to six months in duration, the noviciate a year, and sometimes longer, and the vows are solemn. It is not an Order which attracts much notice or admiration in this busy, restless age; but the praise of men is not the object of a religious's life, and the faithful daughters of Mount Carmel are dear in the sight of the angels, as from day to day, and year to year, they follow the teaching of their holy reformer, St. Teresa.

## THE ORDER OF THE POOR CLARES COLLETINES.

The story is too well known to need repeating here,—how the merchant's son of Assissi, touched by an inspiration from Heaven, "sold all that he had," and went forth from his father's house to follow Christ in that literal manner we in these days can hardly understand; and thus, in the little town of Assissi, was planted the seed of that wonderful

Franciscan tree which was to overshadow the whole earth.

And as women were not wanting to stand beneath the Cross and to weep beside the Tomb, so the first St. Francis in his stern poverty, in his utter abnegation, and in his crucifixion of the body, found women as well as men to emulate his example.

Young, gentle, and beautiful was Clare, the daughter of a noble house, when she resolved to be the first spiritual daughter of St. Francis, and she fled from a deluding and dazzling world to lead a life of penance.

We all know the tale—how St. Francis received her that Palm Sunday evening, how and in the vain world raged at her departure, and how, in spite of storms, there arose on the hills of Assisi the Convent of St. Damian, in which was founded the Second Order of St. Francis, called afterwards the Poor Ladies, or the Poor Clares,—for they, like St. Francis, espoused poverty; that stern master, so dreaded, so shrank from by the world, became to them a dear and loving friend.

Around St. Clare soon gathered a number of holy virgins who consecrated themselves to God. Among others, her sister Agnes, and afterwards her sister Beatrice, and her mother Hortulane. For a long time they lived by no written rules, but only by the verbal directions of St. Francis and St.

Clare; but after the return of the Holy Patriarch from Egypt, at the request of St. Clare, he composed the Rule for the Poor Ladies.

It may easily be imagined with what prayers, with what abundance of tears, with what clear insight into the things of God, this Rule was composed by him surnamed Seraphic, for his heavenly light and his supernatural union with our Lord. Conforming her life to these holy precepts, St. Clare advanced rapidly in the way of perfection. For fourteen years she was permitted to enjoy the blessing of intercourse with her holy father, to listen to his teaching, and to see the love with which he was so inflamed that it shone visibly on his face; but this assistance was to be taken from her, for the last days of St. Francis were at hand. From the moment when on Mount Alvernia he had received the mysterious marks of the Wounds of his Lord, his body had been growing feebler and weaker; his eyes were nearly blind with his continual tears, and the hour of his release was at hand. At the beginning of his last illness he was brought to a poor cell near St. Damian, and then he sent for St. Clare, and conversed with her " on the infinite goodness of God for men." He was afterwards removed from thence, and Clare had no longer the consolation of seeing him; but she prayed him to send his last benediction to her and his daughters, and the Saint, too weak to write, dictated to a companion his last loving words. He bade them remember that the Lord had assembled them from all parts of the earth, and that they should strengthen each other in following faithfully the spirit of their vocation. He bade them perfect themselves every day in the virtues of their state. He exhorted those who were sick to be patient, and those who were in health to wait carefully on the sick. He wished that they should moderate their austerities a little, and that they should use with joy and thanksgivings, the alms given them by the faithful. He forbade them to use austerities to such a degree as to render them incapable afterwards of fulfilling the duties of their holy state. He exhorted them above all to interior mortification, to sweetness, to mutual support, to resignation to all the events of life; and finally, he promised that they should see him again, but they were not to be impatient as to the moment, for all that was arranged by God, and they should submit themselves entirely and in all things to His Will.

They did see him again; but it was after his beautiful soul had left the prison of its body and gone to the great reward. Then that sacred body, so worn with fast and penance, and marked with the tokens of his Saviour's love, was borne into the

Chapel of St. Damian, and St. Clare and her nuns came to venerate the form of him they had loved so much.

Years had fled by—years which brought so much of changes and storms over the face of the earth, but which brought none to the daughters of St. Clare, save that they had advanced so much nearer to their destined end; and they had seen convent after convent of their Order founded, not only in Italy, but in many other countries. At length the sound of war pealed even to their calm retreat; and the brutal Saracen soldiery, in their rage against the Holy See, attacked the States of the Church, and in them the town of Assissi. One night they attempted to spoil the Convent of St. Damian. What task so easy as to besiege a building defended only by a few weak women, whose Abbess, herself, lay extended on a bed of sickness? Already they are scaling the walls, and the terrified nuns have fled to the cell of St. Clare. "Fear not, my beloved daughters; confide in Jesus Christ, He will save you," said she; then rising from her bed, she went into the chapel, and taking from thence the Ciborium containing the Adorable Sacrament, she placed It on her bosom, and falling down before the Lord, she said, "Divine Jesus, cast Thy merciful eyes on Thy poor servants, whom I have nourished until now with the milk of Thy Divine Love. Wilt Thou then abandon them into the hands of the heathen? Preserve pure those who are consecrated to Thee, and whom I cannot defend myself. Deliver not to these ferocious beasts those who confess Thy name, but guard those whom Thou hast redeemed by Thy Precious Blood." She ceased her prayer, and then she heard the voice of a little child, who said to her, *"Yes; I will keep you for ever."* "Lord," she answered, "deign also to take under Thy Protection this town, which supports us for the love of Thee." And the voice answered, *"It is true this town will suffer much, but it will be defended by my protection, and by your prayers."* Then Clare, turning towards her trembling daughters, said to them, "My beloved ones, you can now dry your tears; the victory is ours, because God interests Himself in our behalf. Have only a lively faith and a fervent hope." In a moment she was transported to the walls of the monastery, and showing the Ciborium to the infidels, a sudden terror seized upon them, and they were blinded by the celestial light which flowed from the hidden God, and fled before this unseen Power, not only from the convent, but the city. Assissi was saved! This miracle is the solitary event to be justly called so in the life of St. Clare. She employed her remaining years in obtaining a confirmation of her Rule from the Holy Father, and to see secured to her children for ever the right of utter and absolute poverty, to hold no property, and to depend entirely on the alms of the faithful.

So supernatural a desire did this appear, that towards the close of St. Clare's life, Pope Gregory the Ninth, when asked by her to confirm her loved privilege, tried to dissuade her from it; and thinking that she was restrained from complying by the vow she had made, he said, "If you are restrained by your vow, dearest daughter, we will absolve you from it." "Holy Father," replied the saint, "I desire, with all my heart, absolution from my sins; but no absolution from following the counsels of Christ." Long bodily illness was allowed to try St. Clare's later years. One Christmas night she lay alone and suffering in her cell, while her nuns were in the choir, welcoming with the angels' song our Infant Lord. "O Lord Jesus Christ," said St. Clare, "see, I am deprived of the joy in which all beside have a share. They are all assembled round Thy crib; and I am here alone on my bed, and far from Thee." Quick came the answer. Suddenly she began to hear the joyful chants with which the Franciscan friars were making their church to ring; the words of the Office, the deep voices of the brethren, and the harmonious tones of the organ. Whether it were that she was transported in spirit to St. Mary of the Angels, or that He to whom distance is nothing had miraculously opened her ears, she knew not; nor was this all, she beheld the stable at Bethlehem, with the Divine Infant wrapped in swaddling clothes and lying on the straw, as He appeared to the shepherds when the angel brought them good tidings. One of St. Clare's employments on her sick bed was to spin corporals for the poor altars in the village churches which had been lately despoiled, and corporals of snowy whiteness were wrought by those feeble, wasted hands. When the hour of her death drew near, her sisters prayed for her blessing. She complied in these words:—"In the name of the most Holy Trinity, Amen. My beloved sisters, may the Almighty God bless you; may He cast upon you the eyes of His goodness and mercy; may He give you peace, and grant it not to you alone, but to all those who are absent, and to all who after you shall enter into this Order, and persevere unto the end in their vocation, whether it be in this monastery, or in any other following the same Rule. I then, Clare, the unworthy handmaid of Jesus Christ, and the little worthless plant of our father St. Francis, your sister and your mother, beseech our Lord Jesus Christ, and conjure Him by the intercession of the Blessed Virgin Mary, His Most Holy Mother, of the Archangel St. Michael, of all the Holy Angels, of our Seraphic Father, and of all the Saints, to be pleased to give you His blessing, and so to confirm in heaven that which I give you on earth. May He shed upon you here below the abundance of His graces, that He may exalt you one day among the saints and the blessed above! Yes; I give you my blessing now and as long as I live, and I confirm it also as far as I may for the time when I shall be with you no more, and I leave you all the benedictions which I have power to bestow upon you." Suddenly her spirit was lifted up from the things of earth, and her face was lighted up with joy, and she exclaimed, " Come, my soul, rejoice that thou hast a good Viaticum to accompany thee, an excellent guide to show thee the way. Fear nothing; be at peace; for He who created thee has sanctified thee, and unceasingly watched over thee with the tender love of a mother for her child. Blessed be Thou, O Lord, that Thou hast created me!" Then a sister asked to whom she spoke so lovingly. "Dear child, I speak to my happy soul! Do you see, my daughter, the King of Glory, whom I behold?" And then to one religious it was vouchsafed to have her " eyes opened," and she saw a glorious train of virgins, and at their head *Mary* herself come as a true Mother to the death-bed of her child, and bending over Clare, she kissed her with the kiss of welcome into her Father's house, and the other virgins put on her a royal robe; and so

Clare laid aside the coarse heavy Franciscan habit, and went to wear a robe of that exceeding whiteness "such as no fuller on earth can white them."

St. Clare had left the flock on earth she had loved so much and watched over so tenderly. She went to join her beloved father in heaven, at the feet of their dear Lord. Yet still Francis and Clare watched over their children on earth, and unceasingly ascended their prayers for the preservation of their Orders. And if we had told men so a century after St. Clare's death, they would have mocked at our words; they would have pointed to relaxation and abuses which had crept in; they would have said, "Francis and Clare attempted more than mortals could do; they laid down a Rule only to be followed by saints like themselves." They would have shown the dispensations which even the Blessed Isabelle of France, sister to St. Louis, herself of saintly memory, had prayed Pope Urban to grant for her monastery of Longchamp, near Paris,—dispensations which so altered the Rule, that the community used to take the name of Urbanistes instead of Clares. They might, we say, have remarked all these things, and yet we now can believe that God permitted the partial decay of the Franciscan Order only to show forth fresh miracles of His mercy in restoring it. Miraculous indeed, and the work of His own Right Hand, was the reform wrought by St. Collette. She was not even, like St. Teresa, a religious of the Order she sought to reform. A carpenter's daughter in the little town of Corbie, not far from Amiens, without education, and withal of such a tiny stature that it grieved her parents, who would have dreamt that God would choose her as an instrument of His great work? Yet we cease to wonder as we read further. We read of her kneeling before the Image of our Lady, and asking, with a child's simplicity, that to please her parents she might grow taller, and in a very short time she was as remarkable for height as she had formerly been for the contrary, and with this height was given all those intellectual gifts necessary for the labour she was to accomplish. We see her making astonishing progress in the ways of prayer and penance, and obedience to her spiritual guides. Feeling drawn by God to religion, she entered first the Congregation of Beguines, who served the Hôtel Dieu at Corbie; and then feeling that an active life of charity was not for her, she went to a convent of *Urbanistes*, hoping to find rest under the shadow of St. Francis and St. Clare; but, alas! there she found that the glory had departed, and the children who bore their name were no longer faithful to their laws. Quitting the Urbanistes, she made a further essay at the Benedictine Convent;

but although it would seem these religious were true to their Rule, Collette did not feel called to be among them; she therefore returned home, and after waiting some years to determine what her vocation really was, she took the habit of the third Order of St. Francis in the world, and shortly afterwards retired into a hermitage, and began the extraordinary life of a recluse. At first the world mocked and called her mad; then it said she was a Saint, and besieged her door. Collette was indifferent to both one and the other; she lived so continually in the Presence of God, that she had a contempt for the tongues of men we can hardly understand. From her hermitage she was called to reform the Orders of St. Francis. Can we not easily imagine the storm, even among the good, such a step would raise? It seemed incredible and impossible; but Collette, urged on by that Divine impulsion which conquers all things, persevered, till from the hands of the Holy Father himself (Benedict the Thirteenth) she received the habit of the Poor Clares, made her profession, and was appointed Abbess over the Order.

The new Abbess commenced her work without a single subject. She was mocked and insulted wherever she went; Hell did its worst against her, but God was on her side.

It must not be supposed that Collette had received

any power to interfere with existing convents, however relaxed. The Holy See, in its perfect justice, only gave her the opportunity of creating convents of the Reform, and thus, it was hoped, of inducing the present communities to follow her. Gradually and slowly, as all God's works are wrought, was Collette's established. Novices came; convents, one after another, were opened. She who had been despised and hated, and chased from her native place, was sought for here and there. Not only did she establish the reform among the nuns, but also the monks of St. Francis. Who could resist those burning words of love, or the power of those constant miracles? We see at her feet a king's daughter asking to be received into her noviciate (Isabeau de Bourbon, daughter of the King of Naples). Collette asked if she knew the kind of life her religious led. "Yes," she replied. "Fear not, my Reverend Mother, to terrify me by the picture of the austerities that are practised in your Order. I know that your life is a life of immolation, and that the most austere poverty is found everywhere, in food, clothing, and in sleeping; but nothing of that repels me. Other women, as delicately brought up as I am, have entered your Order, and they carry with joy the yoke of Jesus Christ. He Who has given me the desire for this vocation knows well how to give me the grace of fulfilling its obligations, as well as He has done for those whom I wish to imitate."

It was in 1447 that St. Collette ended her life. On her bed of death her zeal for God's glory seemed to consume her, and to swallow up, as it were, those passionate aspirations of love which generally burst from the lips of the dying Saints. "If I can yet," exclaimed she, "spite of my unworthiness, serve for the good of souls, leave me on the earth; I refuse not agony, nor sorrow, nor torment, *be it what it may*, if I can at this price procure Thy glory." But she had served long enough, and God took her to His celestial joys. Since that day the children of St. Clare and St. Collette have been faithful in their strict observance. There have been storms, there have been troubles; days came in which the fury of war sweeping over kingdoms, levelled convents, and made the religious fly before them; but the storms passed, and the convents were re-filled.

It is now time that we should describe more particularly the kind of life led by the *Clares Colletines*. The *Rule of St. Clare* is divided into twelve Chapters. The first speaks of the kind of life to be followed by the nuns, and that the Rules are in general those of the Monks of St. Francis; that they consist in observing the three vows of poverty, obedience, and chastity, in all their perfection. The second Chapter treats of the reception of novices, and the conditions required from them—the clothing of the novices, the qualities of the novice mistress, and of her duties, and says that the Profession must be preceded by a total relinquishment of all the goods that the Professed possesses in the world, and that all be given in alms. The time of profession is fixed at the end of a year's noviciate. St. Clare shows to what point she wishes poverty carried, not only in regard to the goods they possess in the world, but to the very clothing which they wear in religion; and she exhorts her daughters, for the love of the Infant Jesus, and of His most holy Mother, to content themselves with the very poorest. The third Chapter treats of the Divine Office which is said by the Choir Sisters—of the fasting, which is perpetual, and of the frequent confessions and communions. The fourth Chapter speaks of the elections of the Abbess, of all the other officers, and of the discreets who compose the council of the Abbess. *She* is told by the Rule to strive to be the Superior of the others, more in virtues than in office, so that the Sisters, excited by her example, be obedient more by love than by fear. She is to have no particular affection for any one; she is to console the afflicted and be their refuge; she is to share alike with the community in all things—in the church, the dormitory, refectory, infirmary, and in clothing; and the vicaress (who is next in authority) does the same. The Rule forbids any debt being contracted without the leave of the whole community, and without a great necessity. The fifth Chapter prescribes the silence, and the rules to be observed when speaking. No one can go to the parlour without leave, and she must be accompanied by two sisters to the *grille,* which must have a curtain inside. The Abbess herself is subject to this law. The parlour is forbidden to the Sisters during the two Lents,—the first called the Lent of St. Martin, which begins from All Saints and lasts till Christmas; the second begins Quinquagesima Sunday; but it is permitted to speak to a priest alone on spiritual matters, or for manifest necessity. The Abbess can, however, always receive persons on business, or strangers. No conversation on vain or frivolous matters is permitted. The sixth Chapter concerns the practice of holy Poverty; no one is to have anything of their own, and St. Clare implores all succeeding Abbesses never to suffer, under any pretext, that this rule be broken through, but that they always observe holy and rigorous poverty. The seventh Chapter prescribes that all the Sisters, except the sick or infirm, employ themselves in work of the hands. The time for work begins after Terce; the Sisters must acquit themselves of this duty faithfully, and in a manner by which they must avoid idleness, and preserve the spirit of devotion. They must work for the common good, and not for their own. An account must be given in Chapter of all the alms that are received, so that the benefactors may be prayed for. The eighth Chapter forbids the Sisters to be ashamed to beg for alms. No letters must be written or received without leave, and any presents that may be made are to be given to the Superior for the community. The same rule recommends the exercise of a tender charity towards the sick, and permits them to have a feather pillow, and even a mattress in case of necessity. The ninth Chapter rules the penances. The tenth the duties of the Abbess towards the Sisters, and of the virtues the Sisters ought to practise—entire submission, patience in affliction, and union of hearts. The eleventh speaks of the office of Portresses, and it forbids any one entering the enclosure, except doctors to see the sick, workmen for necessary repairs, priests to give the Sacraments to the sick, the Bishop, and the Ecclesiastical Visitor. The twelfth Chapter rules the times for the ecclesiastical visits. The Rule of St. Clare was solemnly confirmed by Pope Innocent the Fourth.

Beside the Rule, St. Clare also left the following touching recommendation, which is called her

*Testament:*—" In the name of our Lord Jesus Christ. In thanksgiving for our vocation, we ought then to keep, in the state to which our Lord has called us, the Commandments of God, of holy Church, and of our Seraphic Father, in order that, aided by God, we may multiply the graces He has given us. If our Lord has raised us to the dignity and excellence of serving as examples and models for others, how much are we not obliged to bless God, to praise Him, and to rest firmly in our Saviour by always practising what is right! If we live holily and observe our rules, and if we give good examples, we shall certainly acquire, by a very short labour, the reward of eternal beatitude."
" I, Clare," she continues, " servant of Jesus Christ and the poor Sisters of the Monastery of St. Damian, and the unworthy little plant of our holy Father, in regard of our sublime vocation, and of the commandment of our Seraphic Father, I am engaged with my sisters to guard inviolably holy poverty, and I wish that those who succeed me in this office *be firm*, by the grace of God, to keep and to cause to be kept this poverty. We bow the knee, and we humble our mind and our body before the Roman Church, our holy Mother, and before the Pope, who is her chief, and in particular before the Lord Cardinal, who will be given for protector of the Religion of the Friars Minor. It is to him

that I recommend my sisters, those who are now and those who will be hereafter, in order that for the love of God, Who was born in the stable of Bethlehem, and Who died naked on the Cross, he will have care of this little flock which God has created in the holy Church, by the words and examples of our Blessed Father, St. Francis; and that, following the poverty and humility of our Lord and of the glorious Virgin, His Mother, he may make them observe the holy Poverty that we have promised. I supplicate also my Sisters, those who are now and who will be for the future, to lead a life accompanied by simplicity, humility, poverty, and holy conversation, such as our Lord has taught us. By the charity of Jesus Christ let us love each other, and make known the love we carry in our hearts by the works which appear, so that our good example may excite and help the Sisters to advance in the love of God, and in the charity and union which ought to be between them. Finally, let us consider that the road to Heaven is difficult, and the gate to enter in is strait; that there are few that enter; that if many enter for some time, few persevere; that those are truly happy to whom God has given the grace to enter, and to persevere until the end. Let us take good care not to withdraw from this way if we are already entered; not to injure our Lord, His holy Mother the Virgin, and our father, St. Francis. To obtain these graces I bow my knees before the Father of our Lord, in order that, by the merits of the glorious Virgin Mary, His Mother, and of our Seraphic Father, St. Francis, and of all the Saints, our Lord, who has given a good commencement, will give us the accomplishment, and give us also in time final perseverance. Amen."

St. Collette did not wish for a moment to alter the Rule of St. Clare, she endeavoured only to develop it by her "Constitutions." These Constitutions are divided into fifteen chapters.

The first speaks of those who enter the Order, and of their reception. Unmarried women and widows can be received, and a married woman, if her husband be also determined to go into religion. Those who from want of health, or of intellectual capacity, cannot fulfil the obligations, are excluded; also any one with a remarkable deformity, or those who are in debt, of bad reputation, or aged persons; persons over forty must not be admitted, except in particular cases; neither are those to enter who wish to avoid some misery in the world, or who are constrained by their parents. She directs that postulants applying for entrance are to be told all the rude austerities of the Rule. The manner in which the Sisters are to dispose of their worldly property is also touched on in this chapter. The second Chapter speaks of the dress of the Sisters, and orders the tunic to be of the same colour as the habit and mantle; all the clothing must be poor and humble, the stuff very thick and of low price, and all worldly appearance to be carefully shunned. No distinction is to be made for the Abbess or any of the Superiors. The Poor Clares are barefooted in the house, and are allowed wooden sandals when they go into the garden. In very cold countries the Mother Abbess is permitted to give additional clothing to those who require it. The third Chapter exacts that the Sisters go to the choir at night as in the day, at the first sound of the clock, and keep themselves in a perfect spirit of recollection, in order to prepare their souls for prayer. No Sister can be absent from Office without permission; all are obliged to recite the Offices. Besides the Divine Office, the Poor Clares say the Office of the Blessed Virgin, and that of the dead. The extern Sisters who have to beg for the community recite a number of prayers instead of the Office. St. Collette speaks also of mental prayer, and assigns two hours a day for this holy exercise. The fourth Chapter speaks of the perpetual fasting, and enforces the Rule, giving directions for its dispensation in case of sickness. The fifth Chapter speaks of the times for confession and of the confessors, of whom there are two,—the ordinary confessor, who comes weekly, and the extraordinary, who comes four times in the year. The sixth Chapter treats of the enclosure. St. Collette rules that there be only one parlour; that the *grille* be so arranged that the Sisters can neither see any one nor be seen, and that there be a *tour* near the *grille* to receive anything that may be given. The enclosure is perpetual, and can only be broken when a Sister goes from one convent to another, or in case of some grave accident. The seventh Chapter speaks of the elections—the officers of the convent are elected by the Sisters in Chapter—*i. e.*, the Abbess, the Vicaress, the novice mistress, two portresses, and eight discreets, who compose the council. The Chapter for the election is announced some days before. During this time all the Sisters ought to offer fervent prayers that the Divine Majesty may dispose all things to His greater glory. The day of the election they should all communicate with the same intention. The confessor and another priest must be present. All the community must assemble in the chapel, the priests being at the *grille;* the *Veni Creator* or other prayers are said; then the Abbess going out of office prostrates herself, and gives up the keys and seal of the Monastery. Then she acknowledges her faults in the fulfilment of her office, and afterwards quits the assembly. The Sisters then give their written suffrages, and it is so arranged that no one should know for whom each has voted. After the Chapter all the votes are burnt. The religious who has the majority is then proclaimed Abbess. In the same manner all the other elections are made. The Abbess must, if possible, be forty years of age, and be professed for eight years; she must never be less than thirty years, or professed less than five years. The Abbess can be deposed from her charge if her health should fail, or should she commit any grave fault. The eighth Chapter speaks of the conventual Chapters, which are held once a week; they must be held at a time not to interfere with the Divine Office or important occupations. In the first part of the Chapter, the names of benefactors, living and dead, are recommended; in the second, the Sisters acknowledge faults against the Rule; the third part consists of consultations on any affair of importance to the community. The ninth Chapter of the Rule speaks of silence, and enforces strict observance on this point. The tenth Chapter speaks of poverty; forbids the convents to be built as large or grand buildings, but they are to be poor, lowly, and simple. The eleventh Chapter speaks of the care of the sick, and shows the tender and benevolent spirit of this Saint, so unsparing to herself. The twelfth Chapter is on the manual labour, its time, its duration, and forbids the Superiors to let the Sisters work beyond their strength; it speaks also of recreation, and of the spirit which ought to prevail, and the holy conversation which ought to be held; and it speaks of books, and directs that the books which are used are those which tend to the spiritual advancement of the Sisters. In the thirteenth Chapter Saint Collette indicates the efficacious means to avoid relaxation in the communities. She says that relaxation does not come so much from the faults that are committed in religious houses, as from the negligence of Superiors in repressing them; and while she desires the Abbesses to reprove the Sisters in the spirit of humility and of sweetness, she warns them to take care not to open the way for abuses by weakness, disguised under a false appearance of gentleness and charity. The fourteenth Chapter speaks of the necessary cases in which persons must enter the convent, as doctors, workmen, &c., and points out the measures to be taken to avoid all kind of infractious to silence, modesty, and regularity. The fifteenth and last Chapter speaks of the ecclesiastical visits made either by the Franciscan Superior, or, in case of those convents under the immediate care of the Bishop, by him or his delegate.

The Rule thus explained by the Constitutions shows us plainly what is the life of a Poor Clare Colletine,—a life which may truly be called *miraculous*, for it is a miracle that young and delicate women should day by day bind themselves to crucify the flesh, and subdue our human nature. It will be interesting to give a brief history of the manner in which a nun of St. Clare passes her day.

At half-past four they rise, and after morning prayers make the "Way of the Cross," which is followed by Prime and Terce of the Divine Office, and the little hours of the Office of the Blessed Virgin, the Litany of the Saints, and various prayers. At half-past six, preparation for Holy Communion; seven, Mass—after Communion an hour's private thanksgiving, then the whole Rosary is said aloud; at nine, they go to work till eleven, then comes examen of conscience, Sext, None, and Angelus; at twelve, dinner (the first meal of the day); after dinner, a quarter of an hour for grace, Vespers, and Compline of our Lady, and a procession in honour of the Sacred Heart; at half-past one work is resumed; at half-past three, Litanies, Matins, and Lauds of the Blessed Virgin; at four, Vespers of Divine Office; at half-past, Office for the dead; at five, meditation till six; at six, collation (which consists of a few ounces of bread and a little beer); at half-past six, recommendation of benefactors, Compline, and prayers; at half-past seven, the nuns go to their cells, and at eight are in bed. They rise at eleven, say Matins and Lauds, and the Chaplet of the Holy Souls; it is followed by an hour's meditation, and at two the nuns go again to bed, to begin the day anew at half-past four. A weary life, it may seem, to read of; but not so to those who bind it in peace and joy, and at the occasional recreations nothing is more remarkable than their spirit of joyous gladness.

St. Collette has been far from the only glory vouchsafed to the Order of St. Clare. Numberless, indeed, are those chosen souls, who in the solitude of their convents have won the crown of saints; but of them even the Church knows nothing. They have been hidden in the recesses of the Sacred Heart of Jesus, and their names will be unknown till the hour when all shall receive their reward, and then it will be known to what height of sanctity they have risen. But some others there are whose deeds have been permitted by God to edify the faithful. Among these we may reckon the Blessed Cunégonde, daughter of the King of Hungary, and niece of St. Elizabeth. She laid aside her royal state for the poverty of the Clares, and in the religious life was distinguished for her poverty of spirit, and her burning love of God. She possessed the gift of prophecy, and many miracles were wrought by her hands, and after her death at her tomb. She was beatified by Clement the Eleventh, and her feast is kept on the twenty-seventh of July. St. Catherine of Bologna, too, is among the children of St. Clare.

The life and virtues of this eminent Saint are well known. She is celebrated not only for her marvellous virtues, but for her remarkable works on spiritual subjects. Perhaps the greatest of these is her " Treatise on Purgatory," in which her close union with God, and her clear insight into holy things, may plainly be seen. Her power of working miracles was most wonderful, and still to this day are they wrought before her shrine at Bologna; for there her blessed body rests, holy and uncorrupt, waiting for the morning of the Resurrection, when it shall rejoin the glorious soul.

Then again there was the Blessed Louise, daughter of the Duke of Savoy, who became a Poor Clare, and led such a life of perfection that she too was beatified. Nor must we forget the name of sweet Veronica Giurgliani, to whom it was vouchsafed to bear the stigmata of our Lord's Sacred Wounds. After a long life of heroic suffering, she could say, " All is little for the love of God: hail sorrows! hail sweet Cross !"

Many more names might be added to our list had we space to dwell on them. In a world of sin and turmoil, where God seems to be forgotten in His own creation, it is consoling to remember such lives as these have passed, nay, more, are passing still, for the life of the Poor Clares is not a thing of the past, but the present.

There are many branches of this Order. Some convents of the Poor Clares follow the original Rule, but without the Constitutions of St. Collette; others again follow the Rule of St. Clare, with some mitigations. In general, these communities have undertaken the charge of schools, and are therefore unable to support the full austerity of the ancient Rule. Some of the houses of the Poor Clares Colletines are governed by a Mother-General, who has the power of removing the religious from one convent to another. Other convents are independent; for a Generalate form of government was not prescribed for them by their founders, and its adoption is quite optional. The Poor Clares were, however, supposed to be under the charge of the General of the Franciscans, and in olden times the Fathers of St. Francis were their directors. Since the Revolution, it has been found better to place each convent under the Bishop of the diocese, who appoints the priests who have charge of them, and is their visitor. The convents of this Order are very numerous in Belgium; they exist also in many other countries, and England has for some years past possessed the blessing of two convents of the Poor Clares Colletines, from whence rises up unceasingly a fervent and acceptable intercession.

## ORDER OF THE PERPETUAL ADORATION OF THE BLESSED SACRAMENT.

The foundation of this Order was the commencement of another branch in the contemplative life. Devotion to the Blessed Sacrament was, indeed, no novelty in religion; on the contrary, it had ever been its mainspring and support, and the source from whence the religious drew fresh strength and vigour. But the seventeenth century brought a necessity for the formation of a new Order, especially devoted to the Adoration of the Blessed Sacrament. All through the " ages of faith" it had not been needed, for the heart of the Church always beat with reverential love for this great mystery, and no voice was bold enough to be raised against It. Those days were ended, and once more men had begun to say, " This is a hard saying, and who can hear it?" and swiftly after unbelief came blasphemy. Then, with the quick instinct of love, the Church came forward to make reparations for the outrages, and thus the Order of the Perpetual Adoration took its rise. While the world stormed and raged, denying this miracle of Divine love, a young girl, in a distant province of France, wept and prayed before the altar, and offered her life to God as a victim to repair these insults. Her name was Catherine de

Bar. There was nothing remarkable about her, and she never thought of founding a Religious Order; but, as she felt a vocation for the cloister, she entered a convent of the Annociades, at Brugères, an Order of nuns strictly enclosed, and devoted to prayer. Here she became a most fervent religious, and having passed through her noviciate, made her solemn profession. In this Order, after profession, the nuns make a ten days' retreat, called "the nuptial silence," during which they do not speak even to their Superior. During her retreat, the ring that she received at her profession broke without any apparent cause; and overwhelmed with grief at the incident, she ran to her Superior, and silently showed it to her. The Superior consoled her, telling her it was only a sign that she should not finish her days in that Order. In 1635, the disastrous wars in Lorraine spread misery around, and Catherine was compelled to leave her convent. The religious were dispersed, and many died of the pestilence then raging. After having spent some time in her father's house, Catherine was offered a refuge in a Benedictine convent still able to contend with the difficulties around; she accepted it, and after residing there some time, she sought and obtained the necessary permission to change her Order. She joined the Benedictine Order, taking as her religious name Mecthilde of the Holy Sacrament.

But not here was she yet to rest. Not long after her second profession, the Benedictines were driven from their convent and dispersed hither and thither, and were in great distress. A refuge was offered for some of them in a convent of their Order in Paris, and Mecthilde was one of those sent thither. Eventually a charitable lady gave them a house in Paris, in which the exiled community re-assembled. In course of time Mecthilde was elected Superior of this house, and her wisdom and sanctity were admired by many. Alas! there seemed no abiding refuge for poor Mecthilde and her nuns. The war of the Fronde brought confusion into Paris itself, and their house was attacked, and they again were homeless beggars. Their sore straits drew on them the compassion of some pious ladies, who provided them with necessaries, and formed ties of friendship with the Superior.

One of these ladies, the Marquise de Beauves, came one day to Mecthilde, telling her she felt the greatest desire to do something to honour the Blessed Sacrament, and she would give her a little money if she could think of any way of accomplishing this; and Mecthilde's instant answer was, it would be well to begin the Perpetual Adoration of the Blessed Sacrament. Many were the obstacles that stood in the way of the great undertaking. First, there was want of more money; then, when that was furnished by different friends, Anne of Austria declared she could not in the then perilous state of affairs sanction the foundation of any new convent, and as the Archbishop was of the same opinion as the Queen, the plan *apparently* fell to the ground.

The scourge of civil war grew still more fierce in France, and the Queen implored an holy priest of the name of Picotté, in whose prayers she had great confidence, to pray for mercy on France; adding, that whatever offering should appear to him in prayer as most likely to be acceptable to God, he might pledge in her name should be given, and Monsieur Picotté found himself drawn to vow for the Queen that she should establish an house of the Perpetual Adoration of the Blessed Sacrament; the priest being, however, in perfect ignorance of the project having been already on foot. The civil war ceased in France, Louis XIV. was seated firmly on the throne, and Mecthilde's loved devotion was at last commenced. To establish her Order perfectly was no easy task; to the extreme rigour of the Rule of St. Benedict was to be added the Perpetual Adoration of the Most Holy. However, with the help of God, Mecthilde accomplished her undertaking. She lived to found another house in Paris, as well as various others in the provinces, and she even saw her Institute spread into Poland. She had her share of the Cross; good people misunderstood her, spoke against her, and censured her to her face. She bore all with meekness; her great endeavour being to prevent her friends from defending her. She who was often before her Hidden Lord so patient amidst neglect, thought little of man's praise or blame. Long bodily sufferings too were her portion, but she rejoiced in them; and at length God called her to Himself, and she ended her long life of eighty-three years the 6th of April, 1698.

We must now give a short account of the peculiar observances of the Order. The nuns observed, as we have said, the Benedictine Rule in its full rigour; they kept strict enclosure, rose at two A.M. to say Matins, sang the whole of the Divine Office, spent much time in meditation and prayer, kept perpetual abstinence, and fasted the greater part of the year. To these observances the nuns of La Mère Mecthilde added, that by day and night a religious should be kneeling before the Tabernacle in the spirit of reparation. Every day one religious takes it, as her turn, to enter the Choir at the beginning of Mass with a cord round her neck and a torch in her hand, and there offers amends for the profanation done to the Holy Sacrament. In this spirit she communicates, "in order," says the Rule, "to unite herself with Jesus Christ, Who can alone worthily repair His glory and satisfy the Divine Justice." And at dinner-time she goes to the

Refectory, still wearing the cord round her neck, and there kneeling in the midst, she says,—

"My Sisters, let us remember that we are vowed to God in the quality of victims, to repair the outrages and profanations which are incessantly made to the most Holy Sacrament of the Altar. I ask the assistance of your prayers, that I may acquit myself as I ought."

She remains in Retreat the whole day to honour the solitude of the Son of God, and as the scapegoat of the ancient law driven into the desert and charged with the sins of the people. In this convent every hour of the day and night the great bell rings five times; and she who rings, and they who hear it, each say, "Blessed for ever be the Most Holy Sacrament of the Altar!" This sentence is further to be, as it were, their *watchword*. Before they speak to each other, whenever they go to knock at the door of any one's cell, their first words shall be this ejaculation of praise; when they go to the parlour, and when they write a letter, it shall be their first salutation. It shall be last on their lips when they go to rest, and the first when they awake; all the Hours of the Office begin and end with it, as well as grace in the Refectory, and their Chapters and Conferences; and each religious wears a large brass medal, bearing a figure of the Holy Sacrament, with these words engraved on its foot.

Every Thursday there is exposition of the Blessed Sacrament, and a general Communion: the Sisters abstain from manual work and from recreation, and a great silence, " in honour of the silence of Jesus," reigns in the house. On the vigils of great feasts recreation is omitted. At daily recreation all boasting of country, rank, or family is forbidden.

A deep devotion is also cherished for the Blessed Virgin, and every Saturday the nuns communicate in honour of her Immaculate conception.

Our Lady is called their only Abbess, and the Prioress is only her assistant; and they have a simple and touching custom of placing a table in the Refectory for their invisible Abbess, and upon it bread, wine, and the best food in the house, and after the meal is over this is given to the poor. The interior spirit which Mecthilde strove to plant in her nuns may be gathered by the following extracts from the Constitutions:—" They shall go into choir as if they were the Angels of God, with respectful love and profound recollection. She who has in charge the regulation of the chanting of the Office, shall remember that her office is like that of the angels who announced to the Shepherds the birth of the Son of God." " It is no longer in Bethlehem that He invites creatures to go and adore Him; it is before the Tabernacles, where He is so often without homage."

"The bell should be as a voice that awakes us to light a new fire in our hearts as victims, and to transport us with a holy fervour that cannot suffer remissness or negligence." "The perfect union of this Divine Mystery should produce charity in us, making us bear patiently with others, and deeming ourselves most guilty." "If they could choose their deaths, they should certainly desire to shed their blood at the foot of the altar; but as, by their vows, they have given up all right over themselves, they must ardently desire to die at the time, and in the manner, that God wishes." When any nun shall be in her last agony, the community assembles, all wearing cords round their necks, and torches in their hands, and kneeling they make reparation for the faults of her who is agonizing; and if it be possible, they put a cord upon the dying Sister, that she may die as a victim, *reparatrice*, and penitent.

After death, the body is watched day and night by two nuns, who pray for her soul. In the vacant place in the Refectory a cross is placed for thirty days after her death, a *De profundis* is said after grace, and the food she would, if living, have eaten, is still placed on her plate, and afterwards given to the poor. The Feast of Corpus Christi and its octave is celebrated in this Order with the greatest solemnity; every year on the Annunciation and during its octave, the community make acts of reparation for any faults and negligences committed by themselves during the year against the Blessed Sacrament, and they make a general communion of thanksgiving on the Annunciation—that day being the anniversary of the foundation of the Order in 1653. Whenever news is brought to the religious of any unusual outrage or insult to the Adorable Sacrament committed somewhere in the world, a public procession is made in reparation by these faithful servants, and each religious can, with permission, undertake some especial act of penance with the same intention. This Order, though practising the Benedictine Rule in all its rigour, cannot be considered strictly part of the Benedictine Order—the form of government is different. In this Order, the superioress is always called a prioress instead of an abbess, and it is strictly forbidden to elect her for life. The constitutions framed by Mecthilde were approved by the Apostolic Legate in 1668, and they were confirmed by Pope Innocent the Eleventh in 1676, and again by Clement the Eleventh in 1705. To the three vows of religion the religious add a fourth of Perpetual Adoration of the Blessed Sacrament.

One of the most celebrated religious of this Order was the Princess Louise Adelaide de Bourbon-Condé; and a brief notice of her life, who was one of the most remarkable of the women living in the eventful era of the great Revolution, will serve further to illustrate the beautiful intention and spirit of the Order of the Perpetual Adoration.

### THE PRINCESS LOUISE ADELAIDE DE BOURBON-CONDÉ, CALLED IN RELIGION MARIE JOSEPH DE LA MISÉRICORDE.

LOUISE ADELAIDE DE BOURBON was the youngest daughter of that Prince de Condé who suffered so much by his loyal devotion to the unhappy Louis XVI. She was born on the 2nd October, 1755. Her mother was of the noble house of Rohan-Loubise. She died in 1762, and for her virtue and piety was called the Saint. After her mother's death, Louise was placed under the care of her aunt, the Abbess of Beaumont les Tours, about sixty leagues from Paris. The day when she entered the Abbey all the nuns were assembled to welcome her, as was the custom, and a great number of people followed her there. After the little Princess had been shown the interior of the convent, she was asked where next she would like to go. "Oh! take me," she answered, "where there is the most noise." And afterwards, being in church, she was told she might retire as soon as she liked; hardly was the first Psalm of Compline ended when she touched the nun who had charge of her, and whispered, "I have had enough of it." Strange commencement of a life which was to end in continual adoration before the Sacrament of the Altar! And though afterwards she scrupulously observed all the outward forms of piety, and even tried to imitate the nuns in their silence and demeanour, she herself tells us that "she does not remember having been really pious in her childhood." After seven years spent in the convent she returned to her father; but before leaving she made her first Communion under the guidance of her aunt, whose holy teaching and preparation sank deeply into the heart of Louise. The seed was then sown which would afterwards produce such abundant fruit. After that first great action, which stamps a young life for so much good or so much evil, she returned to the world. Then there opened before her a contrast so great, that a young and fresh mind might well feel dizzy at the sight. She was presented at the Court of Louis XVI.,—a Court which glittered in all the false brilliancy of sin and worldliness. But the almighty power of grace worked in Louise's heart; her guardian angel walked beside the motherless child as she threaded her way amid the *salons* of alluring splendour. The force of early lessons and youthful impressions gained influence on her mind, and she writes that she had no wish to live like the worldly. "My real inclination," she says, "was to lead a quiet, simple, retired life. It often happened that I was put out, because some party of pleasure would interrupt the routine of my life, and yet I never refused or shrunk from it, because, once there, I found amusement." And yet deep in her heart the voice of God was whispering and bidding her give herself entirely to Him.

At this time she formed a very strong friendship with the Princesses Elizabeth and Clotilde. The latter was her dearest companion, and the strong attraction which Clotilde felt for the religious life doubtless tended to strengthen the same in the heart of Louise. Strange it is now to recal the days when these three young girls, royally born, and surrounded by every softness and luxury, sat together and formed plans for their future. How different was that of each to be! Clotilde, whose heart's desire it was to be hidden in a cloister, was destined to relinquish the desire, to wear a crown, and live in the very midst of the world's dazzle and glare, overwhelmed with the bitterest sorrows and cares a sovereign was ever called upon to endure; and yet through it all, through prospeity and adversity, was so to rule her life that the voice of Holy Church should declare her blessed. Elizabeth's path was to be a swifter and sharper road to a sure and eternal rest; and Louise was to join her beloved friends again, after a long life of tribulations and disappointments, but of unswerving fidelity to God as we shall further see. Time passed on. Clotilde was married to the Prince of Piedmont, heir to the throne of Sardinia, and Louise had her house in the Rue Monsieur, where she lived with the state and retinue suitable to her rank. In her garden there was a grating, to which at certain times the poor would troop, and *Mademoiselle* would serve them with her own hands. And though she mixed among the gay scenes of her father's princely court, she was not afraid to witness against the false maxims of the world. She was accustomed to attend the private theatricals then in fashion, and at which plays were often, if not always, acted, from which Christian ears should shrink to listen. The celebrated Jesuit, Père Beauregard, courageously raised his voice against the impiety of the time, and God had given him the grace of convincing many who came to hear. He preached against the corrupt literature of the day, and when his sermons were ended, many came to lay their evil books at his feet, and promise never to touch them again. He preached against these disgraceful theatricals; and, among others, his words made such an impression on Mademoiselle de Condé, that she resolved never again to be present at this amusement, nor could either anger or sarcasm make her break her resolution. And she was faithful in obeying the commandments of the Church, and while the courtiers mocked and feasted, the Princess ate her fasting fare. But peaceful days for the house of Bourbon were drawing to a close. Heavy were the hearts of those who loved the King; and the Prince de Condé determined to leave France, and to seek from foreign countries the aid he clearly saw would soon be necessary to maintain Louis XVI. on the throne. Louise accompanied her father, first to Brussels, afterwards to Turin. There they separated for a time, and it was while living alone at Fribourg that Louise made up her mind to enter the religious life, and she wrote to her father to ask his consent. " I will open my heart entirely to you. Always, even at those times when I have seemed most easily to give myself up to the pleasures of the world, to follow its maxims and its customs the closest, the *attrait* for the religious life has existed in my heart's depths. This *attrait* has become now not only a desire, but an irresistible *want* of my soul, so that I have finally taken the unalterable resolution to delay no longer the consecration of myself to God. * * * My father, from the depth of my heart, I solicit your consent. Oh! you who, as is fitting, have never hesitated to sacrifice your two sons to honour, will you hesitate to sacrifice your daughter to her God, to your God, to the God whom my good mother loved and served so well? It is He alone who calls me to this state of life. Oh! do not believe that disgust of the world, strengthened by the terrible events which have succeeded each other, influence my decision. If these unforeseen events have produced a change in my position, it is so much the better for my taste for a solitary and retired life. * * * You cannot then attribute my determination to human motives, or to a momentary vexation, or believe even that it is only rest that I seek, and that I wish to sacrifice everything to the tranquillity which I love. No, it is only God who can have the preference over all that is dearest to me; but I should be still more guilty in not giving myself to Him, because I know by experience that I am not of any use to you in the world. I have the hope of being more so to you when I have offered myself in sacrifice to God; if He deigns not to reject me, as I delight to think, without however being certain, because a long probation must precede my final engagement. * * * My father, I throw myself into your arms; I press you to my heart, always, oh! always, be very sure your daughter loves you; but it is at the foot of the Altar that she desires to prove the truth of this to you." She had also written to ask the consent of the King, for the old traditions of French loyalty made the Bourbons look on the head of their family as a clan does upon its chief. Louis replied as follows: " You have well reflected, my dear cousin, on the step that you have taken. Your father has given his consent, I give mine also, or rather I give it to Providence, who asks this sacrifice from me. I will not conceal from you that it is a great one, and it is with extreme regret that I lose the hope of seeing you one day, by your virtues, become the example of my Court, and the edification of all my subjects. I have but one consolation: it is of thinking that while the valour and talents of your nearest relations are aiding me to preserve the throne of St. Louis, your prayers will draw down the benedictions of the Most High on my cause, and, finally, on all my reign. I recommend this, then, to you; and I beg you, my dear cousin, be well persuaded of all my affection for you.—LOUIS."

Swiftly passed away the year of noviciate in the Capuchine or Franciscan Convent at Turin which the Princess entered. An idea had been raised of forming a convent of the exiled religious of France, into which Louise would be received; but she foresaw the difficulties of such a re-union, and she dreaded it for herself.

"There I should fear," said she, "the deference which by habit they would give to my rank. The place that I am ambitious for is the last of all. Ah! what are the thrones of the universe compared to that last place!" The time for her profession as a Capuchine drew near; but not as yet was the longing desire to be satisfied. The revolutionary troops were on the frontiers of Piedmont, and the hated name of Bourbon would be sufficient to bring ruin and devastation into the convent, and Louise was obliged to leave her loved retreat, and go as *Dame Pensionnaire* into a Convent of the Annonciades, in order that she might be ready for flight at any moment, and that she might not involve others in her misfortunes.

These fears were soon realized. She fled in haste from Turin, and took refuge in Bavaria; but the government dared not give shelter to a Bourbon-Condé, and drove out the exile. She then went to Vienna, and claimed an asylum from the Emperor of Austria, which was granted, and she resided for more than a year in a Convent of the Visitation. Her mental sufferings at this time were very severe. She had no attraction for the Order of the Visitation, and though she continued to observe all the rules of a religious life, as far as possible, and lived in great retirement, her heart was oppressed with anguish at the thought of not really being consecrated to God by vow. Her director counselled her to make a retreat; she did so, and we will give what followed in her own words.

"The ninth day of my retreat, my director laid before me the idea, not of a simple act of consecration, which is in reality the work of the Sacrament of

Baptism, but a secret and more particular engagement by the three vows of religion,—Poverty, Obedience, and Chastity. By this, he said to me, you will be truly a religious in the eyes of God, and your ardent desires will be satisfied. Further, it will not prevent you, when obstacles are removed, from taking the religious habit, and making a solemn profession in any Order. This was merely a proposition, and I ought to add, that he did not press me to accept it. But there was no need for him to do so. The continual burning ardour which had so long consumed me answered the question, and the accomplishment was fixed for the next day, the Presentation of the Blessed Virgin. In the interval, one thing perplexed me; it seemed to me that, not being a member of any community, my vow of obedience would be an illusion if I did not promise to practise it towards some person in particular; and I was so anxious to act towards my God with a pure intention, and with simplicity, and, above all, without misusing words, that I asked my confessor to be that person. He made some difficulty, though for a long time I had actually practised strict obedience to him. At last he consented. I ought to observe, that in the form of the vows I pronounced I promised obedience to my present confessor as long as Providence left me under his guidance." The next morning she pronounced her vows secretly at Holy Communion; but her own words best tell in what manner the act was done.

"My heart is very unworthy of you," said I to Jesus Christ, my Love; "but as a wife ornaments herself with the jewels she has received from her husband to please his eyes, so I ornament my heart with the gifts that Thou wilt deign to give me in this day of graces and happiness. I invoked the help of saints also; I asked contrition from St. Peter, an interior spirit from St. Joseph, charity for others from St. John, mortification from St. Francis, zeal for souls from St. Teresa, and Divine love from the Magdalene. With these feelings I heard Mass, begging that some drops of the blood of the Holy Victim might purify my heart. The moment was come! I raised my eyes, and by faith I saw my God in the Adorable Host; then I pronounced, in His Holy Presence, and in that of the Blessed Virgin, the angels and saints, and all the celestial court, the secret vows which consecrated me to Jesus Christ, my Saviour, my faithful Friend, my Father, my best Beloved, my all, and my God. I had nothing to give him; nothing to sacrifice. Then succeeded a rest of soul, which I can only compare to what we feel when, after having run far beyond our strength, we are suddenly stopped, and everything is done to refresh us after our long fatigue. At the end of my thanksgiving I said the

Magnificat and the Te Deum, joining with the Blessed Virgin and the angels, and I said also the prayer *Suscipe*. I did not neglect in spirit the ceremony of the funeral pall. I implored from God the grace to die to all things, and to live only to God and for God."

Nothing displays better the loving and generous nature of Louise de Bourbon than this extract from her papers. Although this sacred act imparted a rest and calmness to her soul, and brought down on her abundant graces, it never prevented her from longing and praying that she might be professed in a regular community; for she knew her private vows, though holy and acceptable before God, were very different from any pronounced in an Order sanctioned by Holy Church. She soon formed a great desire of becoming a Trappiste nun, and of joining the colony of that Order at Valais, whither they had fled when the Monastery of La Trappe was suppressed. She accomplished her wish, and her letters express her joy at being again in community. "Ah! I am going to retake the very of Jesus Christ, my Spouse and my Love This place is not what people think it. I know not where the austerity is which they paint as so dreadful. Here I see fresh and rosy faces, but what is better still, happy, holy, and peaceful faces. * * * I cannot feel *ennui* here, and it seems to me I have all I want, or at least all that is necessary for

Christian souls who have taken Jesus crucified for their Master and for their model; the silence, recollection, and peace, are most touching in this regular and fervent house." Here Louise entirely enjoyed her wish of laying aside her rank; for her companions, from the simplicity of the dress she wore on entering, took her at first for a Swiss peasant, and though her bearing soon undeceived them, it was long ere they knew who she really was. Alas, poor Louise! not yet had she found her resting-place, for where in Europe at that time was there repose for any? Again the storm broke, and the community were obliged to fly. Dom Augustin, the head of the Order, could not see any safe place of refuge for his religious except in Russia, and he begged Louise to write to the Emperor by her secular name, and entreat his permission for their arrival in his dominions.

Long ago, at the brilliant festivities of the Prince de Condé, had the Emperor Paul, travelling under the title of the "*Comte du Nord*," been the guest of Madame Louise, and now she wrote to beseech his protection as an exile. "I pray the amiable Comte du Nord," she wrote gracefully, "to be my interpreter with the Emperor Paul." The most affectionate answer came from the Emperor, and all the Royal Family of Russia, and the colony of La Trappe, after a long and painful voyage, settled at Orcha, in Russie Blanche. After some months, for reasons which do not appear, Dom Augustin determined to emigrate with his community to America. As the Princess was not yet professed, she was free to act, and her director strongly advised her not to go there. She accordingly left the Trappists, and proceeded to a Benedictine Convent in Prussia. The step cost her still more than that of quitting the Capuchins, years before.

"It was necessary to strip myself again of the livery of my Lord," she said. "I did it, and did not die, that is all that I can say."

After residing as a boarder some time with the Benedictine nuns in *Nienoiz*, she heard there was a Convent of the Order of the Perpetual Adoration at Warsaw, in Poland, and she felt God called her there. Thither then she went, and found in this holy institute all that she could desire; and fervently she thanked God, who had led her by a way of sorrow and disappointment to the place whither He called her. Her *third* noviciate was passed even more fervently than the others, and on the 21st of September, 1802, she made her solemn profession.

It was in the convent at Warsaw that one of the sharpest griefs of her life came upon Louise. Her long separation from her family had never weakened her attachment to them, and, next to her father, she cherished most dearly her nephew, the Duc d'Enghien. From his birth he had been her darling, and among her papers was found the following beautiful prayer, which she composed while the little Louis Antoine was yet an infant:—" Oh Mother of my God, who seest the anxiety of my heart regarding the frightful dangers that Louis Antoine will encounter in entering the world, have pity on him, protect his innocence and weakness, surrounded by a thousand snares; pray for him, most Holy Virgin, that God may touch his heart, enlighten his spirit, and calm his impetuous passions; and pray to the God of mercy and goodness never to permit him to lose his faith. Blessed Virgin, be a mother and protectrice to Louis Antoine." And from the Capuchine Convent at Turin she wrote as follows to the young Prince:—

"Dec. 23, 1795.

"Yes, my dear child, it is from a convent I write to you, and wish you a happy new year. I do more than wish it for you, I ask such for you from God, with all my heart. I have the hope that He Who is so good will hear me; that He will pour His benedictions on you, and never suffer those germs of faith and religion, which to my joy I have seen in you, to be trodden down. May they grow, and take firm root, and make you what you ought to be, and what I desire to see you. I will not weary you with repeating how contented I am at finding myself in the position I have so long wished for. It is a sort of happiness which must be tasted to be understood. All that I can tell you is, that I did not find such in the riches, or the joys, or pleasures of the world. Try to send the enclosed letter to my dearest brother. Love him, dear child. I entrust his happiness to you who can so much contribute to it. I say the same for my father: you are all so dear to me. But my God has had the preference, I acknowledge it. Could it be otherwise?"

And ever since her heart's prayers had followed the career of this beloved boy, and the tidings of his gallantry and his loyalty had thrilled her with joy. "I am a Frenchman, sire," wrote the Duc to Louis XVIII., "who is faithful to his God, to his King, and to his oaths." How could a soul like his dream of the base treachery that surrounded him! It was in 1804 that the tragedy of Vincennes was enacted. Who can read without emotion the account of the death of that young and gallant prince, rudely awakened from his sound sleep on a rough bed, and led at midnight before his judges? "I have fought with my family to recover the heritage of my ancestors, but since peace has been made, I have laid aside my arms; I see there are no longer kings in Europe," said he boldly. The judges hesitate, and send to Napoleon to know what to do. Swiftly comes the brief answer: "*Condemned to death;*" and when Cambacérès pleaded for him, the tyrant answered, "Since when have you become so avaricious of the blood of a Bourbon?"

"Never permit him to lose his faith," was the prayer that for long years had gone up for Louis Antoine; and when in the gloom of the night, without flinching a nerve, the Duc stood before his assassins, saying, "At least I shall die a soldier's death," he turned to his jailors and demanded a priest. "Wouldest thou, then, die like a Capuchin?" said they insultingly, "the priests are all in bed now." No indignant reply passed his lips, but he meekly knelt down and made that brief but fervent prayer for pardon, which was doubtless accepted. One last thought of earth as he cut off a tress of hair for his fondly loved wife, and this hope of the Bourbon-Condés was infamously slain, and the name of Bonaparte eternally stained. Such was the news that the Abbé Edgeworth de Firmont, the same who had been the revered director of Madame Elizabeth, and the consoler of Louis XVI. on the scaffold, brought to Warsaw. On receiving the news, the Princess fell with her face upon the earth, crying, "Mercy, my God, have mercy on him!" and soon after she poured out her heart, saying, "Have mercy, Lord, on the soul of Louis Antoine! Pardon the faults of his youth, remembering the Precious Blood which Jesus Christ shed for all men, and have regard to the cruel manner in which his has been shed. Glory and misfortune have attended his life. But what *we* call glory, has it any claim in Thy Eyes? However, Lord, it is not a demerit before thee, when it is based on true honour, which is always inseparable from devotion to our duties. Thou knowest, Lord, those that he has fulfilled; and for those in which he has failed, let the misfortunes of which he has been at last the victim, be a reparation and an expiation. Again, Lord, I ask for mercy on his soul. Oh, young and unfortunate victim! I have reason to hope that in thy last moments thy faith and religion were stedfast. Thou hast shown it. Let us give thanks unto our God."

But from that day forward another name was constantly on the lips of Louise while praying before God, the last that the world would have expected to hear, that of *Napoleon Bonaparte.* Long afterwards she said, " He made himself my enemy by killing my nephew, and from that moment God gave me grace to name him daily in my prayers." About this time also, amongst the prayers which she often composed were some on the seven corporal and spiritual works of mercy; and in the one on praying for the living and the dead, she added, " and for those who persecute us;" and in the prayer she said, " I pray Thee especially, Lord, for those who have sought, are seeking, or will seek, to injure me." We cannot but remark here that forgiveness of enemies was a characteristic of the Bourbons at this time. No one can forget the dying charge of Louis XVI.; and Queen Clotilde of Sardinia, writing to the Princess Louise, said, " The most brilliant crown that a soul can receive in heaven is to see near her the soul of one of her enemies; above all, when it is by her tears that she has obtained the salvation of that soul."

Not long after this terrible blow, it was thought well by her ecclesiastical superiors to send the Princess to England, where she entered a convent of her Order at Rodney Hall, Norfolk. In London she met her father and brother, whom she had not seen for ten years, during which so many heavy sorrows had fallen on their house. It was an affecting meeting, and for some days the long separated exiles remained together. The Princess then entered the Benedictine Convent, where she passed the following nine years. During this quiet period of her life many of her beautiful and edifying writings on the spiritual and religious life were composed. Six years after her arrival the community moved from Rodney Hall to Heath; and while residing in this latter house Louise became acquainted with the Père de la Fontaine, of the Society of Jesus. He became her director, and under his care she made rapid progress in virtue. Her veneration for this holy religious was very great, for she comprehended well the sanctity of his life.

The Père de la Fontaine united a great knowledge of the interior life to the high standard of virtue, which he put into practice. He had long experience in the spiritual life, and understood well how to guide the fervent soul of Louise. All his advice sank deeply into her heart; and that she might not lose any of it, she committed it to writing, and this valuable record was found among her papers. It evidences the extreme simplicity which, we are told, was the characteristic of the holy man. "Never neglect," says he, "the interior reproaches which your heart makes to itself. Ask from God constantly a great delicacy of conscience, and follow it faithfully in all things. Try always to have a sweet, agreeable, and cheerful manner, without being drawn into dissipation." He also recommends to her frequent recourse to the Sacraments, great fidelity to rule, and submission to directors; and he gives many other counsels hardly to be understood by those who have not, like Louise de Bourbon, made great progress in the interior life.

The next event in the life of Louise was her return to France, when the Bourbons were again called to the throne of their fathers. It was Louise's earnest wish to re-establish a convent of her Order in Paris, so that the work of reparation to the Blessed Sacrament might again be continued in a city where such awful sacrileges had been committed. The Princess lodged for some time in the hotel of the Duchess of Bourbon, having her own apartments, and living a most retired life with two religious who accompanied her, while waiting to see what house the King could give her for her convent. The magnificent building of the *Val du Grâce* was first thought of, but it was larger than Madame Louise required.

In the confusion of affairs consequent on a change of dynasty, the choice of this house was a real difficulty, and the Vicar-General of Paris recommended that a *Novena to Louis XVI.*—whom none doubted was in heaven—should be made among those interested in the work. On the seventh day of the Novena, a member of the Council of State suddenly interrupted the discussion on other affairs which was going on, and recalling the subject of Madame Louise, proposed the *Temple* should be given to her. A thrill ran through the assembly; there was not a dissentient voice; and the only doubt remaining was whether Madame Louise would like to spend her life in the place for ever consecrated to such sad memories. Louise hesitated for a moment, and then she saw that for a convent of *expiation* the Temple was indeed the fittest place, and she recognised the designs of God in having crossed her desire both for the Capuchine and Trappist Orders, to reserve her for this especial end. One sacrifice she must at once make on entering; it was impossible that the Duchess of Angoulême could revisit a place in which she had suffered such cruel agonies, and intercourse with this loved friend must be relinquished. The workmen began to raise new walls upon the ruins of the Temple, and preparations were busily proceeding when the *Cent Jours* commenced, and once more the family of Bourbon became exiles, and again did the Princess fly to England for shelter. As it was supposed the fortunes of her house would soon again be in the ascendant, she did not re-enter her convent, but remained in London. Meanwhile, the works at the Temple proceeded. Madame Louise returned to France in 1816, and in December of that year she entered the Convent of the *Temple*. There the remainder of her life was passed, and there she daily displayed the virtues she had acquired in the school of suffering. Here, in 1820, she received the news of the murder of the Duc de Berri; her tender heart was torn with anguish, and she could not be consoled till her friend the Père de la Fontaine came to her, and his few simple words, "The Lord has covered him with the mantle of His mercy," reassured and calmed her. While in the Temple, Louise received many visits from this holy Jesuit. She once related to her Sisters, that being in the greatest distress of mind one day, she was kneeling in a place by which the Père de la Fontaine passed on his way from the sacristy to the Altar to say his Mass, as he went by his shadow fell on her, and at that instant all trouble left her, and her soul was filled with peace: she had long reverenced him as a Saint, and she did not wonder at the incident. The following year this dear friend was taken from her, and on hearing of his death she wrote to the Jesuits begging for some account of his last hours. Her request was complied with, and the simple and touching details of the way in which he ended his life were found among her papers.

The death of the Prince de Condé was another sharp sorrow. During his illness some of her family begged Louise to ask for a dispensation from the Archbishop, and visit her father; but she stedfastly refused. She would not suffer her rank or position to be made an excuse for breaking her Rule. " If our Holy Father the Pope orders me," said she, " I will obey; but I will never ask for a dispensation which can authorize the example of breaking enclosure." Her sufferings were, however, great; her stall in choir was found bathed with tears, and many were the prayers that went up for her dying father. They were surely heard. When the Prince de Condé was asked if he forgave his enemies, he said, " I am certain of salvation if God will pardon me as I have pardoned them." Nothing was more observable in Louise de Bourbon than the contempt in which she held her worldly rank; nothing displeased her more than to see any one forget the religious in the Princess. The Vicar-General of Paris had been raised to the See of *St. Flour.* Writing to him, she had addressed him by his title, and in reply, he remarked he thought it was not the etiquette for French Princesses to do so. "No," she writes back to him, "Princesses in France do not; but when one of them has the honour of wearing the livery of Jesus Christ, when in His infinite mercy He has drawn her from the shadows of the vain glory of this world to make her His Spouse, to place her on the steps of His Altar, feeling, as she does, her infinite unworthiness, and the greatness and majesty of her Divine Spouse, what can she refuse to His ministers? So, since the moment I received the sacred veil I have cast etiquette under foot, and wherever I am I call the Bishops *Monseigneur.*" About this time the news of Napoleon's death came to France. Louise, writing to the same Bishop, says, "Bonaparte is dead; he was your enemy, for he persecuted you. I think you will say a Mass for him; I beg also a Mass from you to be said on my part for this unfortunate man."

One of Madame Louise's greatest cares was to erect a suitable Conventual Church, dedicated to St. Louis. When the bells of this church were *baptized*, a grand ceremony took place, for the King came to be sponsor. On this day, however, Madame Louise unfortunately missed her footing, and fell with some force. She made light of the accident for several days, but fever set in, and it proved to be the beginning of her last illness. It lasted for six months, and she bore it with patience and sweetness. She felt still more keenly the absence from Paris of her director, the Bishop of *St. Flour;* but she murmured not. For some days before her death she could not speak, and she could not take leave of her beloved brother; but her last hours were peaceful, and she calmly slept into death.

Her writings are numerous, all upon religious subjects, and all showing that she had made great progress in the interior life. Her religious also had carefully retained many of her sayings and wise counsels. Once, speaking of the way in which we should receive humiliations, she advised all to say, " Lord, it seems to me that I ought to receive some glory from this; it is refused, I accept this refusal, and I give to Thee, in the simplicity of my heart, all praise, all honour, all glory, *all*. Amen." In her private rules for self-control (found among her papers) are these brief but beautiful ones. "When I am moved to anger, pronounce three times the Holy Name of Jesus. When I feel self-love, invoke Jesus humiliated, praying Him to destroy in me the thirst for esteem. To pray much for the persons who are a trouble to me. In moments of fear, to say, 'What fearest thou? thou carriest Jesus and His Love in thy heart.' In an occasion of mortifying self, to say, 'Oh, Sacred Heart of Jesus! I die to this pleasure, to live only to Thy Love. After falling into a fault,—'Oh, my only Love! pray for your poor creature, and repair the ill that I have done.'" There is a beautiful custom in the Convents of this Order of holding a Chapter the last day in the year, called the Chapter of Peace, at which all the religious ask mutual pardon for any offences against each other. This practice was very dear to the holy Prioress, and the touching exhortations which she made to her religious at these times were carefully recorded by the nuns. In her last illness, she insisted on leaving her bed, in order to attend the Chapter of Peace. The convent founded by the Princess Louise is still a large and flourishing community. There are two convents of the Order in England; and thus for two hundred years, while loud voices have argued and blasphemed against the Most Blessed Sacrament, in the convents of this Institute of Mectilde a perpetual offering of reparation and love has ascended on high.

## ORDER OF THE VISITATION OF THE BLESSED VIRGIN.

ALTHOUGH the Order founded by Mectilde du Saint Sacrament was especially intended for the wants of modern times, in its spirit of peculiar reparation for the unbelief of the age, it still retained all the observances of the old penitential Orders. And now a new era had commenced in religious life; as the battle increased in fury, and the "foes of her own household" ranged themselves against the Church, so did her army of faithful souls multiply; and those who could not have consecrated themselves to God in the existing Orders, had new Institutes founded, in which they could serve Him with glory and gratitude. St. Francis of Sales, says Father Faber, introduced a new school of theology into the Church. He would seem, therefore, the very man marked out to found a new Order.

Let us look for a moment then at that most beautiful portrait, the character of St. Francis de Sales. He was a son of an illustrious house, the darling child of pious parents, who spared nothing in cultivating his talents, and training him to shine among the men of his time. When he turned away from the professions and chose the priesthood, there seems to have been no opposition. He passed rapidly from the priesthood to the episcopate; and was thus, as a young man, placed on a somewhat giddy eminence. Not only had he the gifts of birth, wealth, influence, and position, but it was given to him to possess one still more wonderful—power over the hearts of men.

He preached, and his hearers turned from an evil life; he heard confessions, and his penitents came away penetrated with compunction and with love. When he asked a favour, nothing could be refused. Wherever he went he was loved and honoured. How difficult it seems to us, in the midst of all this, to follow so closely a crucified Lord. St. Francis had found the secret. He loved his Saviour with an intensity and a fire that broke through all barriers. All worldly advantages were consecrated to His glory; all human love seemed poor and faint in the echo of the Divine whisper. St. Francis de Sales lived and died to teach us that it is not only in sackcloth and penance that we may win heaven.

And the Order of the Visitation is a reflex of his spirit.

As the Visitation was an Order for women, it was necessary St. Francis should have some coadjutrice in the design. A great number of holy women were under the Saint's direction, but this Order was to bear the impress of the Holy Spirit from its very foundation, and therefore it was revealed to Francis by Divine inspiration whom the first nun of the Visitation should be.

Jane Frances de Chantal was one of those whom God chooses for His very own by an unfailing token. She had been called to suffer early and long. The husband of her youth was shot by the blunder of a friend, in the midst of the careless sport of a summer day. Her bright happy home was then exchanged for one in which she was the very slave of one of her father-in-law's menials. Besides this, her soul was tried by long successions of those agonising interior sufferings, often worse than external martyrdom. Thus was the spirit perfected. God at length threw her in the way of the Bishop of Geneva, and under his wise direction she obtained great peace and tranquillity of mind. He singled her out for the foundress of the new Order. Great and sore were her trials in leaving her father and family; of her children, some were settled in life, others went with her.

On the 6th of June, 1610, the day being Trinity Sunday, and the Feast of St. Claude, Madame de Chantal, with three other Sisters, received the Rule from the hands of St. Francis, and began their noviciate.

The original intention of St. Francis was that the religious should only take simple vows, and go out of their convent to visit the poor, and therefore he dedicated them to the *Visitation* of our Blessed Lady to St. Elizabeth; but in a short time his wish was overruled, and St. Francis yielded to the advice of others, prescribed strict enclosure, and when in due time the Order received confirmation from the Holy See, the nuns made solemn vows. The leading idea of St. Francis de Sales in the Rule of the Visitation was this: he wanted an Order into which the aged and the infirm in health might enter,—persons who could not have been received into strict and penitential Orders. St. Francis fixed on the "Rule of St. Austin," as the one by which his religious should live, and he composed Constitutions, and a "Directory," adapted for the peculiar end of his institute.

In the Visitation, then, there were to be no severe penances, no long fasting, no rising at midnight, no laborious toil; but as the members of it had entered to bear their cross and follow their Lord, they were to practise the mortifications St. Francis knew well how to follow and to teach. The spirit and the soul were to be kept in absolute subjection, the interior mortification was to be so constant and so universal, that it is said many deem the penitential Orders, in reality, less severe to human nature.

The Constitutions of the Visitation say, "Many girls and women, by Divine inspiration, aspire very often to the religious life, who, either from the weakness of their health, or from age, or from not being drawn to the practice of austerity, and exterior rigour, cannot enter as religious, where they are obliged to undertake great corporal penances, as do most of the Orders now, and so have to tarry amid the toils of the world, exposed to danger of sin, or at least of losing the fervour of devotion, in which case certainly they are worthy of great compassion; for a generous soul is to be pitied who desires to retire from the noise of the world, to live only to God, and who cannot do it because she has not a body strong enough, or health good enough, or the freshness of youth." "Widows can be received, if they have no children, for whom it is their duty to live in the world and provide."

The Visitation was not founded in peace. There were storms without, and calumnies and misrepresentations. When it was seen that among the first ten sisters there were not two who were really strong, people told St. Francis he was founding an hospital, not a convent. "What would you have me to do?" replied the Saint. "I am the partisan of invalids;" and he went fearlessly on with his design. He says again in the Constitutions, "Those who from ill health are refused by other Orders, can enter if they have a mind ready to live in profound humility, obedience, simplicity, sweetness, and resignation, only excepting those who have contagious maladies, or who have such pressing infirmities that they are altogether incapable of following the Rule, or the ordinary exercises of the congregation." The whole of these directions seem, in truth, to breathe the true spirit of St. Francis de Sales, by the union of sweet gentleness with firmness, and by the lofty aspirations they inspire.

The Order of the Visitation was not intended *only* for the aged and sickly, but simply it should be wide enough to admit them. Thus the Constitutions go on to say, "Those who are strong and well can enter, as called by God to the succour of the infirm; and while the feeble enjoy the benefit of the health of the robust, those enjoy equally the merit of the patience of the weak. The Superioress shall take care that no corporal austerity be introduced by rule, so that, like the parable, there can enter into the religious state as the nuptial feast of the Celestial Spouse, not only the healthy and strong, but also the infirm, lame, and blind, so that the house be filled with guests." There is hardly an Order in the Church which possesses a Rule carried to such minutiæ by the Founder himself. Everything was regulated by him, every difficulty was foreseen and provided against. The Sisters of the Visitation are divided into three classes: the Sisters of the Choir, who are obliged to sing the Office; the

Associate Sisters, who are not under this obligation; and the lay Sisters. The Choir Sisters are obliged to say the Office of the Blessed Virgin: the proper chanting of the Office is much insisted on, the words are pronounced very slowly, and the chant is a most simple one, so that the chanting of the Visitation Office is to the taste of many of unearthly beauty and sweetness. The Associate Sisters are persons who are unable to chant; in all other respects they live like the others, and can hold any of the offices of the house, even that of Superioress, but not that of Assistant, because this Sister must always see that the Office be properly chanted. Each house of the Visitation is to consist of thirty-three Sisters, of whom twenty must be of the Choir. The Superioress must have been professed for five years, and be not less than thirty years of age. She is assisted in the government of the house by a council of four. Two of the Sisters are chosen, and called *Surveillantes*, whose business it is to observe any faults that are committed, and to confer with the Superioress about them. The Mistress of the Novices is bid " to exercise her novices in obedience, sweetness, and modesty, and to clear away from their characters all those follies, tendernesses, and sickly humours by which minds, especially those of women, are often made languid and enfeebled." She is to instruct them in the best methods of prayer and meditation, and other spiritual exercises. Another Sister is called the Aide of the Superioress; her duty is to warn her of the faults she may commit; and if the Sisters have any complaint to make of the Superioress, they can address themselves to this Sister.

The duties of the Sacristan are very minutely laid down, and the Altar is ordered to be as rich and precious as could be, with prudence, done; their images are to be well made, and approved of by the Spiritual Father, and no tawdry ones are to be allowed in any part of the house. Great neatness and cleanliness is ordered in the house, and for this reason silver spoons are permitted, although all other plate is forbidden.

The rules for the Infirmarian are very beautiful, bringing out the especial sweetness and compassion of the Saint. "She is to have a list to help her memory, of everything required for the comfort and good order of the infirmary, and to take care that the rooms be neat, clean, and nicely ornamented with pictures, green leaves, and flowers, according as the season shall permit." The Infirmarian is to be full of charity, not only to serve the sick Sisters well, but to bear with the fancies, distresses, ill-humour, poor sick people often derive from their maladies. She is to "divert their disagreeable impressions in the softest and most dexterous way she can, without ever showing herself disgusted or annoyed." Then, again, appears his spirit in the following direction to the lay Sisters:—" The Sisters employed in the kitchen, and the other household service, will do it with cheerfulness and consolation, recollecting what St. Martha did, and representing to themselves those short but sweet meditations of which St. Catherine of Sienna made use, who, in the midst of such tasks, did not cease her ecstatic contemplations of God. Thus ought the Sisters, as far as possible, to hold their hearts recollected in the goodness of God, Who, if they are faithful, will one day declare before the whole world that what they did for His servants was done for Him." How *like* St. Francis himself, too, is this direction: " In lying down to rest, think of our Lord and of the Saints who slept on the ground, and thank Him for the Fatherly love by which He gives you these comforts, how much you ought to love and serve Him."

The Order is governed, first, by the Bishop of the Diocese, for each House of the Visitation is separate, and there is no Mother-House or General Superior. Next to the Bishop, each house is governed by the " Spiritual Father." This priest is appointed by the Bishop, and he is to take care that the rules are well observed. He is the Visitor of the house, and is present at the elections. There shall be an ordinary Confessor, but the Sisters have full liberty of confessing to any priest of known character.

Thus was the Order of the Visitation founded, and before St. Francis's death he saw the Institute flourishing and increasing. The Order was confirmed by Pope Urban the Eighth, in 1626. Its brightest ornament was its Superioress and Foundress, St. Jane Frances. There is not in all the lives of the Saints a more lovely history than that of this holy woman. We do not read, indeed, of marvellous penances, or great miracles, or varied works of love, as we do in the lives of other servants of God, but we read of a marvellous obedience, of a great humility, and of a sweetness and piety, with which her life was adorned. Not long after the foundation of the Order, St. Jane Frances was attacked by so violent an illness that all believed her dying. St. Francis said to her, " Perhaps, my child, God is contented with our essay and desires to erect this little company, in like manner as He was contented with Abraham's will to sacrifice his son; if such be the case, and it be His will that we should retrace our steps, let it be so." "Yes," replied St. Jane Frances; "His Will be done in time and eternity. If God does not will us to go further, He will at least have seen that we are willing to accomplish the work with which He has inspired us." Her sufferings were intense, but she only exclaimed,

"Yes, my God, make this too eager nature suffer." A Protestant doctor who attended her, used to say she must have some celestial consolations which supported her. For the first few years of her religious life, St. Jane Frances, living in her convent at Annecy, enjoyed the blessing of constant intercourse with St. Francis of Sales; but as time went on, and the Order increased, this privilege was withdrawn. Madame de Chantal had to go hither and thither founding houses of the Order. Long and painful journeys in the depth of winter, or the heat of summer, and the constant fight with difficulties ever attendant on a new foundation, were her portion, and thus it came to pass that towards the close of St. Francis's life three years and a half had passed without their meeting.

At length, she met him at Lyons, in December, 1622, but he was so pressed upon by crowds of visitors, that for a long space he had no time to spare for her. At last she was sent for, and, said the Saint, upon whose face was even then written the tokens of his coming death, "We have now a few hours to ourselves; which of us shall speak first?" St. Jane Frances had in her hands two papers: one was the memoranda of her own spiritual wants; the other concerning the government of the order. So she answered eagerly, "I shall, if such be your will; my heart has great need of being reviewed by you." But he, so near the Beatific Vision, could brook no eagerness even in the holiest things, and he answered, "What are you still eager, and have you a choice of your own? I hoped to have found you altogether angelic. We shall speak of ourselves at Annecy. Let us now finish the business of the congregation. Oh, how I do love our little institute, because God is so loved in it!" Without a word's reply St. Jane Frances put aside her private papers, and opened those of the Order, and a conversation ensued which lasted for four hours, and then she was dismissed with the Saint's benediction, never again to meet him in this life. While on her road to Grenoble the next day, the thought of not having been able to open her heart to her director, pressed on her with anguish. Instantly she cried, "The Lord is my light," and she repeated over and over again the verse, "When my father and my mother forsake me, the Lord taketh me up," till her soul was perfectly resigned. In such a spirit did she bear the trial of St. Francis's death, desiring only so to follow him in life as to see him again in heaven. When the body of St. Francis (who had died at Lyons) was brought to Annecy, St. Jane Frances, remembering his words, that at Annecy he would hear the account of her soul, with a beautiful love and simplicity, went to the chapel, and, kneeling by the corpse, she spoke to him who could no longer answer with his earthly lips, but who, doubtless from his throne in Heaven, interceded that the lights and graces which she needed might enter that loving soul. And from henceforth so passed her life during the nineteen years that she survived St. Francis of Sales: as she had obeyed him, so did she the next Bishop of Geneva, and her other superiors. The election of Superioresses in the Visitation being a triennial one, she was frequently out of office for three years, and never failed to obey the rule which prescribes that the Superior going out shall take the lowest place in the choir, and her obedience to the Superioress was perfect, both in letter and spirit. On the 4th of August, 1632, the tomb of St. Francis de Sales was opened by the persons engaged in the process of his canonization, and the body was found fresh and uncorrupted. St. Jane Frances, bending her head, placed upon it the hand of the Saint, and he who had so often blessed her in life extended his hand and pressed her head with the fingers. The veil which St. Jane Frances wore has been preserved ever since, as a twofold relic. It was ordained that nearly all her first companions and loved friends in the Order should die before her, doubtless to wean more perfectly her soul, which had such an immense capacity of love, from too human affections. Her son was killed in battle, dying the death of a Christian soldier; friend after friend, her confessor, the next Bishop of Geneva, her brother, the Archbishop of Bourgoes, were called from earth, and yet she lingered behind; they were, she said, "ripe fruit, ready for the table of the great King, while she was yet quite green, or rather rotten and worm-eaten."

At length she whose life had been a practice of her own words, "We must put no bounds to our spoliation of self," was drawing to her end. On the morning of the Feast of the Immaculate Conception, her last illness began; the Sisters urged her to leave the chapel, and go again to bed, but she begged to remain, saying it was thirty-one years that day since St. Francis had permitted her to begin daily communion. Her communion over, she was taken to her bed, which was to be that of her death. They brought her next day her Viaticum; she exclaimed, "I believe firmly that my Lord Jesus Christ is present in the blessed sacrament of the altar; I have always believed and confessed it; I adore and acknowledge Him to be my God and Redeemer, Who has ransomed me with His precious blood. I would willingly lay down my life in defence of this belief, but I am not worthy of it; I confess that I look to be saved only by His infinite mercy." When taking leave of her spiritual children she said, "Pay strict obedience to your Superiors, regarding our Lord in them; be perfectly united one with another, but with the true union of hearts," repeating these last words several times, and, she added, "Live in great simplicity." She embraced them all, whispering to each some word to help them on in the road to Heaven. From that time all her thoughts were in God. They read to her the Passion, and the Creed of Pope Pius, to which she expressed her firm assent. She often repeated the verse—

> "Mother of grace, O Mary blest,
> To thee, sweet fount of love, we fly.
> Shield us through life, and take us hence
> To thy dear bosom when we die."

The hour was come, and the community were kneeling round, when her confessor told her the Bridegroom was at hand,—would not she go forth to meet him? "Yes, father, I am going. *Jesus! Jesus! Jesus!*" and the soul was with Jesus, never to know suffering or disquiet again.

Thus lived and thus died the first nun of the Visitation, the first-fruits of the new Institute; although the most distinguished in virtue, there were others among her companions who did much to advance in the way she marked out for them. Such was Marie Jacqueline Favre, the second religious of the Order. She was the daughter of the President of Savoy, and by her position obliged to mix in the gay world,—an occupation she was far from disliking, for she was beautiful and accomplished, and fond of admiration. She had great force of character, and was of so independent a nature that she not only disliked the idea of becoming a nun, but she declared herself unable to endure the yoke of marriage. Widows were the only people she envied, and "If one could be assured," she would say in fun, "that one's husband would die two hours after the ceremony, one could then consent to the marriage." Still, though she loved the world, she did not neglect her religious duties; she often thought of death, and was constantly to be found assisting the dying in their last agony; she was under the direction of St. Francis de Sales, and gradually his holy influence was softening her heart. Among other accomplishments she danced with exquisite grace, and had such a reputation for it that the ladies of Chambéry, when she was staying in the town, gave a ball on purpose to see her dancing, and Jacqueline, naturally elated by the compliment, went to it, determined to excel. The Governor of the country led her out to dance, and her triumph was complete. Suddenly Jacqueline recollected a rule given to her by the Bishop of Geneva, "to look often into oneself," and the frivolity of her occupation struck her in a new and forcible light, "What reward shall you have for all these efforts? What fruit will you draw from it? People will say she dances very well; behold your recompense." A horror came over her of the kind of life she was leading, and she left the ball-room determined to be a nun.

Her beauty and her talents, together with her original and striking character, induced many men to seek her as their wife. Among them was one of the brothers of St. Francis de Sales. "Brother," said the Saint to him one day, "you have a terrible rival, and to Him you must resolve to relinquish this lady." The young man impetuously answered, that except he Duke of Savoy himself, no one should dare to cross his path. The Saint replied smiling, that his rival was so great one dared not even look upon His face, and then he declared to him that Jesus Christ was the only spouse whom Jacqueline's Favre would accept. It was not likely that such a disposition as Jacqueline's would easily find peace in the religious life. Hers was a soul capable of enduring much suffering, and God gave her this portion. But He gave His grace also, and faithfully did she correspond with it. No one would have guessed, when they saw her strict observance of her rule, that every act cost her a sacrifice; or those who came to the parlour, and were converted from heresy or an evil life by her powerful words, that her soul was plunged into profound darkness and desolation. St. Francis de Sales even had no power to relieve the anguish of her spirit. She fulfilled many different offices of the community, and so changed was she, that she, who had been proudly independent, became a model of obedience, and she who had been very haughty, became so meek, that when she was once recalled by St. Jane Frances from the superiority of the convent at Dijon, she imagined it was from her bad government, and that it was intended to send her into the noviciate again, to be further instructed in the religious life. Her sorrows and her trials lasted the whole of her life, but her death was calm and peaceful, the names of Jesus and Mary were constantly on her lips, and death seemed to be "a foretaste of her eternal rest."

Another remarkable nun of this order was Anne Jacqueline Coste, a lay sister. She was a servant at an hotel in Geneva, and her honesty and industry made her so valued and respected by her masters that they endured her being a Catholic, in a town so infected with heresy, in which all public Catholic services were prohibited, and priests had to go about in disguise. St. Francis de Sales could only appear publicly to hold a disputation with the Protestant minister De la Faye; and afterwards the holy Bishop had to come to his own episcopal see in disguise. On one of these occasions he went to stay at the *Hôtel de l'Ecu de France*, where Anne Coste was servant. She knew him. As soon as she could speak to him alone she said, "Oh, Monseigneur, for a long time I have asked our Lord to let me speak to you; be so benevolent to me as to tell me what I ought to do to serve God well." St. Francis, surprised and overjoyed at such a request, conversed with her, encouraged her, and after hearing her confession, he asked her if she would wish to receive the Holy Communion. "Alas!" she replied, "that would indeed be a consolation, but how can I possibly have it, seeing that mass is forbidden in Geneva." And then the saint told her that always there rested on his breast the Blessed Sacrament, whenever he went about on such a mission as he was then engaged in. Still Anne was perplexed. "But, my Lord," she continued, "you have no clerk here to assist you; what can you do?" The saint replied with his accustomed smile of sweetness, "My child, fear not; my good angel, who is between you and me, and yours likewise, who is present at your side, will serve as clerks, for it is the especial office of the angels to stand around the holy table."

From this moment a miraculous communication existed between the guardian angels of the holy Bishop and the poor servant girl, and each was wont to invoke the angel of the other, with that simple and perfect faith which belongs to the Saints of God.

Anne continued to live at Geneva, serving her Master by her fidelity in her daily work, and by endeavouring in her quiet humble way to gain souls. She drew many from heresy to the true faith. She succeeded before her mistress's death in bringing her to the truth, and having contrived to get Mass said in a cellar, she was able to receive the last Sacraments. After her death, Anne went to Annecy; she had longed to be under the direction of the Bishop, but she was too humble and modest to hasten to him. Patience in waiting was her especial virtue, and St. Francis used to say afterwards, she was a model of it.

The joy of being in a Catholic city filled Anne's heart; she was continually in the churches admiring everything and adoring the Holy Sacrament. The sound of the church bells was music to her, and her heart swelled with delight at the sound of the *Angelus*. It was the custom of St. Francis to explain the catechism to the poor and ignorant as often as he could. On the first occasion of this being done, Anne came with the crowd; instantly the keen eye of the pastor knew his sheep, and looking at her earnestly he pressed his hand on his breast, reminding her of the precious gift he had given her one morning long ago at the Geneva Hotel. From this time he took Anne under his especial guidance, and employed her in various works of charity among the poor. She gave him great satisfaction in her good works; once only we read of her erring, when she repulsed a person who had an infectious disease, and who wished to see the Bishop. On telling this to St. Francis, he said, "It was a great fault, my child; know you not that God has destined me for the service of the poor and sick. Bring this person to me; it is these sort of people that I must have;" and he gave Anne as her penance to go and seek out the most infected and miserable of the poor, that they might have the Sacraments. One day Anne said to St. Francis she desired greatly to enter religion. He proposed to her the different convents in the town, but she refused them all, and St. Francis then asked where she wished to go. "Monseigneur, I wish to serve those religious whom you will found." "Who has told you I am going to found an Order?" "No one," she answered; "but I feel continually this conviction in my soul, and so I tell you."

St. Francis at that time had spoken of his design to no one but Madame de Chantal, and he was greatly struck by this incident.

As soon as the first Convent of the Visitation was opened Anne entered as lay sister.

She was not less holy in the religious than in the secular life; she edified her companions, and gave great glory to God. When in November, 1622, St. Francis left Annecy for Lyons, Anne threw herself at his feet, weeping bitterly. "My child," said the Saint, "I have made other journeys, and I never saw you weep when I went." "Oh!" she answered, "my heart tells me that this will be the last, and we shall see each other no more." "My child," replied the Bishop, smiling, "my heart says, that if I return not we shall see each other sooner than you think. Keep yourself in peace, near our Lord; pray often for me, and send me every day your good angel." He then gave her his blessing and a picture of the Blessed Virgin. Anne could not be consoled, and from that moment she wept her father as if dead?

On the Feast of Holy Innocents, at the moment when St. Francis was dying at Lyons, his loving daughter was praying for him, and begging her good angel to go to him and render him all kind offices. Suddenly she saw a great light, and heard a voice, which she thought was that of her father's guardian angel, saying, "We are carrying the soul of thy father: praise God!" And Anne went to tell her Superior the news of the Bishop's death. When, a few weeks afterwards, Madame de Chantal returned to the Convent overwhelmed with grief, there was none who could console her so well as Anne. St. Francis's prophecy was fulfilled; one short six months, and the child went to see her father again. She asked to be buried with his last gift of a picture of our Lady, and after often invoking his guardian angel, she died pronouncing the names of Jesus and Mary.

But there is one more glory attached to the Visitation which we must not omit to mention. From the hidden retreat of one of their convents sprung forth the beautiful devotion to the Sacred Heart of Jesus. Great truly is their glory, that one among thêm should have been chosen by our Lord Himself, to make known to men the burning love of His Divine Heart, and to have a new Feast dedicated to His honour in His Church.

Margaret Mary Alacoque entered the Visitation Convent at Paray le Monial, in Burgundy, in May, 1671. There was nothing striking about her, nothing that the world saw and admired. She had not the talents of St. Teresa, nor the beauty of St. Clare; her great characteristic was apparently intense human affection and a very sensitive nature. None of God's servants have been called to do any especial work for His glory without having to bear peculiar suffering; and such was Margaret's lot. Our Divine Lord led and directed her Himself in a most wonderful manner. He gave her the charge of making His Divine Heart to be known and worshipped, and not only did He vouchsafe to her visions and ecstasies, but on one occasion He seemed to her to take out her heart, place it within His own, and then return it to her all inflamed with love, and as a token of this grace there was from henceforth a burning heat and pain about her heart.

A severe portion of contempt and suffering was in store for Margaret. All the traditions of the Visitation were against any new devotion, or any extraordinary ways. The great desire of all Superiors was to lead the nuns in the road of simplicity, humility, and obedience, and they naturally suspected the visions and lights of Margaret. To her sensitive and loving nature, no pain could be so hard as the suspicion and distrust of her Sisters, and to her profound humility it was terrible, to be, as it were, put as the teacher of those she deemed so much above her; but she endured all with heroic patience, sufferings long and bitter, which we cannot recount here, but which can be found at length in her life. She was but a feeble instrument in an Almighty Hand. After a long course of contradictions she conquered. The devotion to the Sacred Heart took its rise in the humble convent, and spread into the whole world. A Feast was instituted, in obedience to our Lord's own commands to Margaret Mary. The Friday after the Octave of Corpus Christi was set aside to honour the special mystery of the Pierced Heart of Jesus. Confraternities in Its honour sprung up, and there are few of the faithful who do not cherish this devotion as dearest to their hearts. Margaret Mary became at length as much honoured in the community as she had formerly been despised, and filled for a long time the office of mistress of novices, and afterwards that of assistant. All this honour was hateful to her; her greatest efforts were to be forgotten, to be " buried in the Heart of Jesus Christ," as she would say. In October, 1690, she was called to her reward. One of her last sayings was, " What a happiness to love God! Oh! what a happiness! Love then this Love; but love Him perfectly;" and she died in a transport of Divine love.

The strictest spirit of poverty is observed in the Visitation Order, and every year the Sisters change not only their cells, but their rosaries, medals, and pictures, so that the most entire detachment shall be attained in the smallest matters. Their day is spent as follows:—Five A. M., they rise; at half-past, adore the Blessed Sacraments, and make their meditation; at half-past six, Prime; at eight o'clock, Terce, Sext, and Mass, followed by None, examen, and work; ten, dinner and recreation; twelve, work, but half an hour's repose is allowed for those who wish; at half-past two, spiritual reading, and "if the mind be drawn to prayer, it can follow the attraction;" three, Vespers, then work, during which they may converse of the spiritual books they have read; five, Compline and Litanies; half-past five, Meditation; six, collation, recreation, obedience (*i. e.*, assigning the duties for the following day); half-past eight, *strict silence* begins; a quarter to nine, Matins and Lauds, examen, points for tomorrow's meditation; ten, in bed. No fixed time is given for the completion of any work in which they are engaged, in order not to interfere with the interior spirit, but they are left to their own spiritual diligence. The time for the exercises may differ in various places.

St. Francis of Sales tells the Superiors not to take "women obstinate and rebellious, or giddy and frivolous, nor those with too much compassion for themselves, for people who are tender over their body are sure to be also over their soul; fervent charity, and strength of intimate devotion supplies austerity." The words with which the Saint concludes the Rule are singularly beautiful: "Come, O daughters of benediction eternal, and as it was said to Ezekiel, and to the dearest loved of your souls, come, hold, take and eat this book, digest it and keep it in your bosoms, and it will nourish your hearts; let the words of it dwell day and night before your eyes, to meditate on them, and on your arms to practise them, and in your heart to praise God. It will give bitterness to your interior, for it conducts you to perfect mortification of your self-love; but it will be sweeter than honey to your mouth, because it is incomparable consolation to mortify self-love, to make the love of Him, Who is dead for us, live and reign in us. Thus our greatest bitterness will turn itself into the suavity of a most abundant peace, and you will be filled with true happiness. I pray you, my Sisters, I supplicate and conjure you, my beloved daughters, behold, see, and consider you have been instructed until now in these observances; you have received the sacred veil under them—by them you have been multiplied, and have had an holy increase in age, number, and piety. Be then strong, firm, constant, immoveable, and live so that nothing may separate you from the Celestial Spouse Who has united you together, nor from the union by which you ought to be united to Him; so that, having in all things but one heart and one soul, it may be your only soul and your heart. Blessed is the soul who observes this Rule, for she is faithful and true; and to all the souls who follow it, be for ever abundantly grace, peace, and consolation of the Holy Spirit."

The vows of the Visitation nuns are renewed as follows:—" Oh, Heaven, behold what I say! earth, hear the words of my mouth. It is to you, O Jesus, my Saviour, to whom my heart speaks, although I am but dust and ashes. Oh! my God, I confirm and renew with all my heart the vows that I have made to your Divine Majesty of living in perpetual chastity, obedience, and poverty, according to the

Rule of St. Augustine and the Constitutions of the Congregation of our Lady of the Visitation, for the observance of which I offer and consecrate to Thy Divine Majesty, and to the Sacred Virgin Mary, Thy Mother, our Lady, and to the said Congregation, my person and my life. Receive me, O Eternal Father! into the arms of Thy pitiful Paternity, that I may carry constantly the yoke and burden of Thy holy service, to which I have dedicated and consecrated myself. Oh! very glorious, very sacred, and very sweet Virgin Mary, I supplicate you by thy love, and by the death of your Son, to succour me beneath thy maternal protection. I have chosen Jesus, my Lord and my God, for the only object of my dilection—I have chosen His holy and sacred Mother in the Congregation, and for my perpetual direction. Glory be to the Father, and to the Son, and to the Holy Ghost. Amen."

The Convents of the Visitation being all separate foundations, it is difficult to know their exact number; they are, however, numerous in France. Two large and important convents exist in Paris. To both these convents *schools* for young ladies are attached; but it is an error to reckon the Order of the Visitation as an educational one. St. Francis permitted his nuns to educate when necessity called for it, but not otherwise. The large and beautiful

Convent of the Visitation at Boulogne, is without a school, as also the English convent of the Order at Westbury, near Bristol. The nuns of this Order keep strict enclosure behind a *grille*, but it is not curtained, so that they can be seen.

It is said that the idea of the Order of the Visitation was revealed to St. Francis de Sales in a vision, and there is no reason to doubt that it was so, for most certainly has the promise which is said then to have been made to him been fulfilled, that his new Order "should edify the Church by their virtues, and perpetuate his spirit and his maxims."

## ORDER OF THE GOOD SHEPHERD; OR, OF OUR LADY OF CHARITY OF THE GOOD SHEPHERD.

WE have already noticed that the Orders of the Perpetual Adoration and the Visitation had been called into being by the peculiar necessities of the time. The wants of modern ages were rapidly increasing, and the ancient Orders of cloistered religious were not sufficient to meet them all. Sublime as were their lives of prayer and penance, for the conversion of others, it became necessary to have those who should more directly minister to the suffering and the sinful. The spirit of charity had always existed in monastic life. The convent of the olden time had given shelter, and food, and clothing, —there wounds had been tended and hearts consoled; and to the service of hospitals many religious women had devoted their lives, while from those afflicted with the awful scourge of leprosy, the religious had not shrunk. And now devoted hearts were called to new fields of labour. The sixteenth century had seen the foundation of the greatest of all modern Orders, and the spirit of the Society of Jesus not only made its own body the glory and defence of the Church, but it cast its reflex around, and kindled up zeal in many a heart, and induced many to hasten "where the harvest was great and the labourers few." The Order of the Good Shepherd was founded to obtain the conversion of sinners. Its members were to devote themselves to the rescue of women or girls who had been leading, or were likely to be led, into an evil life. They were to keep enclosure, but were to attach houses to their convents, in which they could watch over and instruct these objects of their care.

Its founder, *Père Eudes*, was born at Rie, in Normandy, in 1661. From his childhood he showed a great devotion to the service of God, and at fourteen he bound himself by vow to belong only to Him. At twenty-three he entered the congregation of the

French Oratory, and as his talent for preaching was remarkable, he was much employed in this office; but his disappointment was great when he found that the Oratorians had given up a work which they had undertaken to perform, *i.e.*, the foundation of seminaries for the education of the clergy. The Oratorians are secular priests, living in community, and not bound by religious vows. Père Eudes therefore withdrew from them, and founded a congregation which was dedicated to Jesus and Mary, and which undertook the training of young men for the priesthood. Many and various were the trials which were permitted to come on Père Eudes. Calumnies and misrepresentations beset more or less his whole life, but they served but to perfect him in humility, unalterable patience, and great confidence in God. While residing in Caen, his attention was forcibly drawn by means of a poor woman, called Madeleine l'Amy, to the sad condition of fallen women, many of whom she had been trying to assist. Père Eudes took a house in which some of these poor creatures were received, and a number of charitable ladies undertook its guidance. But the task was soon found too arduous for secular persons, and the inspiration entered Père Eudes' mind to found an Order of women who would devote themselves to the task of seeking the lost sheep of their Master's flock.

It is always the same story. Of course, its beginning was slow and feeble; of course, it met with opposition, with calumny, with fiery trials. It was God's work, and the devil hated it. We may say he hated it with a peculiar hatred; for worse to him than the Carmelites' penance, worse than the Sister of Charity with her orphan children, were they who would go fearlessly into his own domain, to snatch away his prey, to snatch away those whom even the *world* calls *lost*, whom even the world scorns and loathes and turns from, but whom he does not despise; and blessed be God there is One also who does not despise them, and He inspired His children with the same charity, and a community of women rose up ready to carry out Père Eudes' designs. The prudent founder saw the necessity of forming the Sisters first to the religious life, and he procured for them a holy religious of the Visitation, who became their Superioress, and remained with them for several years.

He then adopted for the Order the Rule of the Visitation, which is founded on that of St. Augustine. He drew up Constitutions, which adapted the rule to the especial end for which the new institute had been begun. The Order was confirmed by the Holy See, January 2nd, 1666, after having been twenty years in existence. Up to this time the vows of the religious had been annual only; as the

Pope's brief permitted them to make perpetual vows, the sixteen nuns of whom the community was composed made a solemn retreat, in order to consider seriously before God the further engagement they were to undertake. Not one wished to draw back, and on the Feast of the Ascension they all made their solemn profession, adding to the three vows of Poverty, Obedience, and Chastity, a fourth, "to employ themselves in the instruction of the penitent girls and women who submit themselves voluntarily, or shall be forced by legitimate and competent authority to submit themselves to the guidance of the religious of this congregation, to be converted and to do penance."

Fourteen years afterwards Père Eudes was called from earth. Before his death the calumnies and misrepresentations that had hung over him so long were dispersed. He was as indifferent to praise as he had been to blame. "I wish," he said, "for no other reward on earth than that which my Saviour chose for himself—the Cross." Calmness and serenity and *waiting* for God had ever been his characteristic through life, and death seemed to him truly only a going home. "Come, Lord Jesu," he whispered, and so passed into eternity.

The Order flourished and increased, and was founded in various places. It of course suffered greatly at the time of the Revolution, especially the

Convent in Paris, called St. Michel. The Commissioners drove out the nuns by force. The greater part of them were enabled to live together in a small miserable house, keeping their rule as far as they could. They were so poor that they had to work day and night to gain a bare subsistence. Some sat at home and sewed, and others went out to pick up wood, and in the summer to glean.

A charitable man, seeing from the calm faces and recollected manner of these poor labourers that they were religious, gave them flour, bread, and vegetables, and told them to come to him every week. The Superioress of the community, "Mary of the Infant Jesus," used to sally forth to the market, carrying a large pannier. The fishwomen would give her some of their worst stores, other vendors would add butter and vegetables, and as they gave her these things they whispered to her, "Pray for us, for we can see very well you are a religious." One day the whole wealth of the community consisted in *thirty sous*, and no food was left in the house. Mary of the Infant Jesus began to consider what to do. At the market she already owed for articles of food, and to go again in her wretched ragged clothing was not a likely way of getting further credit. She remembered, however, Him whose name she bore, and His poor cradle, and so she went forth to the market. Scarcely had she entered when the market-women ran to her crying out, "Come, *ma cocotté*, it is a long time since we have seen thee. It is because thou hast not money to pay us, is it not? Come all the same; thou shalt owe us nothing; since we gave to thee we have sold our goods all the better." And they loaded her with presents. On her return home she found an unknown benefactor had left bread, meat, and eggs, and soon after a lady came to offer to pay their rent. Thus did God protect his servants through their bitter trials. After the Revolution the nuns resumed their work, and they procured the convent formerly occupied by the Visitation nuns, and which had been honoured by the presence of St. Francis de Sales and St. Jane Frances de Chantal. To this house they also gave the name of St. Michel. They had a narrow escape from further trouble, for a conspirator against Buonaparte, having fled for concealment to them, the merciful Superioress could not turn him out, and he remained a day in the outer part of the convent. Her arrest soon followed, but she was acquitted upon some legal quibble of which the judges were glad to avail themselves. The capricious Napoleon ever afterwards showed her great favour, and the house received money from Government. This convent still exists; it is an immense building, and contains, besides the religious, three hundred inmates. They are divided into classes. A "Preservation" class of young girls who have been removed from dangerous positions; a second of those suspected of immoral conduct, and placed in the convent by Government; and the third the ordinary class of penitents.

The Order of the Good Shepherd had originally no General Superioress, but in 1835 the religious of the convent at *Angers* obtained a brief from the Pope allowing them to elect a Superioress-General, and to keep all their future foundations under her obedience. Of course the existing houses of the Order were in no way affected by this brief. Since that time the Order has greatly increased, and the Mother-House at Angers has sent out a large number of foundations. From it was sent the first foundation for England, and the incidents respecting it are truly worthy of record.

It was in 1840 that the Mother-General at Angers, Sister Mary of St. Euphrasie Pelletier, determined to make a foundation in England. To worldly minds the project seemed a wild one. She had hardly any friends in England, little money, and no Sisters who could speak the language. She, however, fixed on one to begin the work who was admirably suited for it. Sister Mary of St. Joseph (*née* Jeanne Marie Regandial) was born at Royaume, near Lyons, in 1809. At twenty-three years of age she devoted herself to God, and entered the Order of the Good Shepherd, and she it was whom the Mother-General selected for the arduous undertaking. With one companion, Sister Mary of St. Celeste Frisson, she set out on St. Martin's Day, 1840, and proceeded to St. Malo, intending to proceed by steamer to England. Anxiously did they watch the signal for going on board, but they did not hear it; and while they were wondering, persons came to tell them the vessel was gone. It was a great disappointment, but they bore it patiently, believing it to be all in God's especial arrangement for them. What were their feelings when they found afterwards a storm had come on, and every soul on board that vessel had been lost! After waiting four days at Saint Malo they set out in a small vessel laden with hides, in which there was but one wretched cabin. After a long, weary, and dangerous voyage, they reached London, and as soon as possible went to present their only letter of introduction to the Abbé Voyaux de Trarrons, a priest, at Chelsea. In him they hoped to find a father and a friend. When the servant opened the door to them, she burst into tears; they did not understand her words, so she beckoned them to follow her, and led them to a room where lay the body of the Abbé, arrayed for the grave. Truly were they meant to learn to look to God only for help. They knelt beside the corpse and prayed;

prayed doubtless for the soul of him whose labour had ended, and for themselves for strength and help in the dim future before them. They next proceeded to the Bishop (then Dr. Griffiths). He received them with much kindness, but did not look encouragingly on their enterprise. The Catholics in England then were a small and struggling body, and the prospect of support for a new and extensive work of charity was not promising. The Bishop sent them to the Benedictine nuns at Hammersmith, who took them in at once, and treated them with all possible kindness.

A convent was then in course of erection at St. Leonard's-on-Sea, and it was offered to the French nuns. Accordingly they went thither, and remained there for some months; but they found the distance from any large town an insuperable objection to the success of their work, as the expense and risk of sending the penitents a long journey would be a serious obstacle. In February, 1841, they returned to the hospitable Benedictines, and remained there till the 3rd of May, when the Order of the Good Shepherd in England was really founded. It had no grand or striking beginning. Some kind friends took for them a small house in King-street, Hammersmith. The work prospered, and in two years' time it was necessary to remove to a larger house. Subsequently, new buildings were joined to this residence, to which large grounds were attached. For nine years more did the Mère Marie de St. Joseph continue to work for her Lord. She spared no labour, and was ready to make any sacrifice. Simple and humble as a child, she yet possessed the most wonderful influence over all who came within her reach. Her manners were most graceful and winning. People in the world who came to see her were so impressed by her, that they were accustomed to say she was a saint. Well and wisely did she govern both the community and asylum, as may be evinced by the rapid increase of both. She who, in 1840, had arrived in London lonely and without a prospect of success, saw, in 1852, a flourishing community in that city, another house of the Order at Bristol, and both asylums filled with penitents.

She had a painful illness, which she bore with saintly patience; and the picture that was drawn of her at this time shows the unearthly peace that illuminated her wasted features. She rendered her soul to her Creator, January 24, 1852, aged forty-three years. The Cardinal Archbishop of Westminster desired the community to have her body interred in the midst of the choir. He came himself to her funeral, as well as almost all the London clergy, and His Eminence placed the monumental stone to her memory with his own hands. But her best memorial is in the living work she has left behind her. Many are the souls rescued from sin's lowest depth by her means. How many will thank her in Heaven—who can tell?

The Order of the Good Shepherd has houses at Bristol, Glasgow, Liverpool, Limerick, and Waterford. The Noviciate House for England is at Hammersmith; for though governed by the Superioress-General of Angers, the novices are not obliged to go to Angers.

In 1854, a convent of the Order was founded, from Angers, at Vienna, for the purpose of receiving prisoners. As soon as the nuns were settled in the house provided for them, six prisoners were placed under their charge. The nuns give a most interesting account of the commencement and progress of this work. "These poor children did not know we were religious, and were seized with horror, thinking we were ghosts, and their gestures of terror were desperate. We cannot express the impression their first arrival made on us; the pale disfigured countenances, bearing the marks of vice and misfortune, excited our deepest compassion. It was terrible to us to hear the sound of their chains, which they carry night and day, and which jangle at the least movement. Alas! we soon found the chains of their souls were stronger and more horrible." At the end of three weeks six more prisoners were brought, and the number was gradually increased till a hundred and sixty were under the charge of a few religious: there were less than a dozen in this new foundation. The prisoners were most desperate characters; they had been condemned for frauds, stealing, *arson*, and even some for *assassination*. The Government had great fears as to the possibility of the Sisters' success, and had begun the work merely as an experiment. In the prisons the soldiers had often to be called in to quell outbursts of rage and rebellion. Many gentlemen interested in the community declared they could not sleep for fear some harm might be done to the nuns, shut up alone with these wild creatures; but the religious themselves were tranquil. " The most High God was in the midst of us; how could we fear?" they said afterwards. " Our God is He Who has often changed wild beasts, and made them gentle as lambs. At the foot of the Altar we prayed, and kneeling before the Tabernacle we recalled those consoling words, ' Fear not, little flock, I have conquered the world and the Prince of Darkness, I will keep you as the apple of mine Eye.' We had put our work under the protection of the 'faithful and powerful Virgin,' and knew that She would show herself to be our Mother, and the Refuge of Sinners."

We cannot do better than give in the words of the nuns themselves the history of their labours. " Our confidence increased as we saw the operations of Divine grace, although the devil did not easily give up the souls of which for many years he had been the peaceful possessor, and whom now he was obliged to relinquish to the Powerful God. The poor creatures wish to become better, but their will is very, very feeble; they cannot even believe in the possibility of their improvement; their fall has been so complete, that their faith has been shipwrecked. Religion they scarcely know, and it is as strange to them to hear of it as it is to us to hear fables. Nearly all have been away from the Sacraments for many years, or else they have received them only to profane them horribly. Many of them from childhood have drunk in vice like water; they have been slaves to sin and their passions. From the first the order and quiet of our house did good, and seemed to re-awaken human feelings in their minds, and the dew of grace began to soften and penetrate the long closed up hearts."

The religious began their work in the month of January. In Easter week, which fell in April, a "Retreat" was given to the prisoners, and then write the Sisters, "The grace of God was very visible. The ceremonies of Holy Week had touched the most hardened, and the great truths of our religion began to make a deep impression on them; the faith of their childhood woke again, and they began to believe in a God Who had created them for Himself. Hell was opened under their feet, and for the first time they raised their eyes to Heaven, and wished to be there; and then the angels carried many prayers from contrite hearts, many tears from repenting sinners to the throne of mercy, and the silence of night was often broken by their weeping. Their sobs often obliged the preacher to stop. Nearly all threw themselves at the feet of God's minister to make the sorrowful confession of a life full of iniquity. Oh! most holy Spirit, let us relate the miracles of mercy which Thou then did work. Let us exalt the God of mercy, Who pardoned their sins, because they were great. All glory be to God, our prisoners are so quiet that people cannot understand, or hardly believe it. Those who were used to talk, cry out, and dispute the whole day, now keep the hours of silence perfectly. Those whom the word of an armed soldier could scarcely control, obey the least sign of a feeble servant of God. Our dear children, who are much attached to us, cannot understand the change in themselves. Let us bless Him Who has calmed the troubled sea, Who has commanded, and the wind is still." Wonderful, indeed, to these poor creatures must have been the sight of the self-devotion of their new governors. High-born and refined ladies had left their native land, and shut themselves within four walls, for the sole purpose of waiting on them, and bringing them back to God, and hard indeed must be the heart which remains insensible to a sacrifice like this.

As regards the temporal management of the prisoners, the Sisters were not left to their own choice, being obliged to follow the government rule for prisons. The prisoners slept on a palliasse with two sheets and one covering, in sickness as well as in health. They had one pound of bread served out *per diem*, and *one meal* only, consisting of soup and vegetables; and on Sundays only, six ounces of meat are allowed. The Superioress then sought and obtained leave to give them a little soup for breakfast. The gratitude with which this boon was received was excessive. "Nearly all," say the Sisters, "had their health injured by the severity of the *regime:* the poor married women are the most grateful. Although we are obliged to execute the rigour of the law, the government leaves us much liberty in directing the prisoners, and it is very good for the poor children to feel that they depend solely on the religious. We employ them in making shirts for the soldiers or for shops; they are not yet as industrious as our penitents in France. When those whose time has expired go out, they never omit going to the Sacraments; and although they are glad of their freedom, they are sorry to leave their mothers who have become dear to them, and to leave the asylum where they have found peace. Some, and they are the crown of our work, prefer sacrificing their liberty rather than exposing themselves to fresh temptations, and eagerly ask leave to stay with us for ever. We have five of these, and soon hope to have more; they are entirely distinct from the prisoners, and wear a costume of their own." On the Feast of Corpus Christi a procession took place in the convent grounds, which must indeed have been pleasing to the Most Holy One Whom they carried amongst them. A Cardinal had come to see the religious and carry the Host; the prisoners went in front, then came the clergy; the nuns preceded and followed the Blessed Sacrament; the voices of the prisoners were stifled with weeping, as the triumphant chant to welcome Him, their Saviour and their Lord, swelled in the air. Those who were sick insisted on rising to take their place, and " follow the train of the Divine Physician." On the fête of the Superioress, the prisoners tried their best to do her honour, and composed some verses to sing in her praise, and when she spoke to them in answer there was a universal burst of weeping. One of them had very much dreaded the day of her release, fearing again to be led from God—for some reason she could not voluntarily choose to remain for life. God had mercy on her, and she was taken from earth's temptations and sorrows on the very day on which the prison doors would have opened for her. At the close of 1854 the religious prepared to follow their annual retreat. At its commencement, the priest who was giving the exercises bade them prepare for sorrow, for he felt certain it was coming on them. It was a strange presentiment. The very next day cholera broke out, several of the prisoners died, and the disease was not subdued before it had taken from the community one of the most beloved and valuable of their members, and finally the priest who had given the retreat, and who was their ecclesiastical superior, and a kind and a true friend to the nuns. But He who could never be taken from them did not forsake them, and the work continues to progress until the present day.

A convent of this Order exists at Tripoli, for the purpose of rescuing slaves sold in the public markets. At Bangalore, East Indies, a convent was founded, where, in addition to their usual works, they received a class of little Indian children thus saved from idolatry. One of the community, writing of these, says, " The Archbishop has collected them; Sister —— has the charge of them, and has begun to learn Malabar. I wish you could see the devotion of these children; it is charming to hear them say the Ave Maria. This class of children rescued from idolatry is a great consolation to us, and we increase it as much as our means will permit. On the fête of our Père Eudes we ornamented his picture with flowers, and he rewarded us directly by sending us an Indian prince to visit us. His ancestors had been converted by St. Francis Yavier; he has preserved the faith of his fathers in all its purity, and always protects the Christians. He has a great regard for our house, and we hope by his means to do much good. Next day we were visited by a lady and her daughter, who remained under the palanquin, because, according to their laws, Indian women, though Catholics and princesses, cannot enter a house where a priest is, or sit down in his presence, and at that moment priests were in the house."

The mother-house at Angers is the largest convent of the Order. In the class of inmates called that of "Preservation" are 200, and another class has been formed called St. Germaine, which consists of girls from the prison or reformatory who wish to remain for life in the convent. The convents and asylums of the Good Shepherd are quite separate, and only communicate by a door, always kept locked. The Penitents' Chapel is separated from the choir of the religious. The penitents are called *children* by the nuns, who in return are called *mothers*. The "children" are never left alone. Religious are with them in the work-room, at recreation, in the dormitories, wash-house, and laundry. The penitents are employed in work, both in order to assist in means for their support and to employ their time and thoughts. Besides this, much of the nuns' time is occupied in giving individual help and instruction.

None but those who have had experience can form an idea of the difficulty of restoring these poor creatures to their place in society. A thousand bad habits have been added to the sin for which they are outcasts. They have learnt to use vile words, they have often been used to dram drinking, their minds have been darkened, and they have lost all idea of self-control. Any kind of rule is a yoke to them, and they are ready to yield to every impulse; they will suddenly want to leave the asylum; the Sisters know very well the next day the step will be bitterly repented; nevertheless, as they can use no coercion, their only means are sweet and winning words, and unwearied patience. Hard and unremitting is the toil of the nuns of the Good Shepherd, and blessed indeed to them is the rest of a return to their convent exercises, when their hours of labour are over, and they are relieved by others of their Sisters.

It is impossible for any one who has been an inmate of the asylum ever to become a nun of this Order. The Constitutions strictly require the nuns to be persons of unstained reputation; but if the penitents be really converted, and shrink from again entering the world with its snares and trials, these are the means of escape open to them:—First, they may become "consecrated;" they will then go through a little ceremony, wear a different dress from the penitents, and, in due time, make a profession, and thus remain in the asylum for life as "consecrated penitents." There are many of these, and they are of great use in promoting a good spirit among the other penitents. But if there are those who desire a stricter life even than this, who want really to do penance, they can enter the Order of the *Magdalenes*, who live as a separate religious community, only that they must always be governed by religious of the Good Shepherd. They live a most retired and penitential life, and it is to them chiefly the religious turn for consolation in their trying work, for they are true imitators of the life of her whose sweet name they bear, and "whose sins were forgiven, for she *loved much*."

Most of the convents of the Good Shepherd possess some of these true penitents. At the convent at Avignon there are a large number; and the nuns speaking of them, said, " They could not praise sufficiently their fervour and humility; they are souls eager for sanctity; and with gratitude we remark the improvement in our works, since they began their life." These are the consolations which from time to time the religious encounter along their difficult path, when they see those who have been among the outcasts, weeping tears of true repentance at the Cross of Jesus, or when appeals are made to them like the following :—To the convent at Loos one day came a girl of eighteen—" Take me," she said ; " it is true I have nothing to bring, but my soul is of great price." Another girl was placed in this convent by her father, who was quite unable to control her, and when provoked, she used to swear most horribly. In time she was completely cured, and became gentle and quiet ; she left the asylum, married, and made an excellent wife. At the convent at Lille a girl of twenty-four had been received among the penitents. After having made a general confession, she said to the nuns, " I have beautiful hair ; it has often been the means of offending God, I beg you to cut it off ; " and another made the same request, saying, " Cut it, that I may not be tempted to return to the world."

In another convent in France an incident is related of a girl who had defied all efforts for her improvement, till at length, for the sake of the others, the nuns were obliged to dismiss her. Soon after she fell ill, and was taken to an hospital. Being in danger of death, nothing would induce her to receive the Sacraments, until she was taken back to the Good Shepherd asylum. Yielding to the entreaties of the hospital chaplain, the nuns received her ; but for some days she still refused to make her confession, but kept continually complaining of the *black form* which was creeping about the room, but which was, of course, quite invisible to others. After some days she at length consented to make her confession, but when the priest, having given her absolution, proposed bringing her the Blessed Sacrament, she stedfastly refused. Day after day passed,—death was rapidly approaching, and yet nothing, she said, should induce her to receive the Viaticum, and her whole mind seemed taken up with watching the "black form," as she called it, which continually beset her, while she gave no evidence of being otherwise delirious or wandering. Her last agony had begun,—the figure was on her bed, she said, and she implored the Sister beside her to remove it. The Sister, who had been praying most fervently for the unhappy girl, said to her, "Are you sure, my child, that you made a good confession, and kept back nothing?" "Yes, there was something," she answered, "and so I did not choose to receive Holy Communion." "If I fetch the priest now, will you confess it?" said the nun. "Oh! it is too late now," returned the dying girl. But, thanks to the mercy of God, time was yet given; the priest came, and when the confession had really been made, contrition appeared to touch the heart. She received the Viaticum, and turning to the Sister, said, "The black figure has gone away now," and immediately after breathed her last. To those little accustomed to deal with the impenitent and fallen, such a history may seem a strange one; but others, whose lot has lain amid such scenes, can well believe it. The nuns are allowed by their Constitutions to undertake the charge of five different "classes" of inmates in their asylum. First, the penitents; secondly, prisoners; thirdly, reformatory children; fourthly, the preservation class; and fifthly, orphans. Besides these, there are the Magdalenes, and also a certain number out of each class, who may choose voluntarily to remain for life in the convent. As all these classes are kept quite separate one from the other, it is very seldom that the religious of any one community preside over them all. It is done, we believe, in the Mother-House at Angers, which is a very vast building, with a great number of religious.

The very dress of the Good Shepherd nuns is typical of their work. They wear a habit and scapular of white serge; a blue cord, in honour of the Blessed Virgin; a silver heart, bearing the image of Him who gave "His life for His sheep," rests on their bosom; and a black veil, covering their heads, speaks of death to the world, and death to self.

After a two years' noviciate, they bind themselves by perpetual vows. They have no great austerities or long fasts. Truly they need it not; their life is one in which they find the cross, but in it they also find consolation; and great, doubtless, will be their reward in the day when they who turn many to righteousness shall shine as the stars for ever and ever.

## ORDER OF THE SACRED HEART.

No time could have been conceived as more unfavourable for the foundation of a new Order than the close of the eighteenth century. Europe had been shaken to its centre, and was still trembling with the blow; and of all the ancient institutions overthrown, none had suffered more severely than Religious Orders. But the Church, beaten down for a moment, speedily arose with fresh vigour, and seeing that many of her old Orders were gone, determined to fill the breach with new ones. The Society of Jesus was suppressed, but a congregation of priests arose, whose endeavour was faithfully to imitate the life of the Jesuits, and to hold themselves ready to join the ranks of the Company when (as they doubted not would one day happen) it should be restored. The founder of this congregation was a young priest called the Père de Tournely. Besides his congregation of men, he ardently desired to see the foundation of one of women, who should devote themselves to the education of their own sex. The convents for education were swept away, and besides, the spirit of the age was so peculiar, that it needed the self-devotion of minds who would, by new and as yet untried ways, endeavour to counteract its pernicious teaching. It was the hope of the Père de Tournely that the Princess Louise de Bourbon-Condé would become the foundress of an Order for education. As we have already seen, her vocation was a different one; but the good priest was not discouraged, and he said to his companion and friend, the Père Varin, " Sooner or later this society will exist."

A few years later the Père de Tournely died, but the Père Varin, who succeeded him in the government of the Pères du Sacré Cœur de Jesus, or, as they were afterwards called, the Pères de la Foi, cherished the idea of a new Order for women, and often sought for one whom he thought would carry out his idea. Strange to say, the foundress he finally chose was a young girl of eighteen, with " delicate health, extreme modesty, and great timidity," and yet the young Madeleine Sophie Barat was indeed destined by God to be the foundation stone of the new Institute. Two companions at once came forward to join her, and they consecrated themselves to the Sacred Heart of Jesus, on

November 21st, 1800. The devotion to the Sacred Heart had always been a chosen one in the Society of Jesus. When Margaret Mary Alacoque was suffering and praying in her convent, unable to see how she was to accomplish the mission with which she was charged, and misunderstood and chided by those around her, the Père de la Colombière, a Jesuit father of great holiness, came to the town where she lived and became her director, and God revealed to her that the Father was to be a great instrument in spreading the devotion to His Sacred Heart. And from thenceforth the Jesuits took the charge as an especial heritage, and following this instinct of the Order he so revered, the Père Varin dedicated the new Institute to the Sacred Heart.

The chief work of the religious of the Sacred Heart is the education of young ladies; their Rule permits them to teach poor schools, to allow ladies to make retreats in their convents, and in various ways to influence others for good. "The end of this Society," says their Rule, "is to glorify the Sacred Heart of Jesus by working for the salvation and perfection of its members, by the imitation of those virtues of which this Divine Heart was the centre and model, and to consecrate themselves as much as can be done by persons of their sex, to the sanctification of their neighbours, as the work dearest to the Heart of Jesus."

The religious at their profession make a fourth vow, of devoting themselves to the education of youth; and their Rule is full of holy instructions as to the manner in which they should fulfil their obligation. "They are to endeavour to inspire in their pupils the spirit of faith; this spirit should animate themselves, should make them consider and esteem only in the pupils the qualities and titles which make them truly great in the eyes of God; they are children of God, redeemed by the Blood of Jesus Christ, destined to reign eternally with Him; they should look on them as the most precious charge that the love of Jesus Christ could confide to them, and should have a maternal love for them in the Heart of their Divine Spouse. They must weigh every day the account that they must render to Jesus Christ of the souls that have cost Him so dearly. They must labour to lay firmly in their souls the solid foundation of faith, fear of God, and horror of sin, and then it will be easy to turn their young hearts to the sweet devotion of the Sacred Heart of Jesus; they must devote themselves with their whole heart to the salvation of these dear children, and to that point they must bring all parts and branches of education. When obliged to apply to worldly studies for the sake of teaching them, they must be on their guard against the vain pretensions of this haughty age, and never pass the bounds that humble and wise discretion prescribes to their sex. Although all the souls confided to the cares of the spouses of Jesus Christ seem to have the same title to their affection, they are permitted to have one particular *attrait, i.e.*, to the children of the poor. All that is revolting in them, ignorance and rudeness, should give them only new claims to tenderness and zeal. With them there is more merit to exercise, they may without danger love these souls so precious and dear to Jesus Christ whom the world disdains and despises, and in giving this kind of teaching they are more like to their Divine Saviour, Who, possessing all treasures of wisdom and science, was pleased to teach the poor and ignorant; and they should humble themselves, considering that while they who have made a vow of poverty lack nothing, these poor children, who have no such engagement, often lack all."

They are to "strive by humility, sweetness, and gentleness, to gain the hearts of their pupils; by love, not a feeble and familiar love, but a love, noble, tender, pure, and disinterested, striving by this love to gain them to the Heart of Jesus."

In speaking of the way in which they ought to glorify God by their intercourse with the world, they are told that "they may be well assured that if dead to themselves, and united to their Lord, the interior spirit which will animate them will suggest to them what is fitting under all circumstances for the position and spiritual wants of various people. Persons ought not to leave the house without edification, and that certain taste for virtue which inspires them with the desire of becoming better." The Rule of the Sacred Heart is that of St. Ignatius. Their Constitutions, which adapt this Rule to their use, were compiled by the Père Varin, and were confirmed by the Holy See in 1826. It is little more than half a century since the poor and feeble beginning by the youthful Madeleine Barat, yet she has lived to extreme old age to see her Institute a large and important body, having numerous houses in all parts of the world. The form of government is a Generalate, and the Mother-General holds her office for life, and is assisted by Provincials for the different branches of the Order. The noviciate lasts two years, and the novices then make the three vows for three years. They next proceed to a branch house, to be employed in the works of the Order. At the end of this period they again pass some time in the noviciate, and then make perpetual vows, adding the fourth of education. The vows are made as follows:—" In the name of the Father, Son, and Holy Ghost, and to the greater glory of God, of the Sacred Hearts of Jesus and Mary, I, ———, humbly prostrate at the feet of the most Holy Trinity, in presence of the most Holy Virgin,

Mother of God, of all the celestial court, and of all those who are here witnesses, promise to the allpowerful God, and to you, my Rev. Mother ———, and all those who shall legitimately succeed you, perpetual poverty, chastity, and obedience; and, according to obedience, to consecrate myself to the education of youth, conformably to the spirit of our Institute, under the authority of my Lord Bishop ———, and of our legitimate ecclesiastical superiors. I make, further, the vow of stability, such as is understood in our Constitutions. Signed ———, at ———."

These last vows are made before receiving the Blessed Sacrament. The Sisters are taught to unite their will and judgment with that of their superiors, and so with the Will of the Sacred Heart of Jesus. Those who present themselves as postulants must be "of honest birth, and with a good education, an unsullied reputation, and a decent exterior, good health and right mind, a simple and docile character, and an aptitude to acquire what is necessary for the virtues of their vocation."

Although the Order of the Sacred Heart is of recent foundation, at least one instance of a saintly life passed under its Rule is on record. Susanne Geoffroy was one of the brightest ornaments that a religious Order could desire. She had been destined by Almighty God in the most remarkable way to be a religious of the Sacred Heart. "You are destined," said her director to her in the year 1787, "to enter a society which will arise in Germany;" and when she begged for further details on the momentous subject, the priest continued, "My child, I can tell you nothing more, except that the person who is to be the foundress of this Congregation in France is still engaged in the care of her dolls." Many long years were indeed to pass before Susanne could realize her desire; years of woe and terror in the world around, such as had scarcely any parallel in history, and years with no common share of sorrow and suffering for Susanne herself. But never was a spirit more fitted to meet trials. She was endowed with an indomitable courage, and with a generous and noble heart. Her parents were very poor, so much so, that being unable to bring her up as they desired, she was adopted by a rich uncle and aunt, who resided at Poitiers. She was very anxious to remain with them, and hearing it said, that to obtain a favour from God it was a very good thing to make a novena to our Lady, she went, child as she was, for nine successive days before an image of Mary, in the parish church, and said to her, "Dear Holy Virgin, I am very happy with my uncle, obtain for me the favour of remaining there; I salute you with all my heart." It was the beginning of a long life of childlike confidence. When Susanne grew to womanhood, dangers and temptations beset her path. She was not gifted with beauty or grace, neither was she highly educated; but the wit and vivacity so frequently inherent in her countrywomen made her very attractive, and surrounded by friends ready to flatter and admire, she ran great peril of losing the high vocation reserved for her.

But God spoke to her heart in clear and forcible accents, and Susanne listened, and resolved to give herself entirely to His service, and it is supposed that at the age of twenty-one she consecrated herself by a vow to our Lord. From that time she began to lead a retired and mortified life, and spent much of her time in prayer. Her future had not as yet been prophesied to her, and the director she was under was not the one who was to mark out her destiny. The one who then guided her was a Capuchin, a man of great wisdom and sanctity. In all her after life she loved to recall the counsels he had given her. "My child," said he once, " there is no harm in wishing to gain the esteem of good people; indeed, we ought to do all we can to deserve it. Act in such a manner that in your dress, as well as in everything else, you may give no occasion for any remarks. I mean to say, let no one be able to observe, ' Oh, how well she looks! Oh, how ill she looks!' but try as much as possible to pass everywhere unperceived."

Susanne had learnt the habit of making her confessions in a short and concise manner, but perceiving one day that a person whom she knew to be very pious, stayed a long time in the confessional, she felt alarmed, and told her confessor of her feeling. "My child," replied he quickly, "confessions are not like pieces of cloth; the longest are not always the best;" and these few words quieted and reassured her. Her director, who was an old man, grew so infirm that he was unable to continue his priestly functions, and he advised Susanne to place herself under the care of Father Draut, a Jesuit, whose character was greatly venerated. It was from him that Susanne received the remarkable prediction which we have recorded above. Father Draut had passed his noviciate under Father Nectou, who had imparted to him most striking predictions of future events. He foretold to him the French revolution, and that after it "one bearing a hated name would be placed on the throne." He foretold many other circumstances which were fulfilled afterwards. He died in 1772. Father Draut having told Susanne of the predictions of Father Nectou, she was in some sort prepared for the awful events which a few years afterwards took place around her. The fury of the Revolution was not felt in Poitiers in the same degree as in Paris. However, all churches were closed, convents broken up, and priests obliged either to fly or disguise themselves. The nuns were all dispersed and in hiding; the poor were, of course, neglected, and misery was all around. Suddenly a thought occurred to Susanne, and turning to some of her intimate friends, she said, "The religious communities are to be suppressed; suppose we form one!" It needed an ardent spirit like hers to make such a proposal at such a time; her friends, inspired by her example, responded to her call, electing her as Superior; which office she accepted readily, "Because," she said, "they were all more holy than I was, and I did not think the office would be a difficult one to fill." For some time these ladies all remained in their families, but afterwards they took a house and lived together, wearing of course their ordinary dress, and appearing to the outward world as usual, but endeavouring to lead, as far as possible, a religious life; and, eventually, they were rewarded for their generosity in being called to be really religious. In this house they afforded refuge to disguised priests, and Mass was said secretly in their chapel.

One of their chief duties was to carry relief to the priests and nuns who had been driven from their convents; they supported all the religious in Poitiers. Besides this, they went to teach the catechism in the worst parts of the town, and the austerity of their life may be guessed by the fact, that they "ate only at three o'clock, and our food consisted of some soup, which we put on the fire when we went out, and into which we dipped some bread on our return, whether it were cooked or not; for the fire often went out, and the vegetables were half raw, and the broth cold." " But," adds Susanne Geoffroy, " we were hungry, and could eat even our bad fare with relish. We denied ourselves the use of animal food, and even butter, and we practised several other austerities."

Time passed on, the fury of the Revolution abated, but fresh trials for Susanne commenced. Her community, devout as they were, were not religious; they were not under the government and protection of the Church, and had no settled Rule. Naturally, then, when dissensions arose, there was no one to decide them; and Susanne, seeing this, resigned her office and withdrew. The community subsequently grew into a congregation, known as the congregation of the Sacred Hearts of Jesus and Mary of Picpus.

God had other designs for Susanne, and until these were accomplished He permitted all she did to fail eventually, in order to purify and discipline her soul. After leaving the first community, she was urged by some who had left with her to begin another; and accordingly she began a house known as "*La*

*Providence,*" in which she carried on good works; but here, again, storms arose, which caused her most terrible grief, and at length she saw it was best to quit this second work and retire into a convent in La Vendée. Just before she did so, the Mère Barat, the foundress of the Order of the Sacred Heart, came to Poitiers to begin the third house of her new congregation. Here, then, was the institute so long since pointed out to Susanne as a haven of rest. But she did not eagerly rush thither. She knew if God called her He would make the way plain, and in her prudence and consideration for others she feared to do harm to the Mère Barat's new foundation if she appeared to take refuge there from the storms in her own house. So she went to Chavagne and became a novice, with some Ursuline nuns. The community were charmed with her, and would willingly have retained her; but when the Mère Barat saw that she had really left Poitiers and " La Providence," she wrote to invite her to the Sacré Cœur. Susanne laid the whole matter before the director of the convent, who said the will of God was clearly manifested, and greatly as he regretted it, she must go.

The noviciate of the Sacré Cœur was then her next place of refuge, and here, says the Mère Barat herself, " though she was forty-four years of age, and had been Superioress fourteen years, she fulfilled all her duties as a novice with the most exemplary humility and obedience." After her profession she was sent to found a house in Niort, and trials and contradictions again pursued her, though of a different kind from her former ones. She had no longer dissensions within her household, for not only did the union which reigns in all fervent communities prevail in hers, but her assistant, the Mère Emilie Giraud, was bound to her by a peculiar affection and similarity of character. But the house at Niort was poor, unable to find pupils, and a constant source of anxiety to the Superior. She laid all the blame on herself, saying, "I am more fitted to destroy than to found houses."

However, after a time matters improved, pupils came to the convent, and when once the ice was broken, a tide of success set in, and the Mère Geoffroy was able to buy one of the largest houses in Niort for a new convent. A great grief awaited her, in the departure of her assistant, Madame Emilie Giraud, who was sent for to the house at Grenoble. When Susanne fixed her affections on any one, it was with a firm and clinging hold; and though she had never allowed herself to manifest more marks of love to Madame Emilie than to others, their hearts were knit together with a very close tie. Added to this, the abilities of Emilie made her the greatest help to the success of the house. But it was the will of superiors, and thus the will of God, and Susanne submitted, and made her sacrifice with that cheerfulness which God loveth. On the night following Emilie's departure, she was heard to say, when passing her now empty room, "Oh, my God! would that I had an Emilie to offer Thee every day!" After a short time this well-loved sister was restored to her; but the first separation had been a preparation for a longer one which was at hand. The Mère Geoffroy was summoned to Paris to assist at the general council of the Order, held at the Mother-House every six years, and at which all the Superiors of branch houses assist. After this council she was ordered to proceed to Lyons, and there found a house of the Sacré Cœur. Such was the respect in which the Mother-General held her opinion, that a single objection on her part would have sufficed to countermand the order; but Susanne said not a word, and went readily to meet the trials and difficulties inseparable from a new foundation. Here she passed the last eighteen years of her life, growing daily in virtue and heavenly grace, in every one's estimation but her own. Her humility was very deep, as well as her conformity to the will of God. She wrote to the Mère Emilie in May, 1833: "When I was young, I wrote down the resolutions I made in my retreat; now I only make one, conformity to the will of God in everything and in every place. In this word is contained the perfection of every state, of every employment, and of every situation." It is from her letters to this loved and trusted friend that we gain an insight into her noble character, for she was not given to speak much of herself. She writes thus one day: "I give continual thanks to God that I was born at a time so favourable to my salvation; everything turns to our advantage in conformity with the will of God. Let us show our gratitude to Him all the days of our life; do not let us merely thank Him for what is pleasant to us, but, above all, for what is painful to nature. Nothing can happen to us without the permission of God; let us, then, live in continual thanksgiving."

She had no love of praise or notice, and was free from that fault so often to be found in religious, of boasting of their Order; not that she was anything but a loving and loyal subject of the Order of the Sacred Heart—she loved and esteemed it beyond all others, and spoke of it in these terms to her Sisters; but she did not bring it forward to others, did not try to exalt it before men, and was always ready to speak with admiration of other religious institutes.

She had a great respect for the Order of the "Visitation." "We owe much to them," she said; "we are indebted to them for the beautiful name we bear." She was fond of reading the lives of the first nuns of this Order, and had much devotion to St. Francis de Sales and St. Jane Frances. "They were saints to be imitated," she would say, "for they sanctified themselves in common life, without appearing to do anything extraordinary." But her chief veneration was for the Society of Jesus, and she could not find words to express the regard and reverence she felt for the sons of St. Ignatius. To them, indeed, she had owed much,—a heavenly light as to her vocation, and a training in that spirit of patience and courage which had enabled her to withstand the storms and trials of her secular life.

Thus did she live, and thus did she prepare to die. Towards the end of her life she had a great dread of death, and a painful fear of God's judgment; but when the hour came, all was peace. For some days she lost her speech, but her smiling, serene face showed the joy within. She was unable to swallow food; but when the Holy Communion was brought to her, she was able to receive It. On the 13th of May, 1845, she breathed her last, without a sigh, aged eighty-three years—thirty-nine of which she had passed in religion—and leaving behind her a bright example and encouragement to the religious of the Order of the Sacred Heart.

No Order founded in the present century has spread more rapidly, or has more evidently the blessing of God, than this Society, devoted to the honour of the Heart of our Divine Lord; and doubtless among them there are many souls advancing in the same path which was trodden by this saintly religious.

## THE CONGREGATION OF SAINT CLOTILDE.

ALTHOUGH this community possesses a comparatively small number of subjects, the circumstances of its foundation, and the peculiarity of its Rule, are not unworthy of notice. When the fury of the Revolution was past, many religious institutes sprang into being. It has sometimes been asked, why so many of similar character were founded at the same time; but a moment's reflection gives the answer. The wants were too universal and too urgent to wait till the new Orders had acquired strength and stability, to enable them to form numerous branch houses; and therefore, in various places, and to meet different requirements, men and women at once joined themselves together. Previous to the Revolution, there had existed a community of women, called "The Perpetual Adoration of the Sacred Heart of Jesus." They were dispersed in the Reign of Terror, and the Superior, Madame Desfontaines, with some of her companions, were thrown into prison, and were only liberated on the 9th thermidor. On their deliverance, they wished to emigrate to America, and endeavour to re-form their community there. But God had other designs for them; they were no longer to watch before Him in continual adoration, but to work hard for souls, and gain back to Him the country He seemed to have lost. He made His Will known to them by the advice of an aged priest, who had been in the same prison, and whose sanctity had inspired their confidence. "The temple," he said, "has been destroyed, and it is the duty of faithful souls to press round its ruins, and try to rebuild them." "You are free," continued he, "to go and seek rest in another hemisphere; for my part, I shall remain by the ruins of Jerusalem."

This language deeply impressed them, and they gave up the idea of leaving their country. Madame Desfontaines resolved to begin a boarding school, trusting in help from God, for she and her Sisters were quite destitute. A friend came forward and offered to lend sixty francs. Nine pupils were promised, and they began the school. God's blessing was with them, and the school rapidly increased in number; and Madame Desfontaines now thought of forming her religious into a community dedicated to education, which should be adapted to those new wants, and that development in female education, which the great changes in society had brought forth. Her ardent desire also was to gain the confidence of parents who had unhappily followed the spirit of the time, and were estranged from God. She thought much and deeply over her project, and prayed fervently for light; and one day she went a pilgrimage to the Calvary on *Mont Valerian* to offer up her petition for Divine guidance.

From very early ages Mont Valerian had been a favourite place of pilgrimage; it had often been the abode of hermits; and a Calvary, with numerous chapels, had been erected, whither the faithful were accustomed to go to make the Stations of the Cross. During the Revolution, this old sanctuary was awfully profaned, and one of the chapels of the Calvary was dedicated to *Venus*. After the Restoration of the Bourbons, Louis XVIII. gave it to a new society of priests recently founded by the Père Rauzan, and called the Missionaries of France. They restored the Calvary, and kept the Octaves of the Feasts of the Invention and Exaltation of the Holy Cross (May 3rd, and September the 14th) with great solemnity. Sermons were preached on these days, and many Masses were offered up.

It was during the Novena of September, 1820, that Madame Desfontaines went to pray at Mont Valerian. Just as she was leaving the spot, she was attracted by the sound of a voice preaching. Entering the little Chapel of the Missionaries, she found an old priest speaking to some soldiers, in a simple, familiar way, of the happiness they would taste in the service of God; with touching sweetness he spoke of a Christian's duties, and showed how easily they can be fulfilled. Madame Desfontaines listened for a few minutes, and a voice seemed to speak to her soul, and say, "This is the guide from God for you." She had no doubt he was the Père Rauzan, the Superior of the Missionaries, and she determined to lay her designs before him. On the 29th of September she accordingly did so, telling him also of the inspiration which she believed to have had in the Chapel on Mont Valerian.

Père Rauzan listened attentively, and said, "For thirty years, Madame, I have wished to see the foundation of a new community devoted to the education of the young. Every day I pray for it; and I believe it is necessary in order that we may secure the fruit of our missions. We have learnt by experience that the men who quickly obey the call of grace during the holy exercises, are always those who in their early years received their first lessons of the faith from a holy mother. The Archbishop of Bordeaux and I have often considered together the grave question of the education of women. This good Bishop said to me one day, that if he had to choose between a seminary and a congregation entirely dedicated to this work, he would not hesitate to give the preference to the congregation. I know that during the last few years many congregations have been formed for this purpose; they produce a great deal of good, but they do not entirely carry out my views. I will therefore examine your proposition before God."

The result of his prayers and reflections on the subject were afterwards related by the Père Rauzan himself to the religious of St. Clotilde. "I could not believe, my very dear daughters, that you would entirely enter into my views; and yet, the more I prayed, the more it seemed to me that to do all the good that you could to the pupils, you must devote yourselves entirely to them. I waited then; I confessed and directed the nuns, and even gave a Retreat to them; but I made no definite announcement. Madame Desfontaines urged me to do so; she went to the Archbishop of Paris (Cardinal de Périgord). His Eminence much wished me to proceed, but I told him I must take a longer time for counsel with God. Time passed; my thoughts were the same. Again Madame Desfontaines spoke to me, and I said, 'Madame, I have reflected upon your proposal, and upon the conditions under which I can accept it. I am still convinced you will not entirely accord with my views.' 'And why?' she answered, 'we are entirely in your hands; try, and you will see all that you wish will be done.' But I said, 'You do not know what I shall exact; it will require an unreserved devotion. According to my views, the religious will have to give themselves entirely to the children, to teach them their daily duties, their exercises of piety, and the habits of their whole life. They will have to become pupils with the pupils, live for them, with them, as them. I will not authorize a single practice which can distract them from their work. They shall recite no Office; their office shall be day and night to watch over the children, to instruct them, or to endeavour earnestly to attain the knowledge which they have to impart. They shall not have cells, nor a refectory of their own; they shall sleep in the dormitory of the pupils, take their meals with them, and even their recreation. All the religious must live this life in common with the children, not excepting the Superioress-General. The greatest of all evils, and the way in which children learn so much that is wrong, arises from the negligence in education. Enough care and devotion is never given to this work. But,' I added, 'who will ever subjugate themselves to the life which I want to see established, and which I should exact from any community that I took charge of?' Madame Desfontaines was not discouraged. 'Father,' she said, 'you have reflected, you have prayed, you have asked prayers from others, and you have thought deeply on this subject. On our side, we are disposed to enter into your views; doubtless it is the Will of God that this community should be as you have planned it.' This is the sense at least, my dear daughters, of the conversation I had with your foundress. I then consented to try, and I guided the community according to the rules which I had drawn out. I had begged inspiration from God for them, and had submitted them to several holy and enlightened priests, and to Monseigneurs Zalabert and Frayssinous, who had approved of them. Nevertheless, I still hesitated. I went to see the Cardinal and Monseigneur de Quélen, and as soon as they said to me, *It must be*, I no longer thought of withdrawing, and watched anxiously over a work which, I believed, had been inspired by God."

The Rule which the Père Rauzan drew up for the new congregation omitted some of the outward observances of the religious state, and some of those practised in community; but it retained the spirit and the virtues which characterize the true Spouses of Jesus Christ. They were to be, not so much religious who vow themselves to education, as instructresses who, to assure the success of their work, vow themselves to the religious life. They were to have no grating or enclosure. Their dress was to be a simple one—of purple merino, with a small cross on the breast; a white cap, over which in chapel only a black veil is thrown; there were to be no extraordinary mortifications; and in *appearance* it was an easy life. But there was required from them obedience, forgetfulness of self, application to their work at all times, and not a minute of solitude or of liberty. They live only for the children whom they have to guide. For their sake, they were to apply themselves to difficult studies, so as to be able to give a brilliant and yet solid education, which will please the world, and yet be a safeguard to virtue. The children would thus be constantly watched in their walks and their words, none of which can pass unobserved.

Such were the wishes of Père Rauzan. We can understand why he hesitated in imposing rules which exacted so absolute an abnegation. Madame Desfontaines and her religious willingly accepted the arduous task, and they soon had the happiness of seeing themselves approved by ecclesiastical authority. Monseigneur de Quélen, whose advice had been often asked by the humble Père Rauzan, proposed the nuns should take the name of Dames de St. Clotilde, because, as they were to re-animate the faith in France, they could not have a better Patroness than she to whom the first foundation of that faith in the land was due.

The Congregation was approved in 1821, and in August of that year the religious made their vows in this Order, although most of them had, as we have seen, been long since vowed to God's service. Père Rauzan was appointed Superior, and Madame Desfontaines Superioress. This excellent nun only lived three years after the accomplishment of her wishes, and Madame Fraissinet was elected Superioress. For two years Père Rauzan watched carefully over the new community, till he saw it thoroughly penetrated by the spirit he wanted to prevail there. Then another of the Missionaries assisted him in the charge. When he was away from France, he constantly wrote to the religious wise and loving counsels. "One thought," wrote he, "is always with me; it follows me everywhere, and even when I wake in the night,—it is the immense good that holy mothers can do. Yes, my dear daughters, in travelling over the provinces, I have found it to be a fact, that in places where the faith has been preserved, there are a great number of good mothers living. The good they can do is wonderful. Perhaps, in this age, it is the only means of regenerating France." The union of the two virtues, sweetness and firmness, were most necessary to the nuns of St. Clotilde, he often said, and his daily anxiety was to encourage his spiritual daughters to make rapid steps in the way of perfection. "I do not know how to express to you," said he, "to what a point I desire the community of St. Clotilde to arrive. I want to see firmly rooted there the spirit of prayer, humility, and fervour, and a zeal for the salvation of your pupils, which you must place far above all human advantages; these, however, you ought carefully to provide for them also. Certainly, I have nothing to reproach you with, but I wish things to be always better and better. How can we avoid a pious eagerness in the matter of our sanctification, and that of so many pupils, who one day will do infinite good in the world, if you know how, with God's help, to plant solid virtues in their hearts?" The spirit of the Père Rauzan was like that of St. Francis of Sales; he would have everything done gently, and without disquiet. He writes thus to a Sister:—" No thought, you tell me, is so useful to you, or brings you so near to God, as *confidence*. Follow that *attrait*. Can we count too much on a Father Whose greatness, power, and goodness are infinite? But He does not only permit you to hope in Him; He commands you."

The novice-mistress having some fears about the difficulties of her charge, he wrote to her: "We cannot imagine a greater happiness on earth than to do all the good we are capable of, with the hope of drawing greater good from it, and this is what is reserved for you; this inestimable good is more especially attached to the functions which you fill. A humble and fervent prayer is always heard. Ask all you want from God, and He will not refuse you. Ask the grace to inspire in your novices the forgetfulness of self, and our miserable personal interests, the desire to sacrifice themselves entirely to the glory of Jesus Christ, and those sentiments of zeal, of renouncement, and of love, which ought to establish in your house one spirit and one mind, and an intimate union with Jesus Christ." And to the Superioress he wrote these beautiful words:— "Strive, my daughter, to become very holy, for the spiritual prosperity of a religious house depends much on the fervour of the superiors. I cannot say this without making a sad reflection on myself; but we ought not to be discouraged, all can be obtained by prayer." To a Sister, who wrote to tell him of the death of one of the community, he replied: "I can hardly tell you how much the news affected me; I was overwhelmed! In four years to lose three excellent subjects, when your number is still so small; and such good Sisters, such holy religious! However, hope and courage return at the remembrance of their dispositions for death: their resignation, their contempt of life, their ardent desire to be united to their Divine Spouse, and to the most holy Virgin, their Mother. God does not abandon a house where He has deigned to form these holy souls; it is not until their deaths that He leaves the seeds of new life." Another time he wrote:—"Arm yourselves with a holy courage, my daughter; our all consists in doing the Holy Will of God. A single day of resignation has often more merit than many years."

Instructed in such a manner, no wonder the community of St. Clotilde advanced in the path of perfection. As the infirmities of age increased on the good Father, he was seldom able to visit the community. One December morning, in a bitter frost, the astonished nuns beheld him enter. The roads were so slippery, that the carriage which brought him had been two hours and a half coming from the Rue de Varenne to the Rue de Reuilly. "My dear children," said he, "I wished to be once more among you and your dear pupils, for perhaps I shall not see you again. It is an old man's fancy. I wanted so much to come once more." However, it was not his last visit, for he came afterwards to the profession of Mademoiselle de Brissac, a member of a noble and pious family who were very dear to him. When he could no longer leave the house, the religious used to visit him occasionally. Constantly he said, "What good you are called upon to do, my dear children, if you remain as God has inspired me to found you!" His life of holiness and labour drew to its close. On his deathbed he blessed his sons, the Fathers of the Missions of France, and one of them said to him, "Father, will you also bless your daughters at St. Clotilde?" "Yes, yes, yes," he answered, and they were his last words; a few hours after he breathed his last, in the ninetieth year of his age.

Since his death, the nuns of St. Clotilde have been faithful to the Rule he laid down for them. A lady who was educated there thus describes the life they lead:—" I do not suppose there is any other house where the mistresses and pupils live so much together. Dormitories, meals, and recreations are all in common. As the nuns were numerous, and they always played with us, it was impossible to have any conversation which they did not hear. Particular friendships were forbidden; hence the union which reigned in the house. I have heard it said that school life produces jealousy; I do not believe St. Clotilde's could ever be reproached with this; we were too well watched for a girl of bad habits to gain any influence. As to punishments, I never saw them given; all was so organized, there was no need for them; the hope of obtaining a reward, or of entering a confraternity, was sufficient to make us submissive and studious."

No one can visit the Convent of St. Clotilde without being struck by the especial brightness and gaiety of spirit that seems to pervade the house; nor can any fail to be impressed by the graceful courtesy of the nuns, and their consideration for others. The convent and grounds are spacious, the chapel simple and elegant. The community is a large one, and so is the school; but there is but the one convent in Paris belonging to the Order. For our part, we confess that we do not think the Order of St. Clotilde will spread rapidly, or become a very large body. The life of abnegation required from the nuns is so absolute, that the vocations must necessarily be rare. Their work, like that of all the educational Orders, is generally hidden; the merry, careless girls who leave the convent remember, in hours of trial and temptation, the lessons they learnt of faith and love; but the conflict and the victory are often hidden ones, and the nuns who taught them do not know the result of their care at least not on earth. Nevertheless, a work began as theirs was, and blessed as its first increase has been, is certain to hold a place, though not perhaps a prominent one, in the Church on earth, and a high and glorious one in the Church in Heaven.

## THE CONGREGATION OF THE SISTERS OF CHARITY OF ST. VINCENT DE PAUL.

No community in the Church of God is perhaps so widely known as this Congregation. The vast number of their subjects, their extension into all parts of the earth, and the success of their numerous works of charity, have necessarily tended to bring them before the eyes of the world.

Before them the infidel even has shown respect, and men are forced to admit they are indeed one of "the glories of France." The name of their great founder is better known than any other saint, and they who can scorn a St. Francis or a St. Teresa can hardly make a scoff of a Vincent de Paul. Great praise is oftentimes showered upon this society, but it falls generally on the body, not on the individual members; and in the great crowd the countess is side by side with the peasant, both equally unknown.

It is hardly necessary to do more than glance at the life of St. Vincent de Paul, for it is well known to all classes of readers. He was the son of a poor peasant, and his early childhood was spent in keeping sheep—a fitting type of his after life. Touching anecdotes are told by his biographers of his charity to others, of his giving away his few hardly-earned pence to those poorer than himself. Friends who saw much future promise in him assisted his parents in means for his education, and a vocation for the priesthood soon became visible, and was followed. His first Mass was said in a solitary place, that he might unobserved pour out his soul in gratitude to God. His great devotion to the work of the priesthood drew notice upon him, and those who knew him learnt to love and value him. Once, on making a voyage by sea, he was taken prisoner by pirates, and sold into captivity. He served his masters with fidelity, and was passed from one hand to another as valuable property. His third master was an apostate Christian, who had married a Turkish woman. The wife was attracted by the calm and joyful countenance of the slave as he sat at work. All the eager emotions and stormy passions which darkened the faces of the men she knew, were absent from that face; and so, turning to him, she asked him to sing, and clear and sweet in that heathen country rose the inspired hymn, "How shall we sing the Lord's song in a strange land;" and then, his thoughts soaring beyond the memory of the old Jewish captivity to the desire for freedom from earth's chains and burdens, he sang to Her, the Mother of Mercy, " that after this our exile ended, she would show unto him Jesus, the fruit of her Womb." And then Vincent spoke to the poor heathen woman of Jesus Christ and His dear mother, of their love and their pity; and the wife, running to her husband, said, " Is *this*, then, the religion thou hast renounced?" Repentance began to soften the hardened heart, and finally Vincent returned to Europe with the man and his wife both converted.

Seeing that the great evil of the Church of France was at that time the want of good priests who would devote themselves heart and soul to their work, and who would go and give missions in desolate places, he founded his Congregation of the Missions, consisting of priests who would, though remaining secular priests, live together in community a strict and mortified life. The house of the Congregation was at St. Lazare, formerly an hospital for lepers, dedicated to St. Lazarus. From thence it arose that the sons of St. Vincent are often called Lazaristes. Here Vincent commenced the good work of giving retreats to men of the world—for this holy exercise, conceived and brought to perfection by St. Ignatius, was most highly esteemed by St. Vincent. It was astonishing the number of people who availed themselves of this means of grace. Men of all ranks, the noble and the artisan, the man of letters and the peasant, might be found in St. Lazare. Gradually did Vincent change the whole moral aspect of Paris. He reformed the Hôtel Dieu, the largest Parisian hospital. He formed a confraternity of Ladies of Charity, who were to visit and relieve the poor. He founded the hospital for old men and women, also that for forsaken children. He might be seen in the streets of Paris on perishing nights in winter, when the house-tops were laden with snow, bearing in his arms some little miserable infant, left by an unnatural mother to die, and that without baptism. The streets of Paris then were dangerous at night, being infested by groups of robbers. At times they rudely stopped the saint. He drew aside his cloak and showed *his* treasure, and the men fell back. "It is *Monsieur Vincent*," they exclaimed with awe, and they slunk away. No cry of human distress ever appealed to him in vain. Incredible is the sum of money he collected to send to the relief of those suffering by the war in Lorraine. He loved to assist in various delicate ways the rich who had met with reverses, saying, they were like our Lord, "who was very noble, and yet very poor."

At the feet of Vincent the gay and accomplished Abbé de Rance poured forth his sin and sorrow, and went, fortified by his counsel, to found the austere order of *La Trappe*. Vincent was trusted by the Queen Regent with the distribution of much of her church patronage, yet never did his visits to Court, or his influence with the great, disturb his humility. For six years he lay under an accusation of having stolen a miserable sum of money. He never attempted to clear himself, but thanked his accuser. On the death-bed of his enemy, the truth came out. When any sought to flatter him, he reminded them indirectly that he was peasant born; and once, having momentarily felt ashamed of some poor relation who came to see him, he accused himself of his fault in the full Chapter of the Fathers of the Missions.

We might speak of his love for prayer, of the hours that he stole from sleep to pass with God; we might speak of those sharp penances, of the daily discipline with which he remembered his Lord's sufferings; but pages would but faintly shadow forth the record of him " who has filled the whole world with the perfume of his name, which, like the name of Jesus, from whence its greatness is borrowed, is as ointment poured forth."* The foundation of the Sisters of Charity seems well to fit in, as it were, with all other parts of St. Vincent's life, for the relief of the wants of the poor was his continual and ruling thought. He had bestowed great pains on the management of the *Confrérie* of the Ladies of Charity, and had been aided in doing so by Mademoiselle Legras, of whom, further on, we must speak more in detail.

This confraternity had now existed some years, and had wrought much good; but yet it had its drawbacks, and over these St. Vincent often pondered. He saw that the charity of ladies living in the world at that time was necessarily of a limited nature. They could give money; but time and personal help were often beyond their power. Often when they were intending to go and visit a poor woman, some home call interrupted them, and they sent their alms by their servants. These servants were not of their mistresses' mind; they did not like

* Manning.

climbing into wretched attics, and groping about amid dirt and misery, and thus neglect and rough words were often the portion of the poor. Now it dawned on St. Vincent's mind whether it were not possible to have a class of servants to do this work only for the ladies, and who, being hired for that service, would not be likely to grumble at or neglect it. While these thoughts were recurring to him, and he was always very slow in working out his ideas, he went to give a mission in a distant province of France. In a village he visited was living a young peasant girl, whose occupation was to tend cows in the fields. Reading and writing were unknown to her; but while she wandered among her cows, sweet thoughts of doing something for Him, who despises not a cup of cold water, passed through her soul, and so she began to teach herself to read, and whenever any neighbour more learned than herself passed by, she sought for a little instruction. And when she knew how to read she began to teach the poor village children. The Mission threw her in St. Vincent's way, and he told her how she could serve the sick in Paris. She consented to come, and was placed under the care of Mademoiselle Legras, and thus became the first Sister of Charity. What was her end? Obscure even as the beginning; she was "sent to serve the sick in the parish of St. Nicolas du Chardounet," and among them caught the plague, and being taken to the hospital of St. Louis, died there.

Three or four young girls had now come to Mademoiselle Legras, and she took a small house in the outskirts of Paris, and gave herself to the task of guiding and forming them to be "good servants of the poor." No thought of founding a religious order had then, or for years afterwards, entered the mind of St. Vincent, or of Louise Legras. "I declare to you again and again," said St. Vincent, long afterwards, "that you can be certain God only is your founder, for I can say to you before Him, that in all my life I never thought of it, nor Mademoiselle Legras either."

Time went on; the number of servants of the poor multiplied; they were no longer gathered together in one house, but placed by twos and threes in the different parishes. They were completely under the orders of the Ladies of Charity, and were sent hither and thither, as they pleased. They had not to work in parishes organized according to modern rules, with schools and hospitals. The former did not exist—the latter were insufficient: they had to teach little children the catechism, to feed the starving, to dress wounds and sores, to make up medicines for the sick, and clothes for the naked. Years passed; they increased in their numbers and their work, but yet had no Rule or religious dress. They wore the costume of peasant women of the period, and they formed their manner of life upon St. Vincent's oral instructions. They had a daily rule of the most simple description: they were to rise at four, and go to rest at nine; to recite morning and night prayers together, to make half an hour's meditation morning and evening, to spend another half-hour in spiritual reading, to recite their Rosary, to hear Mass, and to examine themselves twice a day. This was all the outward observance St. Vincent asked from them. No monastic silence, no long fasting, were prescribed; and long before St. Vincent began to form them to outward religious exercises, they had been well trained in the practice of the interior virtues, which alone gives those exercises their value. "To quit all things on earth, and not to quit oneself, would be doing nothing," said he to them. "It is not the religious Order that makes a saint, but the care the persons called to it take to perfect themselves. You can have very imperfect people in religious Orders, and this will show you it is not necessary to be shut up in a cloister to acquire the perfection God asks from you." And so, as the years went by, a plan gradually matured itself in the mind of St. Vincent. He saw the demands for the servants of the poor increasing daily; he saw their work was blessed—their labours crowned with success; he saw that they must become mothers to the orphan and a staff to the aged; that they must fear no contagion, weary of no toil, and for all these things he knew well the hardy, enduring spirit of the peasant girl, or her simple, childlike piety would not be sufficient. They must then follow their Lord in His weary march from the cities of Judea. Like Him, they must journey often; like Him, be pressed upon, and wearied, and scarce have time for prayer; and to do this, they must work in His strength, and be *His own*.

The Queen of Poland wrote for three "servants" to be sent to nurse the soldiers. To leave their country, and go to strange, untried labours, required courage; but St. Vincent had no difficulty in finding the number. They were sent, and on their arrival at Warsaw, the Queen said, "Two of you can now go on to the army; but you, Ma Sœur ——, I will keep to console me." The Sister began to weep. "Why these tears?" said Her Majesty; "do you not like to enter my service?" "Your Majesty has many who can attend on you," said the Sister, "and the poor have no one." The answer was sufficient, and the three Sisters went together to their work; and when St. Vincent heard of the incident, he thanked God. When the work of the servants of the poor had gone on for about ten or twelve years, St. Vincent began to assemble them together once a fortnight, at the house where Mademoiselle Legras lived, and which was called their principal house. There he held "conferences,"—an exercise differing a little from an instruction, as occasionally he would question one or more Sisters as to the way in which they performed the duty or understood the subject on which he was speaking. Conferences, St. Vincent taught them, were begun by our Lord Himself, with His disciples; and it was in one of them that St. Peter spoke, when he said, "Lord, to whom shall we go? Thou hast the words of eternal life." Nothing gives such an insight into St. Vincent's character as these conferences. Many of them were written down from memory by some of the Sisters, and have been ever since carefully preserved among the private books of the community. A few copies, though rare and difficult of access, are still left to the student, and it is from one of these that the following extracts are taken. In reading them we forget the great founder of glorious works of charity, the man who had a voice in the councils of state, or rather we see the depth from whence sprung that wonderful influence Vincent possessed. He was not a man of genius or talent, nor of great learning, nor of eloquence. His instructions were of the simplest kind, in the plainest words; but his love for God was intense and unwavering. In the middle of his conferences a sort of transport of love would possess him, and he burst forth, as we may say, into prayer. "O Saviour of my soul!" was his most frequent expression; his devotion to our Blessed Lady was like that of all the saints, most filial and confiding. "Oh most holy Virgin," said he, one day, "who declared in thy canticle that it was because of thy humility that God has done great things for thee, obtain for this company grace to imitate thee; to obey, because obeying is to practise humility. This is the grace I ask from Thee, my Lord, and my God, with all the tenderness of my affection. It is by thee, oh holy Virgin, that we hope to obtain it of thy dear Son, whom we wish to obey all our life. Refuse not thy mediation, and grant that, aided by their good angels, all our Sisters may endeavour to practise what they have been taught, for happy are those who obey."

At length a day came when the Sisters, being all assembled together, St. Vincent thus spoke: "Until now, my daughters, you have laboured by yourselves, and with no further obligation towards God than of complying with the order prescribed to you, and the manner of life that was given to you. Until now you have not been a distinct body and separate from the Ladies of Charity; but now it is the will of God that you become a particular body, which, without being totally separated from that *Confrérie*, has its peculiar exercises and functions.

Until now, as I have said, you have had no obligation; but now God wishes to ally you in a stricter manner by the approbation which He has permitted to be given to your manner of life and rules by the Archbishop of Paris. Here is the request that has been made to him; here are your Statutes and Rules, and his approbation, which I will read to you. Your title will be 'Sisters of Charity, Servants of the Sick Poor.' Oh, beautiful name! beautiful employment! Oh, my daughters, what have you done for God to merit the glorious title, Servants of the Poor? It is as if we said Servants of Jesus Christ, because He reckons as done to Himself all that is done for His members."

The conferences were now kept up regularly, and a great number were given to explain and draw out, as it were, the meaning of the Rules. "Your Rules are reasonable," said St. Vincent, "for I have spent much thought on them before giving them to you." Every part of their obligations was carefully explained to them, and golden words were spoken, to be treasured up by future generations for ages yet to come. Long since has every one present in those assemblies passed from earth. Dynasties have changed, wild storms have swept over the length and breadth of fair France, great men have arisen, great names have echoed in the Sorbonne, and in the national assemblies; but they all have passed away like shadows, and their deeds are almost forgotten; while the work of St. Vincent has endured and grown, and multiplied, and flourishes at this moment. St. Vincent's design for his daughters was a bold one: he was going against all the traditions of the conventual life. The cloister, the *grille*, the veil, and the cell,—where are these, people asked, in the new institute? St. Vincent had not forgotten them, and how must the hearts of the Sisters have thrilled, when he first spoke to them the words which have become so celebrated, and which were to be the keystone, as it were, of their Order!

"The streets of the city, or the houses of the sick, shall be your cloister; hired rooms shall be your cells; your chapel shall be the parish church; obedience shall be your solitude; the fear of God your grating; and a strict and holy modesty your only veil." And he went on to explain his meaning further:—"You ought to comport yourselves with as much recollection, purity of soul and body, detachment from creatures, and edification, as true religious in the retreat of their monastery." And then, with the fervour which always made the Saint eloquent, he added, "How beautiful it will be to see in paradise a Daughter of Charity, who has lived in the world in this manner, whose cell has been a hired room, and whose cloister obedience!

If you have, my daughters, an obedient and supple spirit to the Will of God; if you have His fear for your grating, and for your veil holy modesty, you will be better cloistered than religious, and you will be truly professed in your Order; and take care, my daughters, to keep yourselves closely in your cloister, that is, in the most perfect obedience, and in the practice of other virtues." At another time he spoke to them of holy obedience, and the indifference to place or work, which a true practice of this virtue brings in its train; and as he spoke, he looked around on the group of simple, gentle faces by whom he was surrounded, and he said, "It seems to me, my dear Sisters, that I read in your hearts an ardent desire to imitate the Saviour of your souls. But shall you not say, 'Must I go six hundred leagues from home; must I go beyond the sea?' Oh! I see indeed that you will; and I see indeed that you will go where obedience calls you, and that though you think you will never return again, you will not delay a moment. I am assured there is not one of you who has not made this act of resignation in her soul, and many of you have done so often. Oh, yes, by God's grace, I see you are all disposed to do whatever it may please the Divine Goodness to order for you; and it seems to me that I hear you say, 'Yes, my Lord Jesus Christ, I give myself entirely to Thee, with all the affection of my heart, and all the strength of my soul, to live and die in obedience, as Thou hast done. All will be the same to me, my God, whether I am sent to one place, or recalled to another, for a short time, or for long, to live or to die. I am content with all the events Thou hast ordered, provided Thou givest me the grace of obeying all my life for love of Thee.'"

Another time the conference was on the sense of the presence of God; and he taught them that it is not only in the stillness of the cloister, or in following a perfect routine of duty, that this can be preserved. Amid the noise and confusion of the world, amid the distractions of a multitude of employments, the heart can still be united to God. He had learnt to do it himself, and he would fain have them follow his example. He taught them how to pray as they walked along. "Oh!" said he, "how many poor people have I confessed while walking along, when I am giving Missions! They run after me—'Father, I have not confessed; I pray you to confess me; I hope God will pardon my sins;' and then I heard them, and in this way we can also pray and meditate." This instruction was especially necessary for an Order whose rule obliges them, *in case of necessity*, to leave their spiritual exercises for the service of the poor. After speaking of the practice of the presence of God, St. Vincent ended thus: "I ask pardon for myself, a miserable sinner; I ask it also for the company. Regard not, O Lord, the voice of the sinner who speaks to Thee, but regard the hearts of our poor Sisters who, by my voice, ask pardon. Fill their souls with an ardent desire of pleasing Thee, give them Thy spirit of sweetness and of strength, so that, imitating Thee, our Sisters can glorify God, and correspond with Thy designs for them, so that they may gain others to Thy service, and live in union together. I ask this grace for our Sisters present and absent. I ask it by the intercession of Thy holy Mother, and of all the Saints who glorify Thee in heaven, and of those who are living on earth. I ask it by the intercession of the guardian angels of our Sisters, who desire to be faithful to Thee. I trust, my God, Thou wilt grant my request; and in this confidence, miserable sinner that I am, I, who have so often gone against the commandments Thou hast given me, the inspirations Thou hast sent me, and the obligations that I have to practise virtue, still will not refrain confiding in Thy infinite mercy to pronounce the words of benediction on this community. Make them efficacious, and fill the hearts of all our Sisters with the spirit of charity."

Another secret of St. Vincent's influence was his wonderful humility. It was entire and unceasing, for it sprung from his deep consciousness of the awful purity of the uncreated God. We are *nothing* before Him, was St. Vincent's feeling, and words of blame and self-condemnation were as great a relief to him to utter, as words of vanity are to others. " We ought, my father," remarked a Sister one day, in a conference, " to hear your words as we would those of God Himself, because you hold His place to us." " Alas! my daughter, I am a miserable sinner, and nothing else," was the instant answer.

Once, after giving a conference on Observance of Rules, he said, " Miserable man that I am, I have not kept faithfully my Rule; I ask pardon of you, my daughters. How many faults regarding you have I not committed! I beg you to ask mercy from God for me, and I will pray our Lord Jesus Christ to give you Himself His holy benediction; and I will not say the words to-day, because my faults towards you have made me unworthy; I pray our Lord to do it Himself." " Here," continues the simple chronicle, " Monsieur Vincent kissed the ground; but Mademoiselle Legras and all the Sisters were so deeply affected that their father refused to give his blessing, and begged so earnestly for it, that at last he said, 'Pray God, then, my dear daughters, not to regard my unworthiness, nor the sins of which I am guilty, but to have mercy on me, and to shed His benediction on you, while I pronounce the words.' " How touching also was this spirit of simplicity whenever he had occasion to speak of himself! " When I went to live with

Monsieur and Madame de Gondi, I resolved to regard Monsieur de Gondi as in the place of God, and Madame de Gondi as the Holy Virgin; and I do not remember ever having received their orders except as coming from God, and I dare to say that, if God has given His benediction to the Congregation of the Missions, it is in virtue of the obedience that I gave to Monsieur and Madame de Gondi, and in virtue of the spirit of submission with which I entered their house. To God be all the glory; to me all the confusion!"

Once, after speaking of sickness, of the way in which to use it to the good of their souls, and the fidelity to rules, which must still be observed, he says, "I pray our Lord to give you grace always to keep your rules, which appear of little importance, but in reality are very great. O Saviour of my soul! Thou that art the true Physician, be so to our bodies as well as our souls. Thou hast taught the animals the necessary remedies for their ills, teach us also how to use those which Thou hast created for us, and teach us how to use them not only for ourselves, but for our poor." We cannot do more than give little fragments of those golden words that were continually falling from the lips of the Saint. He warns them against self-seeking even in the holiest actions. "In this way spiritual persons make shipwreck, because they seek their own satisfaction in confession, communion, prayer, and all spiritual conversations." When he spoke of the poor, and of the honour which it is to serve them: "Ah! they will be the great lords in heaven; to them will the door be opened, says the Gospel." St. Vincent was very fond of repeating a salutary advice again and again, till it had taken root in his hearers' hearts; and one of his favourite repetitions was the saying of Pope Clement VIII., — "Give me a religious who has been perfectly exact to his rule, and without any proof of his working miracles, I will declare him a saint." He was speaking one day of the beautiful spirit of the peasant girls,— one which he had good cause to know thoroughly from his own training amongst them: their spirit, he said, was one of great simplicity; simple, in believing what they are told; never using fine words, never boasting of themselves, and totally without ambition; very sober in use of food, bread and soup generally all their nourishment; and then the Saint remarked, when we hear of our Lord eating, it is generally recorded that he "broke bread." The hard work of the peasants was to be a model also. "Spare not your bodies in serving God in His poor members," he exclaimed. "You are the spouses of Jesus Christ," he cried one day. "If, then, you be faithful, what have you to fear?" At the time of the foundation of this congregation, it brought, as it were, an entirely new element into the Church. The idea of uniting works of charity with the religious life was not indeed new, as we have said; but all these good works were done within the shade of the cloister. It was thought impossible to preserve the religious spirit without an enclosure.

St. Vincent of Paul had witnessed the failure of the first idea of St. Francis de Sales, and he therefore determined to make his congregation a body entirely distinct. He would not have them called religious. "You are not religious," he said often; "and if ever you become so, the company will be at *extreme unction.*" From thence it arose that in St. Vincent's time the Sisters of Charity were far from receiving that admiration, even homage, which is now their well-merited portion throughout Christendom. The Carmelites, just then resplendent with the halo of St. Teresa's life, the Visitation, the chosen Order of St. Francis de Sales, were those which people thought the most of; and the Servants of the Poor, in a dress like ordinary peasant-women, scattered about in twos and threes, and at everybody's beck and call, were rather looked down upon. And this very contempt was a perfect delight to St. Vincent. "Your spirit is that of our Saviour," he said, "humbled, unknown, and despised by all the world. Are you not very happy that He has thought of you, and that you have been chosen from many others to imitate Him in a manner of life so humble and low as yours, by which He has willed you to follow Him in the most difficult thing in the world, which is, really to humble oneself? In reality there is nothing more difficult, nor that costs us more trouble;" and unceasingly did he impress upon them the love of contempt—being unknown, unthought of, counted below other Orders, put in the last place.

"Who would have believed," cried he, " that the Sisters of Charity would be chosen by God to attend upon the army? Men go there to kill, and you go there to give life. Oh, Saviour! be thou blessed for this grace." How little did the Saint dream that in time to come the flag of every Catholic nation going out to war would be followed by a number of his daughters, ready to heal and console? How little did he foresee the time when the Carmelite and Augustine nuns would be unnoticed by the world, and his simple daughters be held in honour and renown throughout the whole earth. Yet even then he looked forward to the increase of numbers, and he was therefore most desirous that the first Sisters should, as it were, lay the foundation of the future edifice by their perfection in the virtues of their state. "You have the happiness to be the first called," said he; "for such a state of life has not been in the Church since the time of the Apostles, and now poor village girls are called to it. Humble yourselves much, and labour to be perfect, and become Saints; for you must not hope those who come after you, and who will mould themselves by your example, will be better than you: generally, like produces like. Take care, then, to adorn your state, or, at least, not to dishonour it, leaving unworthy daughters, because of your example."

There is an anecdote in the relation of the Conferences which, while it makes one smile, serves to show the great simplicity of St. Vincent and his first daughters. He had been speaking one day of the spirit of mortification which should govern them, and one of them innocently remarked, she supposed the custom of scenting the cupboards in which linen was kept would not be right for them. The existence of this luxury was unknown to St. Vincent, and he was so astonished that, adds the chronicle, quaintly, "the astonishment of the holy man was his only reply."

The first Sisters of Charity had indeed many helps to assist them in their arduous life, not only St. Vincent himself, but an example living among them in their Superioress, Mademoiselle Legras. At the first glance at her life she would seem scarcely a fit instrument for the difficult undertaking. She was nobly born, (being a *de Marilac*,) delicate in health, educated in a manner at once solid and refined. From her earliest youth her heart was given to God, but she did not think of a life of toil for the poor, and her longing was for the retirement of a Carmelite cloister. Her health rendered the fulfilment of this desire impossible, and she therefore entered the marriage state. For twelve long years, by the side of a sick, querulous husband, Louise Legras learnt her lesson; learnt to submit to others, learnt abnegation of self, and forgetfulness of her own joys and sorrows in the griefs of others; and thus did the Holy Spirit fashion her soul for a long and arduous future. She became a mother too, and then was infused into her soul that deep and tender love, that wonderful spirit of self-sacrifice, which few practise so perfectly as a good mother.

The world was nothing to Louise; she might have taken her place among the great ladies of her time, and won her share of fame, but she chose a different path. Her only sorrows were the faults and imperfections she saw in herself; and her director, the Bishop of Belley, the intimate friend of St. Francis de Sales, being obliged to leave Paris, besought St. Vincent to receive her under his guidance. Mademoiselle * Legras perceived the sanctity of St. Vincent, and rendered him the most implicit obedience and respect. In a few years, the death of her husband placed her at liberty to devote

* French women of higher rank than their husbands retain this title.

herself to the poor, for her only child was a son; and as we have already said, she was chosen by St. Vincent to guide the new work of the Servants of the Poor,—chosen doubtless by him as the person of most discretion and piety he could find to superintend the untaught girls he placed around her, yet becoming gradually one of the body herself, as it developed more and more the character which Almighty God designed for it. Mademoiselle Legras was the first of the Sisters who made vows, and from the circumstance of her having done so on the Feast of the Annunciation, the Sisters always renew their vows on that day. Mademoiselle Legras never, however, wore the habit, but always retained the black dress and veil usual for widows at that period. She was a living example to the Sisters, and her exhortations were full of the love of God and forgetfulness of self. She writes to a Superior of a branch house: " Those whom God has charged to be over others must forget themselves entirely in everything. We ought to consider that those who are in charge should be as the *mules* of the company. Ask from our Lord this grace for you and me; exercise yourself a little in patience, and with great sweetness, condescension, and discretion. Oh! if we knew our obligations, we should fear the weight of the charges that are given to us, and we should humble ourselves continually. Do not think, dear Sister, that I say this from any knowledge I have of you in particular; I am speaking generally of all those who are in charge, and most of myself, who more than any one has reason to fear. Let us humble ourselves before all to try and keep ourselves in safety; and, above all, let us give ourselves generously to God, to suffer all the humiliations that our pride has need of, that we may not be lost."

Brought up as she had been in riches and luxuries, her love of holy poverty was remarkable. "You have had some necessities," she writes, "and will have some more perhaps. Truly, my dear Sister, does not this give joy to your heart, making your state like that in which our Lord and His holy Mother so often found themselves? Believe me, my Sister, when I see splendid establishments all flourishing at the beginning, I fear for the end. Oh! hasten nothing. The things that are begun quietly are begun solidly. The remembrance that the Sisters of Charity are the servants of the poor is very necessary to keep them to their duty." And another time she exclaimed, " Let not the servants be better off than their masters; let us have His spirit Who said, ' He was not come into this world to be served, but to serve.' " Her love for holy obedience was equally manifest. She was always saying, " Remember our Father's advice." And she wrote to one of her Sisters, " I hope, my Sister, that you have embraced the yoke with great submission of spirit, because Monsieur Vincent has ordered it for you. Enter then anew into your employment with great humility and mistrust of yourself, remembering the teaching that the Son of God has given us, telling us to learn of Him to be meek and humble of heart." " Never think," she writes again, " of beginning any work, hospital or other, without asking Monsieur Vincent; and if any one speaks to you of such, do not give your own approbation. Leave it to God, He will show you His Will by the way of obedience." Once, writing about the admission of novices, she says, " We shall always have enough, having those whom God gives us." Her love for the poor was ever deep and increasing; to serve them was her delight. She would receive those who left the prisons, wash their feet, and clothe them with her own hands. As for her Sisters, her tenderness for them was so great, that when her health was decayed it was necessary to use caution in telling her of their deaths, for her grief would perfectly overwhelm her; and when those in the house with her were sick, she was beside their pillow, and in the hour of death her voice of maternal tenderness did not fail them. Long since, St. Vincent had said to her, " When you are praised and esteemed, unite your spirit to the contempt, the mockeries, and affronts that the Son of God has suffered. In truth, a really humble spirit is humbled as much by honours as by contempts, and is like a bee, who gathers his honey from a bitter as well as from a sweet flower. I hope you will act thus." And this deep truth in humility sank in the heart of Louise Legras, and brought forth fruit. Though by office the first in the community, she might have been deemed the last. Always the first to accuse herself of any fault against the Rule, always seeking the lowest offices, she might be seen serving in the refectory, and washing up the dishes; and weakness and age alone hindered her from performing the most menial offices. Never speaking in a tone of command, her directions were always entreaties, her thanks so abundant and affectionate. The Assistant Superior was entreated to warn her of her faults, and with deep humility she would receive any admonition; seldom, indeed, was it needed, for the Assistant afterwards averred, the difficulty was to find fault in so perfect a soul. Whenever any Sister took a reproof amiss, she was wont to ask the Assistant if she thought it was *her* fault, if she had spoken too harshly, and she was ingenious in finding excuses for any who were in fault. " We must suffer," she would say; " God has chosen us for that. We must give example to the others, and be very courageous in helping our Sisters." All the faults that were committed in the community she imputed to herself, as if God had permitted them to punish her for her coldness in His service. Once she wrote as follows to two Sisters about to undertake a long journey. After giving many minute directions, which evidence her great prudence, she says, "In passing by villages, incline yourselves before the churches, and adore the Blessed Sacrament in spirit, and salute the guardian angels of all who live there, and beg them to continue to assist these people, and to give them holy inspirations to lead them to God. When you pass near a cemetery, pray for the souls of those whose bodies rest there." Her constant prayer was, "Destroy in me what displeases Thee, and grant that I may be no longer full of myself." The infirmities of advanced age, and the yoke of a long sickness, could not subdue her loving soul. She seemed always to keep herself in the presence of God, and her constant admonition was to seek His glory. No word of complaint passed her lips, not even when the feeble frame was sinking under acute agonies or lingering sickness.

Yet even then the spirit was ever bright and joyful, seeking only to make those around her happy. When her agony was extreme, she said, "It is very just that where sin has abounded suffering should dwell;" and again she would say, "God is just, and in His Justice He has mercy." And when a loving friend said to her, "Mademoiselle are you not rejoicing at going to glory?" she meekly answered, "That I do not merit—I am not worthy." And when a Sister bade her take comfort from the afflictions of her body, inasmuch as they made her like our Lord, she again replied, "I am not worthy."

And this deep contrition came from a soul, in whom St. Vincent himself afterwards said, "That for thirty-eight years, during which he had guided her, he had found the greatest purity;" and yet, continued the Saint, "in her confessions she would weep so bitterly over the slightest fault, that it was hardly possible to console her."

One of Mademoiselle Legras's most earnest wishes had been that she might die before St. Vincent, in order to have his assistance at the hour of her death. She died six months before her loved and venerated father, but he was too infirm to be able to come to her; she sent, therefore, entreating to have a few lines from his hand, but St. Vincent did not comply. No doubt he would not have at that last moment any affection of earth, however holy, come between the soul and her God, and Mademoiselle Legras submitted perfectly to his decision. Long since, she had been wont to say to her Sisters, "Look often at eternity, for the hope of its roses consoles amidst the thorns," and now she was on the borders; and

"Perseverance the last flower in our crown," as she had once called it, was all she needed to complete her long and painful life.

They brought her word one evening that she should communicate on the morrow, and often through the night they heard her saying, "What happiness, my Lord! to-morrow, if I live, I shall receive *Thee*." Once her mind began to wander, and she cried out, "Take me away;" and a priest who was by her side answered, "Do you see the Cross?" pointing to a crucifix at the foot of the bed, "Jesus Christ did not ask to leave it." "Oh, no!" she instantly replied, "He remained there.". Soon after she cried out, "Let us go, let us go, because the Lord is come to fetch me." The morning had come of the 15th of March, 1660; the Sisters entered her room, and knelt down beside her. She could hardly speak. "Rise, my Sisters," she said. "Farewell; have great care of the poor." Her voice seemed gone, but a priest beside her bade her give her blessing to her children; and faithful to the last to holy obedience, she complied. "Live as true Sisters of Charity," she said, "and take the Holy Virgin as your only Mother." Her work on earth was done. Soon after, the spirit entered into the joy of her Lord. So gently did she pass from life that no one knew the actual moment. "Adieu, beauteous soul, adieu!" said the Curé, as he left the room. "She has carried with her her baptismal innocence."

The prospect of her approaching death had dismayed many of the community, who could not imagine how she was to be replaced. One of them expressing this to St. Vincent, he answered, "We do what we can to keep her, but it is the work of God, who having preserved her for twenty years against all human appearance, will preserve her yet, if it be expedient for His glory. Serve God, my Sister, as He loves to be served, and let Him do as He wills. He will take the place of father and mother to you, will be your consolation and your strength, and finally the reward of your works."

St. Vincent was not wont to praise those he loved, yet he could not refrain, even during her life, from saying of Mademoiselle Legras, "God has given her a great zeal for His glory." But after her death his lips were opened; praise could no longer be dangerous to her. Although his own sufferings were very severe, he rallied sufficiently to hold a Conference with the Sisters on the example of their late Superioress. The tears of the Sisters often impeded their utterance, and St. Vincent himself could not refrain from weeping. It was then he told them that his absence from her death-bed had been permitted by God for the final purification of this holy soul. So lived, so died, and in such fashion was mourned, Louise Legras. Her body even now rests amidst her children in the Chapel of the Mother-House, and thousands have knelt besides it to pray that a portion of their mother's spirit might rest upon them.

Not long was St. Vincent's care over the community to be given. Those beautiful conferences of his were drawing to a close. No more should they gather from all parts of Paris, eager to hear the words falling from his lips. "Enough for to-day, my dear Sisters," said he once, looking round on them, "I am sorry to have kept you so long here, poor children! who have had so much trouble to come, and will have the same to return; but, oh! how many angels are now occupied in counting your steps! Those which you have made are already marked, and those which you will make will be also, for, says a Saint, all the steps that the servants of Jesus Christ make for His love are counted." On another occasion, when speaking of the joy and satisfaction they should find in their vocation, he told them that being once called to the death-bed of a Sister, she had said to him, "She had no trouble or remorse in looking back upon her works, except that she had taken *too much pleasure* in serving the poor." And when he asked her in what way she had done this, she answered, "When I went to see them I seemed not to walk, but to have wings and to fly, my joy in serving them was so great." Such was the spirit of self-devotion he had inspired in his children. Fearlessly did he look forward to their future without his guiding voice. "It is God who has called them, and it will be He who will maintain them. He will never destroy His work, but will perfect it; and, provided that they are firm in their vocation and faithful to their exercises, He will bless them always in their persons and employments." In March, 1660, Mademoiselle Legras was taken from the Sisters; and in September of the same year, their father, guide, and founder went to his reward. But from heaven he continued to bless and sustain the company of his children, and wise and holy Superiors were raised up to consolidate the work that he had begun.

2.

Among those who came to Paris from the provinces to be received into the community in its early stage of progress, was Mathurine Guérin, a young Breton. She was born in 1631. Her parents were very poor, but pious also, and passionately fond of their beautiful daughter, and they long withstood her constant desire of entering religion; at last they gave way, and Mathurine went into a Carmelite Convent at seventeen years of age. But a violent illness almost immediately seized her, and she was sent home. On her recovery, her father

T

tried to persuade her to remain in the world, but in vain; and some of the Lazarite fathers having come to give a mission in the village, Mathurine heard from them of the "Servants of the Poor," and eagerly desired to enter among them. She left her home, but was not forgotten. Whenever her mother was grieved by any of her other children, she used to say, she would go and live with her daughter Mathurine; and strangely enough it came to pass that Mathurine being sent, in after years, to found an Hospital in her native place, her aged mother entered it, and died there in the arms of her best-loved child, whom she had given up to God. Mathurine was trained by Mademoiselle Legras and St. Vincent, and when sent out among the poor she plainly showed the fruit of their instructions. On her very first mission she encountered a bitter trial. A false accusation of the blackest kind was raised against her and her two companions, and not only did the world condemn them, but they were deprived of that consolation which is generally given to us under the heaviest trial. When the Sisters went to confession, the Curé refused to hear them, telling them that they were hypocrites, and not fit to approach the Sacraments. Four months went by: the Paschal feast was spread for others, but Mathurine and her Sisters were treated as outcasts. Of course they wrote to St. Vincent, but no one can doubt what his answer was. He prized contempt too much to deprive his daughters of it, and he bade them go on in patience. At the end of four months a lady of rank in the place determined to have a full investigation of the matter. She sent for Mathurine, and after questioning her, observed, she supposed she was very anxious to have her innocence brought to light. "Madame," replied the Sister calmly, "I place all my confidence in God, and I hope in Him alone for my justification; it is more His affair than mine, and my cause is His." The lady continued her inquiries, and the truth was discovered. A public punishment was about to be awarded to the calumniators, but Mathurine interposed to prevent it, and she carefully avoided even knowing their names. From this employment she was recalled to Paris, and became Secretary to Mademoiselle Legras, and also she had the charge of training the Novices. It is to her that we owe the preservation of the Conferences of St. Vincent; for it was her attentive memory that retained his words, and committed them to writing. At different times she was made Superioress of various branch houses, and finally, after the death of Mademoiselle Legras, Superioress-General. She showed a bright and fervent example to all, and guarded the Rule with careful fidelity. Accustomed as she had been to the guidance of St. Vincent, his loss was indeed a bitter blow; but she had his true spirit, a great confidence in God, and therefore went on doing all she could to follow out his teaching in letter and spirit. Towards the end of her life she was afflicted by an ulcer, which no remedy could cure.

St. Vincent of Paul had not then been canonized, but none who had known him ever doubted the power of his intercession before God, and his relics had been always guarded at St. Lazare. Before them Mathurine made her prayer, and the ulcer instantly and entirely disappeared. At length her long life was drawing to a close; she could no longer guide others or serve the poor, but her soul was occupied with God. She loved to have hymns sung round her sick-bed, and her great infirmities never prevented her from rising early to communicate. On the day of her death she had done this, but towards noon a change began to pass over her. She received Extreme Unction, and died shortly after, in perfect peace.

She left behind her a Sister of Charity trained by herself, who imitated and even excelled her in virtue. Julienne Jouvin was also of peasant birth, and the youngest child of a large poor family who had lost their father. Her extraordinary beauty and natural talents induced a lady to send her to a good school. From her infancy she possessed that rare and wonderful gift of winning and influencing the souls of others. She had a great blessing in being under the guidance of a wise and holy priest, Monsieur Joisneau, who had in his youth known St. Vincent of Paul, and never lost the memory of the impression made on him by the Saint. He loved the congregation of Sisters of Charity, and prayed and hoped that the little Julie, more like an angel than a child, would be called to that Order. He was not disappointed; and when Julie was eighteen years of age, Monsieur Joisneau had the happiness of proposing her to Mathurine Guérin, then Superioress, and he said to her, " This young girl is a present that God makes to your community; she brings with her the precious treasure of her baptismal innocence, with the best dispositions for preserving it for ever." His words were verified. From the day of her entrance she went on increasing in virtue, "from strength to strength." Her great gifts of influence were sanctified; the Sisters first felt it, and those who lived with her grew fervent also. Numbers of persons were converted by her. Everybody ran to see her, because of her extraordinary and angelic beauty. Praise and admiration were constantly bestowed on her; but she was, as it were, deaf to it. Her eyes were fixed on God, and on the interior beauty which we must labour to attain, and all outward gifts seemed to her nothing. In due time she was made Superioress-General, and never was the community so wisely governed. She studied the characters of the Sisters carefully, and never gave a reproof without acknowledging before God that she was the most guilty of creatures. "Unhappy that I am," she said, "I have to reprove exterior faults, and I have interior ones much more displeasing in the eyes of God." She often spoke to them of purity of intention, and its infinite value in works of charity. Her gift of prayer was very great, and when she spoke of God, she seemed inflamed with love. There was something majestic in her beauty, and people said the sight of her made them wish to become better.

She had a great love for silence, and was most careful in avoiding idle words. "These little violences cost us something," she said; "but at death what consolations they will be to us." Having held the office of Superioress-General for six years, the Rule prevented her re-election; but the question was raised whether in her case it were not possible to infringe it and keep her in office. St. Vincent's words were, however, too powerful to be withstood; and while others mourned, Julienne with joy quitted her elevated post, for she hated authority, and delighted to be more in the direct service of the poor than a Superioress-General can be. Her place, she said, was rather under the earth than above it.

She was placed at Versailles, and was often sent for to Court by the pious Queen Marie Leckinksa, who had an especial affection for her. Julienne loved the Queen; but she did not like being brought into contact with great ladies and Court grandeur. She tried to teach her Sisters to see in it all, types of the Court and King of Heaven. She did not like the sight of grand clothes so much as poor ones, "which teach us better what we are." "Oh!" exclaimed she, "I am dying with desire to see Thee, my God, and to love Thee only!" About this time she wrote to an intimate friend: "I am tired of this world; with all my heart I wish to see the next, and to be in the house of our Celestial Father. I hear our dear Sister —— has knocked at the door. Oh! would to God that I could enter with her, or at least soon after! I envy her; after a moment of suffering, accompanied by so many graces, an eternity of glory! What can there be more worthy to fix our hearts upon? Well, let us be consoled, we shall not be a thousand years after the others who have gone before." But her eager desires for death were tempered by that salutary fear which is always seen in the Saints.

"I desire it, but I fear it, having abused so many graces; but, oh! what a resource is the mercy of my loving Saviour! Let us praise it for ever." She writes again: "There is so much chaff of self-love in me that there must be a great fire to consume it. I am getting weak. Help me to thank

God for it. I have confidence that He will give me grace to purify me from my sins by suffering all the rest of my life."

And, in truth, long and sharp illness was her portion during the latter years of her life. At length the end seemed to be at hand. She received the last Sacraments most fervently, and became ready to die or live, according to the Will of God. Often she cried out, " Oh! may the Divine Will be done. Oh, Divine Will! be my food." " Is there anything you want?" asked those around her. " Nothing but His Will," was her reply. The presence of some friend, perhaps a director, but who it was we are not told, would have been a great consolation to her, but it was denied. " Thy will be done," was her only comment. One of the Court ladies having come to visit her, said to her in fun, " Look what an honour I have done you!" But everything now was very real to her, on whose sight eternity was dawning, and she said, " I feel it, and also how little I deserve it. I acknowledge that among the motives that make me wish to leave the world, one of the greatest is the esteem that is shown me, for it is not due. God sends it for my chastisement, and in that light I receive it." As long as her tongue could utter, she spoke burning words of the love of God, and when she could speak no longer, her gestures showed how great was her love; and her face shone with celestial peace and joy as she calmly passed away from earth, and went to reap the reward of her forty-nine years of devotion to God and the poor. She was in the sixty-eighth year of her age. Her body was followed to the grave by crowds of poor and rich; those whom she had succoured, those whom she had influenced for good. Those who had known her inmost heart firmly believed there was no need of a *requiem* for her.

Among her papers after her death were found many most valuable and beautiful sayings, and those who had lived with her carefully treasured up the advice she had given, and recorded it for the benefit of others. She had always had a great devotion to the Sacred Wounds. "Let us hold fast to the Feet of our Crucified Spouse, and try never to lose our hold. If a single drop of His Precious Blood falls into our hearts, they will become strong, generous, and intrepid; but we must keep very near the Cross, and clasp it to our hearts that it may not escape us." She had also an especial devotion to the Angel guardians. "Let us remember that the Divine Goodness has given us a Prince of His celestial court to guard us. Let us avoid everything that will grieve so benevolent and charitable a guide. Every day let us put ourselves under his protection, and try to imitate him in his punctuality in executing the orders of God, in his indifference for the employments to which he is sent. If he is destined to be near a king or the last of the earth, it matters little to him, so that God be glorified. Let us have this sole ambition in our conduct, and never let us forget in travelling, in the streets, or elsewhere, when we salute people, to have principally in view the rendering of this honour to the good Angels who accompany them." And it may well be conceived how tender was her love and devotion to the Queen of Angels. To the feet of Mary, she carried all her wants, and laid before her all her undertakings. One of her instructions on holy modesty is very beautiful: "This virtue is for all times and all places; it is the silent but efficacious preaching that we ought to give to our neighbours. This virtue, which is recommended to all Christians, ought to be the favourite one of the spouses of our Lord. He inspired our father St. Vincent to give it to us as our veil."

She had a most filial affection for St. Vincent, and loved to dwell on his teaching. "We are the children of saints," she said; "let us not degenerate from our origin." In the days when Julienne lived, Jansenism was spreading its poison in the Church of France, and women were too often seduced by its disguise of holiness and love of perfection. Religious women were found misled enough to prefer the authority of its teachers to the decisions of the Holy See. Let us hear how the saintly Sister of Charity spoke on this subject. "What are we that we should take any other part in the affairs of the Church than that of obedience and submission? Daughters of St. Vincent, who was so humble, so submissive, so attached to the Church, it would be shameful had we any other sentiments and dispositions. We are but poor women; let us hold fast to our Rule and the maxims of our blessed Father. The true character of the children of God is a sincere and blind submission to the rulers of the Church; above all, to the Sovereign Pontiff, Vicar of Jesus Christ in all ages. Those who leave their holy mother the Church always raise themselves up against him who is the Chief, and tear him to pieces in their writings and conversations. They unhappily seduce many souls, who would not have been led astray if they reflected that the Spirit of God is a Spirit Who inspires meekness, humility, respect, and submission. He is a Spirit Who never leads to disobedience, and Who would rather show us we are in the wrong than our superiors." Her prayers were continually offered up that God would give good priests to His Church; for bad ones, she said, were permitted by Him as marks of His anger against His people. With burning words, too, she would speak to her Sisters of their vocation. "Oh, happy obligation to speak of God, and to teach others how to love Him! To give, and it will be given to us. Let us esteem ourselves most happy to be chosen to serve and to help our Lord in the salvation of souls whom He has redeemed with His precious blood." At another time she gave this golden advice: "Hide the faults of others; a little dust often falls on precious stones, but does not diminish their value. God knows of what clay He has made us, and looks on all with compassion. Let us have the same, one for the other, and remember that God's strength is perfected in weakness." "Crosses and afflictions are the wood to feed the fire of Divine love," she cried.

Her first aspiration on rising in the morning was, "What have I in heaven but Thee, and there is nothing on the earth that I desire in comparison of Thee." At meditation she would say, "Oh, Ancient Beauty! too late have I known Thee." At Mass, she exclaimed, with St. Catherine of Sienna, "Oh, Love, too little known, too little loved!" and when she went to her labours it was with the thought: "He came to cast fire on the earth;" and in the refectory she would pray, "Oh, Bread of Angels, Bread of the Strong, sustain me! I eat because Thou willest. I drink because it is necessary to sustain my body and soul." She went to recreation with the thought: "Teach me how to speak, for Thou hast the words of eternal life;" and when the time came to rest her wearied body, she said, and with truth, indeed, "I sleep, but my heart wakes."

And she would speak to her Lord in these tender words: "I wish to love Thee with all my soul and strength, to love Thee with the love of preference beyond all others, as a daughter loves her father, and a wife her spouse." She was never weary of inculcating the spirit of dutiful submission to the Church. "Let us pray for the peace of the Church, and be always submissive to the Holy See, and God will bless us. Such was the spirit of Monsieur Vincent, our most honoured father, and of Mademoiselle Legras, our mother." No wonder was it that Julienne Jouvin was long and deeply mourned in her community, nor that her words were cherished up.

Many other of the Sisters of Charity left behind them numerous marks of the sanctity to which they had attained, but our space forbids our dwelling on them.

More than a century had passed since the time when St. Vincent gave his Conferences and the "Rule" to a small body of poor, simple-minded women, and now they were scattered all over France, and in many foreign countries. Their peasant costume had become a religious dress, and the Order, once so despised and little noticed, was a revered one. But now an awful trial was at hand; and the moral earthquake, of which we have often spoken, overwhelmed France. Monasteries were suppressed, convent gates opened wide, and the unwilling nuns were *driven* from their homes to exile, starvation, often to prison and to death. The Sisters of Charity were compelled to disband, and to put on secular dresses. The Superioress-General was named Antoinette Deleau, and seems to have been a person of remarkable prudence and courage. She contrived to keep up a communication with the dispersed Sisters, and to exhort them to remember that the external accidents of a secular dress and habits took nothing from their obligation of living as the consecrated spouses of Christ. It must have been a strange sight to the eyes of the Angels as they looked down on unhappy France during the fever of the Revolution. Hidden here and there, gliding about the streets, wearing the ordinary dress of the times, and conforming to the usages about them, was many a one whose early life had been spent in the cloister, and who had thought years before to have bid adieu to the tumult of the world, and who now went about as closely united with God as when within the convent walls. Whenever they could, the Sisters of Charity continued their works of mercy; and the necessity of their assistance was so great, that they were, on the whole, less molested than any other Order. Some, indeed, encountered the miseries of the prisons, but the instances were rare. An anecdote is told, but we know not with how much truth, that some of the mob meeting several Sisters carrying food to the poor, stopped them, and said if they were good *citoyennes* they must dance. " Very well," answered they, with that ready wit the inheritance of French-women; " we will dance with all our hearts, but do not let us forget the poor," and the ruffians, laughing, let them pass.

The prayers of the Saints had availed, and the Revolution ceased. Slowly and cautiously did Sœur Deleau gather together the dispersed Sisters. How many a long lineage had become extinct, and how many a noble name had perished in the wreck! How many of the Hotels in the Faubourg St. Germain had been emptied of their inhabitants, and were now filled again with strangers; but the lineage of St. Vincent was not lost, nor would his name ever be forgotten. Sœur Deleau took a house in the Rue Vieux Colombier, near St. Sulpice. The relics of Mademoiselle Legras had been preserved by the Sisters all through the fury of the Revolution, and they were now placed in the Chapel of the community. The Rule was re-established, and though the Sisters dared not resume their habit, they wore a uniform dress of black. When, however, the Holy Father, Pius VII., was in France, he came to visit the Sisters on the fourth Sunday in Advent, 1804, and afterwards he interceded with Napoleon that the Sisters might resume their costume. The Emperor, who knew the *utility* of the Order, gave the permission; and on the Feast of the Annunciation, 1805, the quaint grey dress and the *cornette* were again seen in the streets. Novices began to flow in, and from that day to this the Congregation has gone on making constant and astonishing progress. The house in the Rue Vieux Colombier was exchanged for an immense building in the Rue du Bac, now the Maison Mère of the Order. Houses of the Order have multiplied in Europe, and there are several in Asia and Africa. In 1850, the Congregation was founded in America, and under circumstances so singular that it is well to speak more fully of them.

In 1774, Eliza Anne Bayley was born at New York; her father was a physician of eminence, and as she lost her mother at an early age, she was educated chiefly by her father, who cultivated her natural talents with the utmost care. She was a most sweet, fascinating being, and had a peculiar gift of influencing the minds of others. She was educated as a Protestant, and brought up in profound ignorance of the doctrines of the Catholic Church; but she was most earnest in serving God and fulfilling her duties. At nineteen, she married Mr. Seton, a merchant, and had several children. Her married life was bright and happy in the mutual love of herself and her husband, but she had many cares and sorrows. In them all she endeavoured to draw closer to God, and in her private papers she has left most beautiful evidences of her faith and love for Him. Her husband's health failed, and he was advised to go to Italy for change of air. He arrived in that country only to breathe his last. The desolate widow, however, found loving friends in the foreign land. These friends were Catholics, and seeing and hearing what their faith was, made a deep impression on her. On her return to America, she underwent a long and agonizing struggle with her religious convictions. Her tender and sensitive nature was rent at the idea of parting from her dear friends in the Protestant Church, and of giving them pain; nevertheless, she was too earnest in religion to shrink from investigation, or from making any sacrifice which God required of her. After a long and terrible spiritual trial, light dawned on her, and she became a Catholic, and a most fervent one. Daily did she seem to increase in love and devotion to her Lord. Seldom was the history of a more beautiful and simple soul disclosed than by the record of her diary and letters, for to those she loved and trusted she poured out her whole soul; and her humility was too deep and entire to imagine any one could form an high opinion of *her*, with all the failings and faults she had to weep over. After her conversion, Mrs. Seton was forsaken by her old friends, and plunged into much pecuniary distress. In order, therefore, to educate her children, she commenced a school for young ladies at Baltimore. Gradually the idea of forming a religious community, and of uniting work for the poor as well as the education of young girls, began to develop itself. It was fostered more by Mrs. Seton's spiritual advisers than by herself, for she was too humble to think herself fit to found anything of the kind. Postulants quickly presented themselves, for at this period hardly any religious Order existed in America. The Sisterhood began on June the 1st, 1809. Mrs. Seton, from the very first, wished her community to be exactly similar to that of the Sisters of St. Vincent de Paul. She commissioned an ecclesiastic going to France to lay a petition for union before the Superiors, and to beg not only for the Rule, but also for a number of Sisters to direct and guide the work.

Meanwhile, she endeavoured to form her community to the religious life, and they were called, *provisionally, Sisters of St. Joseph.* The Sisters were very poor, and had often to go through great privations: they lived for a long while on rye bread and *carrot coffee*. Sometimes " we were so reduced, that we often did not know where the next day's meal would come from," writes Mrs. Seton; and one Christmas Day their dinner consisted of " smoked herrings and a spoonful each of molasses." But the fervent Sisters rejoiced in their hardships, and Mother Seton would exclaim, " Oh, my Sisters! let us love *Him;* let us ever be ready for His Holy Will. He is our Father. Oh! when we shall be in our dear eternity, then we shall know the value of suffering here below."

The request of Mother Seton, that herself and daughters might be admitted among the Sisters of Charity, met with a favourable answer from the Superiors in Paris; and they deputed a small body of Sisters, carrying with them a copy of the Holy Rule, to return to America with the priest who had come to fetch them. The Sisters reached Bordeaux, from whence they were to embark for America. While waiting there for the conclusion of final arrangements, they wrote as follows to Mother Seton:—

BORDEAUX, *July* 12*th*, 1810.

MY DEAR SISTERS,

As it is not in my power to leave France, I write for the purpose of proving to you that you are the object of my thoughts. I hope I shall have the pleasure of seeing you in a few months, as the Almighty, who calls you to our holy state, and has inspired me, as well as many of my companions, with the desire of being useful to you, will not fail to prepare the way for our departure. That all powerful God, who made choice of poor fishermen, weak and ignorant men, to become the foundations of His Church, is pleased also in our days to employ the most feeble instruments for the greater glory of His Name, to found an establishment that will be agreeable to Him, since it has for its object the service of His suffering members. Oh! how beautiful is that calling which enables us to walk in the footsteps of our Divine Saviour, to practise the virtues which He practised, and to offer ourselves a sacrifice to Him as He offered Himself for us! What gratitude, what love, do we not owe to that tender Father, for having chosen us for so sublime a vocation! Let us thank Him, dear Sisters, and pray to Him for each other, that He will grant us the grace of corresponding faithfully to this inestimable privilege. Let us have recourse to the Blessed Virgin, to St. Vincent of Paul, our Father, to Mademoiselle Legras, our blessed Mother, that they may obtain this happiness for their cherished daughters. There can be no doubt of our being dear to them, since we love them, and desire to be subject to them. As Monseigneur Flaget will have made known to you the dispositions which his zeal and holy interest for you have awakened among us, I will conclude, dear Sisters, soon to be companions, by assuring you of the sincere and entire devotedness and respect of your very humble Sister,

MARIE BIZERAY,<br>
Unworthy Daughter of Charity,<br>
Servant of the Poor.

But it was the will of God to frustrate for the present this holy and earnest desire of Mother Seton. Napoleon did not choose to permit the Sisters to leave France, and forbade passports to be given to them. All, therefore, that the priest on his return could bring, was the Rule of the Order. It was adopted by the Sisters of St. Joseph, and they endeavoured faithfully to observe it, waiting patiently till the day should come for their perfect union with the Sisters of St. Vincent. Mother Seton was continued in the office of Superior, and admirably did she perform her duty. Her sweetness of disposition, and great power of sympathy, were most valuable aids in her government. Truly did she rule by love, and her letters to her Sisters are full of touching tenderness, yet ever exhorting them to be faithful in forgetting self.

She writes to a Sister sent on a new and difficult

mission: "Try only to keep in mind, as I know you wish, to be very guarded and careful in disapproving or changing anything, until you have been there awhile, and can see through the meaning of everything. We separate, dear child; but you go to do what we stay to do, the dear will of God—all we care for in this poor life." Another time she writes to a Sister: "Look to the kingdom of *souls*, the few to work in the vineyard of our Lord. This is not a country for solitude and silence, but for warfare and crucifixion. You are not to stay in His silent agonies of the Garden at night, but go from post to pillar, to the very fastening on the Cross. If you suffer, so much the better for our high journey above."

Mother Seton's influence over others was quite wonderful. Many were the careless Catholics whom she led to a stricter life. The love of God beamed in her very face. She was always ready for sacrifice, always forgetting self. Though her occupations were numerous, she never repulsed any one. It pleased God to try Mother Seton by many and severe trials. Two of her three daughters died in their early youth; but she had the consolation of witnessing in both, the death of those who pass in their baptismal robe of innocence to "follow the Lamb wheresoever He goeth." And many and deep were the spiritual trials of Mother Seton. Oftentimes the whole future of the Sisterhood was uncertain, and she knew not how to act for the best. Sometimes it pleased our Lord to try her with that mysterious darkness, whereby He teaches those who follow Him to know something of the meaning of that awful cry, "My God! my God! why hast Thou forsaken me?" In this desolation of spirit she was calm and submissive. "In the hour of manifestation," she would say, "when all this cross working will be explained, we shall find that in this period of our poor life we are most ripe for the business for which we were sent. While the ploughers go over us, then we are safe. No fears of pleasing ourselves, no danger of mistaking God's Will. He who works my fate has no need of any other help from me, but a good will to do His Will, and an entire abandonment to His good Providence. Let them plough, let them grind, so much the better, the grain will be sooner prepared for its owner; whereas, should I step forward and take my own cause in hand, the Father of the widow and the orphan would say that I distrust Him. Shall we make schemes and plans of human happiness which we must be so uncertain in obtaining, and if obtained, hush—death, eternity? Oh, *sursum corda!* we know better than to be cheated by such attractions. No; we will offer the hourly sacrifice, and drink our cup to the last drop, and we, when least expecting it, will enter into our rest." Once, writing about her trials, she says, "For them I bless Him most of all. Where should I now be if He had not scourged and bound me? What matters by whose hands? If I get to His kingdom, what matters how? The Captain marches on. Oh, yes; we follow, we follow."

Many of her beautiful sayings are recorded in her life, but we must draw our brief account of her to a close. Her illness and death were yet more lovely than her life. "It seems as if our Lord, or His Blessed Mother, stood continually by me in a corporeal form, to comfort, cheer, and encourage me in the difficult, weary, and tedious hours of pain." Her whole soul seemed to pass into longing for her Viaticum. "*Give Him* to me!" she exclaimed, when the priest entered her room. Almost her last words were that the Will of God might be done. She died January 4th, 1821, in the forty-seventh year of her age; and never, during her life, had her darling wish been accomplished, of being united to the daughters of St. Vincent. Her prayers in Heaven, however, won that blessing for her children. The Sisters of St. Joseph rapidly increased in number, and in their works of charity. Mother Seton's cherished desire for union was shared by the rest of the community, and several petitions were sent to France for affiliation to the Congregation. At length it was accomplished; and on March 25th, 1850, the Sisters of St. Joseph became one and the same body with the daughters of St. Vincent. They had, as we have said, always kept the Rule; but a Rule without the *spirit* of an Order, only to be imparted by living members, is of little avail. Now this was supplied. Sisters came from France, and American Sisters went to Paris, to learn the interior working of the Order. One important alteration was made in the work of the American Sisters. They relinquished the care of schools for young ladies, and devoted themselves entirely to the poor. The necessity there had formerly been for the education of girls in the upper classes no longer existed. Educational Orders had been founded in America which could take up this branch of labour, and the Rule of St. Vincent forbids his daughters from undertaking the education of the rich, *except* in countries where no Educational Orders exist. Since the union with Paris, the Order has gone on rapidly increasing, and its members are very numerous.

The Sisters of St. Vincent de Paul have five years of noviciate. The greater part of the first year is spent in the Seminary, or Mother-House, in Paris; and during this time the novices are not employed in works of charity, but entirely in their spiritual training, in the study of the Rule, and in receiving instruction on the duties of their future life. At the close of the time, they take the habit of the Order, and are then sent to branch houses, to devote themselves to the care of the poor. If the remaining four years of probation be spent in a manner accordant with their Rule, they receive permission from the Superior-General to make the vows of poverty, obedience, chastity, and the service of the poor. These vows are renewed annually on the Feast of the Annunciation. The Congregation is governed first by the Superior-General, who is also the Superior of the Lazarite Fathers, and holds both offices for life. Subject to his authority is the Mother-General, who is elected every three years, and cannot be re-elected more than once running. The Mother-General is also Superioress of the Mother-House, and by her the Superioresses of the branch-houses are appointed.

The Sisters of Charity now number about sixteen thousand; in the Seminary there are generally from three to four hundred Sisters. This vast body are all united under the one obedience to their Superiors in Paris. They wear the same dress, observe the same Rule, in all countries and under all circumstances; they are in constant communication with the Mother-House, and the Mother-General has a number of Sisters employed as secretaries, who correspond in every European language. The Sisters of Charity must always be ready to be sent from place to place, from one employment to another at the will of their Superiors; and wherever the horrors of war are felt, and the Government are willing to employ them, a number of Sisters are immediately sent to follow the footsteps of the army, no matter through what hardships.

Two hundred years have passed since in St. Lazare, in the early morning, the worn-out Vincent of Paul passed to his eternal rest; and the tree which he planted with so much care, which he watered by his prayers, and strengthened by his teaching, has grown to mighty proportions, and those who in his lifetime were so little thought of or admired, are now honoured and revered throughout the whole world. Even in these modern times, souls like to those of whom we have written have been found among them. It was in the chapel of their Mother-House that the Blessed Virgin appeared to a novice, and bade her procure a medal struck in her honour, which has been since known all over the world as the miraculous medal; and a similar grace of a vision of our Lord was given to another novice in that chapel, from whence the Scapular of the Passion took its rise; and the favour of eminent examples of sanctity has also been vouchsafed to them. It is not necessary to do more than refer to the Sœur Rosalie, the mother of the poor, whose long life of sacrifice was brought to its close not many years since. Unknown amidst the great crowd, and employed in an arduous but obscure employment, another Sister displayed most eminent virtues. No press of work or annoyances could disturb her perfect patience; the servant of all, her very countenance was impressed by celestial peace and joy. When lying on her death-bed, she said, "My hands are empty; I have nothing to present but the merits of my Saviour. Alas! I know not what love is, but I have a great hunger to go to my God, and to see how He is loved in Heaven." And when the last moment came, she died, saying, "*Oh! mon bien aimé! oh! mon amour, mon amour!*" After death, her face was radiantly beautiful, and the officer who came to attest the death stood by her side and exclaimed, "What, then, was she an angel?" "Yes, monsieur," returned the weeping Sisters, "she was an angel."

Until very recently, it was England's disgrace that these Sisters, honoured in so many countries, could not find a safe dwelling on her shores. An attempt was made to found the Order at Manchester, in 1848, but proved unsuccessful. Some years afterwards a foundation was made, after some difficulty, in Sheffield, and there are now several houses in different parts of the kingdom.

## ORDER OF OUR LADY OF MERCY.

ALTHOUGH the Order of which we are about to speak is quite a modern one, the name which it bears is of ancient origin. An Order dedicated to Our Lady of Mercy was founded by St. Peter Nolasco in the thirteenth century: this Order was for men only, and the members bound themselves to the work of rescuing Christian captives from the hands of the Moors. As we find to be so frequently the case, women pressed into the good work as far as they could: they could not go forth to heathen lands to offer themselves to suffer instead of their brethren, or even to carry the ransom money, but they could pray, they could beg for alms, they could offer their good works to God, and all this was done by an Order of "Sisters of Mercy," founded at Barcelona in 1265. Another Institute of nuns, bearing the same beautiful name, existed at Seville. Although not a part of the Order of St. Peter Nolasco, they were closely allied to it. They kept enclosure and led an austere life, offering up continually their prayers and penances for the success of the work of the brethren of Our Lady of Mercy. At the profession of these nuns, they added to the three vows of religion a fourth, in these words: "I promise, as much as my state permits, to apply myself to things that regard the redemption of captives, and to give my life for them if necessary." Centuries had passed away, and the cries of Christian captives from Moorish prisons no longer pierced the ears of the faithful; but there were captives in even darker dungeons, and bound by more fearful chains, whom the new "Order of Our Lady of Mercy" rose up to rescue.

Thirty years ago, the need for active works of charity among the poor, the ignorant, and the suffering, was keenly felt, and in both England and Ireland the active Orders then existing could not sufficiently fill the void. More schools, more refuges for the young, more visitation of the poor at their homes and in hospitals, were urgently called for.

All this was apparent, about the year 1825, to a young Irish lady, Miss Katherine McAuley, who then found herself in the world without any close or binding family ties, and the inheritor of a large fortune. Katherine McAuley possessed those charming qualities and that position which were likely to make the world pleasant to her. She could shelter herself from the cares of life, and she could have found in the society she was so fitted to adorn, everything to flatter and delight her. But she chose a different path. One passion, and that an insatiable one, had taken possession of her heart; namely, the love of the poor. Miss McAuley, though born of Catholic parents, having lost her father at an early age, had been brought up among Protestant relations, and had reached womanhood without having any fixed religious principles. Of too earnest a nature to be satisfied with this, she sought for the true religion; she examined carefully both Protestant and Catholic doctrines, and by God's grace became a fervent Catholic. In gratitude for such a benefit, she resolved to consecrate all to God, and to devote herself and her wealth to teach the ignorant and console the unfortunate. Miss McAuley had at this time no drawing towards the religious life, or it might be there was no Order which appeared likely to satisfy her desires. She gathered around her a few friends, like-minded with herself, and she erected a large building in Lower Bagot Street, Dublin, in which to carry on her undertaking. Of course she was opposed, of course she was found fault with. Such seems to be an unfailing token of God's blessing on a good work. The chapel of the new house was blessed on the Feast of Our Lady of Mercy, and on that very day the severest censures were passed on her conduct. Katherine McAuley was profoundly indifferent to man's praise or blame, but her deep humility made her distrust herself. She therefore went to the Archbishop of Dublin, (then Dr. Murray,) and laid her whole plan before him; offering, if he did not approve of it, to resign the whole into his hands to be put under any other government he was pleased to choose; but the Archbishop, seeing plainly in this humility the spirit of God, would not consent. He told her to go on as she had begun. Thus the work progressed and grew to be large and important—still, it had many defects. All felt that its whole prosperity hung on the life of Miss McAuley, and that should she be removed, the time, the labour, and the expense would have been, as it were, useless. A continual storm of censure and disapproval, sometimes even taking an insulting form, pursued her. Calmly as ever did Miss McAuley await the end. She had placed herself unreservedly in the hands of her Bishop, and she knew that obedience always is victorious. One day the Archbishop came to her and announced the decision he had arrived at respecting her and her work: it was, that it should form the foundation of a new Institute, the want of which was felt in the Church, and it should be called the Order of Our Lady of Mercy. Although in many respects similar to the Sisters of Charity of St. Vincent de Paul, it was to contain many distinctive elements. Beginning, as all Orders must, by a simple congregation, it was in due time to seek confirmation from Rome, and become a religious Order. Its members were to unite the religious life to various works of charity. They were to go out from the convent, but only by two and two, and with the express purpose of performing some work of mercy; and they were not to speak in the streets. They were to recite the Office of Our Blessed Lady, to keep the usual exercises of the religious life, and after two years and a half of probation to take perpetual vows. But, like the Sisters of St. Vincent, they were to be exclusively devoted to the care of the poor. The government of the Sisters of Mercy was to be the same as most of the enclosed orders; there was to be no generalate. Each house was to be subject to the Bishop of the diocese, and to have its own noviciate.

It was thought advisable that Miss McAuley and two of her companions should make their noviciate in an enclosed order, in order to learn the practice of the convent life, which was to form so important a part of their Institute. In December, 1829, they entered the Convent of the Presentation, and after spending a year in the noviciate, made their vows, adding to the three vows of religion a fourth, of devoting their lives to the service of the sick and poor. During the time of their absence learned ecclesiastics were engaged in compiling the Rules and Constitutions of the new Order. The Rule was to be that of St. Augustine, modified by the Constitutions as the scope of the new Order required. The "peculiar characteristic of this Congregation," says the Rule, "is a most serious application to the instruction of poor girls, visitation of the sick, and protection of distressed women of good character."

The duties of the Sisters of Mercy are most minutely defined by their holy Rule. They are taught by it how to act in their schools, how to instruct the children, how to visit the sick, and how to guide and instruct those who are inmates of the "House of Mercy." The Sisters are also taught to observe strictly the vow of Poverty, remembering His example who "in His own person consecrated this virtue, and bequeathed it as a most valuable patrimony to His followers." They are told also to obey "rather through love than by servile fear;" and "they shall never murmur, but with humility and spiritual joy carry the sweet yoke of Jesus Christ." They are also instructed how to say their Office with "attention and devotion," and how to practise mental prayer; to "seek in it their comfort and refreshment from the labours and fatigues of the Institute." They are to have "the tenderest and most affectionate devotion towards the Adorable Sacrament." Also, most "tender devotion to the Passion of our Lord and Saviour Jesus Christ; they shall therefore offer the labours and fatigues of their state, the mortifications they undergo, and all their pains of mind and body, in union with the sufferings of their Crucified Spouse;" "in all their fears, afflictions, and temptations, they shall seek comfort and consolation at the foot of the altar." "They shall be devout to the Sacred Heart of Jesus." They are bid to remember that their congregation is under the especial protection of the Mother of God, and that they look on her "as their Mother, and the great Model they are obliged to imitate;" they shall have "unlimited confidence in her, have recourse to her in all their difficulties or spiritual wants," and on the Feast of our Lady of Mercy they make a solemn act of consecration to her love and service. The interior spirit of the Order is most beautiful, and is founded on a deep humility and perfect charity; they are told to strive after the perfection of their ordinary actions, and to attain great recollection. No one could observe the Rule of this Order without making sure and rapid progress in the ways of sanctity. It is governed, as we have said, by the Bishop, or a priest delegated by him, and the Bishop or his substitute shall make the visitation of the convent once a year. The Mother Superior must be thirty years of age, and must have been professed for five years (except in the case of a new foundation). She is elected by the votes of the Sisters; she can only govern three years, but may be re-elected for three more.

The election is made in the presence of the Bishop or his delegate, and the votes are written and sealed, so that no one knows whose are the respective votes. She who receives the majority of votes is led to the Bishop, who declares her canonically elected. The Act of Election is then written and signed by the Bishop. The Superioress shall then propose her officers, who shall be elected by the Chapter. The community consists of Choir and lay Sisters; they all wear the same habit, but the lay Sisters wear also a white apron.

The ceremonies for both the clothing and profession are very beautiful; at the former the Sisters enter in procession, singing the hymn *O Gloriosa Virginum.* After the sermon, the postulant, kneeling before the Bishop, on being asked what she desires, replies, " The mercy of God and the holy habit of religion." " Is it with your own free will," rejoins the Bishop, " that you demand the holy habit of religion ? " If the postulant answers, Yes, the ceremony proceeds.

When the postulant receives the white veil, the Bishop says, " Receive the white veil, the emblem of inward purity, that thou mayst follow the Lamb without spot, and mayst walk with Him in white."

The profession must take place at Mass, and the novice, kneeling at the altar, says, " My Lord, I most humbly beg to be received to the holy profession." The Bishop replies, "My child, do you consider yourself sufficiently instructed in what regards the vows of religion and the rules and constitutions of this Institute? and do you know the obligations you contract by the holy profession?" She answers, "Yes, my Lord, by the grace of God." The Mass continues, and it is always the "Mass of the Holy Ghost." At the time of Communion, the Bishop holds the Adorable Sacrament in his hands, while he stands before the novice, who reads her act of profession: "In the name of our Lord and Saviour Jesus Christ, and under the protection of His immaculate Mother, Mary ever Virgin, I———, called in religion Sister ———, do vow and promise to God perpetual poverty, chastity, obedience, and the service of the poor, sick, and ignorant; and to persevere until the end of my life in this Institute of our Blessed Lady of Mercy, according to its approved Rule and Constitutions, under the authority, and in presence of you, my Lord and Right Reverend Father in God ———, Bishop of this diocese, and of our Reverend Mother ———, called in religion Sister ———, Mother Superior of this Convent of Our Lady of Mercy. This ——— day of ———, in the year of our Lord ———." The novice signs the act after pronouncing it, and gives it to the Mother Assistant, and the Bishop then gives her the Blessed Sacrament, saying, "What God has commenced in thee may He Himself perfect; and may the body of our Lord Jesus Christ preserve thy soul unto life everlasting. Amen." The remainder of the ceremony, and the reception of the black veil, are very touching and beautiful.

Such was the Order Miss McAuley was called upon to found; such the design she was to carry out.

And well did she fulfil her task. The Order spread rapidly. Bishop after Bishop requested the religious to come into their dioceses. To all these foundations Mother McAuley went herself. She spared no fatigue, and cared for no inconvenience. She taught the Sisters more by example than by words; she won the hearts of all who came near her by her winning manners, and by the sweet humility which characterized her. As foundress, she was obliged by the Bishop, against her own wishes, to be Superioress for life, yet she was not ashamed to kneel at the feet of those whom she thought she had inadvertently offended and beg their pardon. She was always calm and serene, trusting only in God; she would say, "All the hopes and fears of a religious ought to be centred in God." She had a great horror of singularity and high-flown expressions, and her favourite aspiration was, "Mortify in me, dear Jesus, all that displeases Thee, and make me according to Thy own heart's desire."

Her greatest devotion was to the hidden life, and from this reason it is difficult to say much of her, for she was always intent on hiding her deeds and thoughts, for she hated praise and shrank from notice. She was far, however, from being sad or silent; she was the life of the community, and all loved to be near her at recreation, to listen to her sparkling words or gay laugh.

She never used to give many positive directions, or, as she called it, "making many laws," thinking this custom prejudicial to good government. She was very earnest in correcting in the Sisters any want of politeness, saying, that such would gradually cool charity and mutual respect in a community, and would be disedifying to seculars, and consequently weaken the influence the Sisters ought to have over them. " Even our nearest and dearest friends," she would say, " expect to find us changed when we embrace this life ; they look for something different from themselves." Mother McAuley was very anxious to attain and to teach others to attain an holy indifference to the events of life; the only thing for which she was really eager was the Confirmation of her holy Rule, and though she only lived twelve years after the foundation of the Order, it had spread and flourished and was approved of by so many Bishops, that Rome granted the favour sooner than ordinary: the Rule was solemnly confirmed by the Holy See on the 20th of June, 1841. Above all things Mother McAuley had learned to love and cherish the religious life, and she followed the example of many holy founders in never rejecting a suitable subject for the Order, because she had no money, if the circumstances of the house rendered it prudent. Before her death Mother McAuley came to London, and founded a convent at Bermondsey. Soon after her return to Dublin her last illness began. Long before any one else suspected her danger she was aware of it, and she prepared herself for her great change with perfect calmness and humble trust in God. She put all her papers in order, took leave of the community, sent messages to the other communities, exhorted all to live in peace and union, promising them in return astonishing joy and happiness, even on earth, and having received the last Sacraments of the Church, she calmly breathed her last.

Since her death her Order has made wonderful progress. It is scarcely yet twenty years since she passed from earth, yet almost every town in Ireland has its Convent of Mercy, and there are many in England, and some in Scotland, besides which many foundations have been made in the colonies. The daughters of Katherine McAuley have not been backward in giving up their friends and country, in parting from dear spiritual relations, in order to carry the news of mercy to far distant and heathen lands.

And we must not pass over in silence their two years of devotion at the time of the Crimean War. In the Hospitals of Scutari and Koulali, and in the hut Hospitals of the Crimea, they did their Master's work. They were not afraid of toil, self-denial, or hardship, so that they could glorify God. They edified, not only by their untiring devotion, but by their religious recollection and their fidelity to their holy Rule; and for long years to come the tall white cross in the graveyard on the Crimean hill will tell the tale of the two devoted Sisters who died in the cause of charity, and whose bodies rest beneath. And in the Order, which now numbers several thousand members, there are many equally self-forgetting, equally courageous. There is always a difficulty in speaking of a modern Order, for we cannot tell of lives of eminent sanctity or heroic deeds. These things are as yet hidden with God, and will be brought to light at the great time of reward, when those who have rescued the slaves of Satan, and broken the bonds of sin and darkness, have taught the ignorant and waited on the suffering, will hear these words of exceeding joy: " Ye have done it unto *Me*."

## CONGREGATION OF THE NURSING SISTERS OF OUR LADY OF HELP.

AMONG the most interesting of the recently founded congregations, are those numerous ones of the *Gardes Malades,* or "Nurses for the Sick," which have taken root in various parts of the Continent. Although bearing different names, and under different governments, they are very similar in character, and it will be impossible to speak of each in detail. We will therefore confine ourselves to a description of the "Nursing Sisters of our Lady of Help."

Besides the usual requirements of a spirit fitted for the religious life, the postulants must bring a certificate of good health from a doctor; their dowry need not be a large one, as their future employment will enable them to earn their bread. Their noviciate lasts two years, and while it lasts their Rule bids them to "seriously examine their vocation, praying often and earnestly that the Lord will not permit them to hastily embrace the religious life." At the close of this time they make vows for two years, renew them again for two more, and, after that, may make them perpetual.

Their Rule prescribes that each Sister be ready at the will of the Superior to take care of the sick in their houses; she must never engage to go of her own accord, but at the first call must go without a murmur, having first visited the Blessed Sacrament, offering to Jesus the act she is about to undertake; she must never stop on the way, but go straight to her destination, modestly salute the inhabitants of the house, and going to the bedside of the invalid, say, " I am here, Sir or Madam, to serve you." The most minute directions are given for her conduct while nursing: 'the cleanliness of the room, the giving medicines, the obedience to the doctor's orders, are stringently enforced; she is bidden to watch the progress of the illness carefully, and to avoid any kind of gossip or interference with affairs of the family, " to be entirely taken up with the care of the sick." Provision is, however, made for cases as among the poor, where it is true charity for the Sister to give leisure time, if she has any, to help in the arrangements of the house. The Sister takes her meals alone, but must always accommodate herself to the hours of the family; she is forbidden to take wine, beer, or spirits.

She must avoid also speaking of the faults and caprices of the invalid, or finding fault with the doctor and advising another to be called in; and if any of the family affairs come to her knowledge, she must guard an inviolable secrecy about them. She is not allowed to ask for worldly news, or look out of the window, or read newspapers, or any kind of book without leave from the Superior. If she is nursing in the same town in which her convent is, she must, if she can leave her invalid, go there every Sunday; but if she is sent to a distance, she returns to her community once a month for a day or two, another Sister, of course, taking her place. In fact, every imaginable difficulty is foreseen and provided against; and while the utmost exactness is taught in her temporal duties to the sick, she is not suffered to forget those of more importance. If her invalid has to receive the last Sacraments, the Sister carefully prepares the room, and has all in order " to receive worthily the visit of the great Master," and she is to endeavour to " draw the sick person to holy thoughts." When the last agony commences, her duty is to encourage the sufferer, " to speak little, but to the purpose," and " to inspire the dying to make acts of faith, hope, charity, contrition, and resignation to the Divine Will." When the soul has departed, she " must adore the Will of God, think of the judgment to which the soul has so swiftly passed, sprinkle the corpse with holy water, and pray beside it." " If a Sister has anything to complain of while nursing, she must bear it with the sweetness and patience of a Spouse of Christ, and submit it to her Superior, receiving with humble submission her rule of conduct." The Sisters are never permitted to nurse in any houses which bear a bad reputation, neither are they allowed to nurse men living alone in lodgings. "The principal virtues," says the Rule, "which ought to accompany the Nursing Sisters in the exercise of their functions are—the spirit of faith, which makes them see our Lord in the persons of the sick; the spirit of charity, which excites them to do their duty carefully with zeal and devotion; mortification, which makes them support with patience the troubles, ennui, and disgusts attached to their vocation; and obedience, which will make them contented with whatever mission is given to them. They must endeavour to give an example of virtue in the houses of the sick; they must never forget that their conduct must be worthy of the veil and habit they wear. If they are modest in their looks, and charitable in their words, they will be an edification to all." "The Sisters, when nursing, are dispensed from fasting, and all corporal austerities are absolutely forbidden; they must be contented to offer to God the labours and sufferings of their holy calling."

The ceremony of receiving the habit of this Order is as follows:—After prayers for the assistance of the Holy Spirit, and blessing of the habit, the Postulant kneels before the Priest, who says, "My Sister, what do you ask?" "I ask the habit of the Congregation of our Lady of Help, and to consecrate myself to the service of the sick."

*Priest.* "Are you quite resolved to wear it with devotion, to live and die in exact observance of the rules prescribed to the Sisters who devote themselves to the care of the sick?" *R.* "Yes, I am entirely resolved, and by the grace of God I will be faithful to my resolve to die to the world and myself." *Priest.* "I bless God, my daughter, for the noble sentiments of your heart; lay aside your worldly dress, and go, dear daughter, to put on the holy habit you have asked for so ardently." The postulant then withdraws to change her dress, and the Psalm *In Exitu Israel* is sung. When she returns, attired in the habit, the Priest says, "You are ready then to die to the world, my dear daughter, and to be destined to carry comforts and consolations to the suffering members of Jesus Christ: are you contented?" *R.* "I feel a lively joy in the depth of my heart, and I bless the Lord."

The Priest then gives the religious name which she has chosen, and she answers, "Blessed be God!" The Priest then concludes, saying, "I thank our Lord, my dear daughter, for the holy resolutions and good sentiments that He has inspired in you. I pray Him to accompany them with His most abundant benedictions. In the

Name of the Father, and the Son, and the Holy Spirit. Amen." The *Te Deum* is then sung.

At the time of profession the novice approaches the altar and says, " In the Name of the most holy Trinity, Father, Son, and Holy Spirit, and of the glorious Virgin Mary, I, Sister——, make (for two years, or for ever) vows of poverty, chastity, and obedience, according to the Rules and Constitution of our dear Congregation of our Lady of Help. To fulfil these vows faithfully I count not on myself, but on the grace of God and intercession of my patroness, holy Mary." The Priest then gives a Crucifix to the Sister, saying, " Take, my Sister, with holy joy the Cross that I give you; bear it with happiness, follow its lessons and teachings, it will render the three vows that you have made easy to you. I give it you as a buckler against the enemies of your salvation, and as the only consolation in all the tribulations of this life."

Perhaps few of the religious Orders are more arduous than the one of Nursing Sisters. It seems to require a *twofold* spirit. There must be a true religious spirit—loving the convent exercises, and flying from the world, and they must also be ready to leave that shelter and mix among seculars continually. They are more exposed than the Sisters of Charity, who never sleep out of their convents, and are required (except in rare cases) to observe their community exercises; therefore their Rule bids them, "having no cloister to shade them from the dangers of the world, to make a kind of cloister by their virtues, and to lead an interior mortified and spiritual life." This Congregation is governed by the Bishop of the diocese in which the Mother-House is situated. Their Superioress-General is elected for life. The local Superiors are appointed by her. The Superiors are charged "to watch most carefully and lovingly over the Sisters, to be united to God, and gentle in commanding, and never to give reproofs till they have been before the Blessed Sacrament and asked for light from Jesus Christ." The life of the Sisters living in the convent is as follows:—At five they rise; the Sister who calls them says, "Let us bless the Lord;" and each answers, "God be blessed for ever and in all ages." At half-past five, meditation; from six to seven, work; at seven, Mass, then breakfast; at nine, the lesser hours of the Office of our Lady are said, then work; at noon, examen, followed by dinner, short visit to the Blessed Sacrament, and recreation; at half-past one, Rosary, and Rosary for the Dead; at two, Vespers and Compline, and then work; at six, Matins and Lauds, then supper and recreation; and at eight, the day closes with night prayers. On every Thursday night to Friday morning, two

Sisters in turn watch before the Blessed Sacrament for an hour. A beautiful provision is made in this Congregation for the Sisters when too much worn by age or illness to continue their work of nursing. "Then," says the Rule, "labours, fatigues, long vigils, are impossible, the body must have necessary rest; but the spirit and the soul have still all the vigour of youth, and the infirm Sisters will spend their last days at the feet of Jesus Christ on the altar. They will pass long hours in the presence of Him whom they have so often nursed and consoled in the sick and poor; they will pray, and ask from the God of Bethlehem and Calvary pardon for the unfaithfulness of their past faults. They can repair their negligences and lukewarmness in His service. They can pray for others—for Superiors, their relations, the members of their dear Congregation, their benefactors, for the families they have known and served, for the whole Church, for the conversion of sinners, and the perseverance of the just."

The Nursing Sisters are intended for the service of both rich and poor. Besides nursing the sick, this Order is allowed to have a Crêche or nurseries for infants by the day, and also to take charge of reformatory schools and orphans; but the attendance on the sick is their principal and most important employment. When attending the rich, they are paid for their services: the money, of course, belonging not to the individual Sister, but to the community; the poor they nurse without any remuneration. But the advice with which their Founder concludes their Constitutions, beautifully expresses what their Institute is intended to be; and we cannot better conclude our notice of them than by giving it. "Love labour; be always the servants of Jesus Christ, whether with the poor or rich; never give up this mission to others, for it is the end of your vocation. Never forget that you are the servants of the sick. You must give to Jesus Christ, through the sick, not only counsels and prayers, but fatigues, vigils, constant and intelligent cares. If under any pretext you discontinue your attendance at the sick bed, administering remedies, dressing wounds, and other assistance, you will fail in your vocation, and no longer merit the sweet name of Nursing Sisters of our Lady of Help.

"Know for certain that you were not instituted to visit sick people, but to nurse them. If ever pride, inspired by sloth and self-love, makes you find the condition of a nurse too low and humiliating, call faith to aid you. It will raise and ennoble all things, and make you find more glory and happiness in the service of the poorest and most revolting sick people, than in the most glorious and striking actions in the world. Be faithful then to your vocation.

If discouragement comes, and your energy for work forsakes you, look at your holy habit and the Cross on your bosom, and say, the combat is not yet finished, the victory is not yet gained, there are still sick to serve, disgusts, sufferings, and fatigues to bear, unhappy ones to console, children to take care of; and recalling the consolations and rewards of faith, thus re-awaken your courage, and march bravely in the path open before you. Love not that which brings praise; the most obscure mission ought to be nearest your heart. Let the desire of being seen be far from you; it is of little consequence to you whether it is the rich or the poor, the great or the little. Jesus Christ is the same everywhere—He always blesses and rewards His humble and faithful servants. Conceal yourselves, desire not, and, above all, ask not, for the employments and functions which give *éclat*. God resists the proud, and gives grace to the humble. Care little for the judgments of men, try every day to become indifferent to blame and praise, to censure or to flattery, for this is the way to have and to keep the peace of the soul. Always, and in all places, place yourselves individually and in a body as last of all. Have a rivalry only in zeal and devotion, and in holy emulation. Never be left behind when it is a question of sacrifices and immolations. Be humble in heart, simple and modest in your dress and your whole conduct. Love the poor, identify yourselves with their wants and sufferings. There are but two things in the world for the Sisters of our Lady of Help, Jesus Christ and the poor. Certainly they are to serve the rich, but they ought to share the wages of their charity and devotion with the poor. Oh, how beautiful is this maxim! preserve it, put it in practice, it will open the Heart of Jesus to you in this life, and will give you His glory in the next. Nothing for yourself, all for the poor. For self—privations, labour, watchings, and fatigue; for the poor—consolation and help. To labour and spend your strength and the wages that you receive in the service of the poor. You are poor now, continue to be so. As you have received, so give comfort; this is the spirit of your Constitutions. Seek out the poor wherever they are; your resources will never be the worse for your love for the poor. Seek aid for them from the charitable. When all we possess is the patrimony of the poor, and we have sworn to God poverty and abnegation for our entire life, we ought not to fear to ask and receive, and in return for alms, make it your duty to pray for your benefactors.

"You have come into community to sanctify yourselves, to devote and immolate yourselves. Jesus, whom you have chosen for your Spouse, looks on you, from the height of Heaven He has His eyes on you; find Him everywhere, ask His grace, and He will assist you, bless you, and reward you. Be proud to be the daughters of Mary, whom you have chosen for mother and patroness; make her the confidante of your troubles, your tribulations, and your combats. Love her, pray to her, and constantly invoke her."

The other Orders of Nursing Sisters are, as we have said, very similar to the one we have described, and we need not do more than mention their names. The Dames de Bon Sécours were founded by Monseigneur de Quélen, Archbishop of Paris, in 1810; they nurse both rich and poor, and also have charge of schools and orphans. The Sœurs de l'Espérance is a Congregation for the same work, but was founded in a distant part of France. The Sœurs de la Miséricorde were founded at Seez, in Normandy, for a similar object, and have a house in London. All these communities possess many hundred members and numerous houses.

The importance of their work is very great; their labours in nursing are far more required by the rich than the poor, for the misery of the dwellings of the latter is generally so great, that in sickness the hospitals are the best refuges they can have, but in sickness the rich are very often greatly to be pitied. In cases of infection, and under many other circumstances, it is impossible for the relatives to take the whole charge, and we need not here dilate on the misery of hired nurses. What a blessing, then, to be able to summon one who will come for the love of God, and will be certain not to spare herself! And how often are the careless or worldly lying on a bed of sickness, and no friend is courageous enough to bid them prepare for their awful change. The bad Catholic who fears or is reluctant to send for the priest of God, is as frequent among the rich as the poor. Here then is a field in which to seek for souls, and the Nursing Sisters of various Orders have not been backward in entering and labouring in it.

## CONGREGATION OF THE SISTERS OF MARY AND JOSEPH FOR PRISONS.

MANY of the active Orders can and do undertake the care of prisons, but we believe no Congregation is so exclusively devoted to this work as the Sisters of Mary and Joseph. They are an offshoot from a large and useful Congregation, known in France as the Sisters of St. Joseph. A number of ladies, headed by one called Mademoiselle Duplaix, entered this Congregation with the wish of being entirely devoted to the care of prisoners. After some years, it was judged well by ecclesiastical superiors that the Sisters for this branch of labour should have a government and noviciate of their own, hence the foundation of the Sisters of Mary and Joseph, of which Mademoiselle Duplaix was made Superior. The Mother-House and noviciate was placed at Dorat, in the diocese of Limoges; subjects soon flocked thither, and the Government requested the community to take charge of some of the central prisons. The end of this Congregation is, says the Rule, "to live retired from the world, but without guarding that strict cloister incompatible with the service of their neighbour."

The noviciate lasts two years and a half, after which they take the vows for five years; at the end of that time they are taken for life. Some extracts from their Rule will show best the spirit in which these Sisters are required to act. Their especial object is, "to assist their neighbour spiritually and corporally, and to consecrate themselves to prisons." "They will devote themselves to pass their lives in these places of penitence, to watch continually over these dear prisoners, to give them the religious and industrial education of which they have need, to teach them habits of order, obedience, temperance, and industry. Happy are they, and too well paid for their sacrifice, if by all this labour they can gain some sincerely repentant souls to the Church and some useful members to society, in order that human justice need no longer punish. It is always with this object, and to complete their work, that they offer to girls leaving prison houses of refuge, in as great a number as the charity of the faithful and their own resources will permit." "And besides having zeal for the reformation of sinful souls, they must be eager to take means to preserve the innocent; therefore they shall have houses of preservation for poor or orphan children, and also *ouvroirs*, where older girls can learn those arts with which they can live honestly."

"This little Congregation bears the name of Mary and Joseph, to make it remember that it is under the very special protection of Jesus, Mary, and Joseph. Placed under such a patronage, what cannot be hoped from the Sisters of Mary and Joseph for the salvation of sinners? These sweet names recall to them that even as Mary and Joseph watched over the Infant Jesus, and provided for all His wants, they ought to see in the prisoners Jesus Himself, according to His own words, bound in His swaddling clothes and captive in our flesh; and further, in them they ought to see Jesus, delivered, mocked, reviled, judged, bound prisoner, and condemned to death for our sins."

"Such thoughts will powerfully animate the

Sisters of Mary and Joseph in their weariness and painful watchings.

"They must remember that, being vowed by their vocation to the service of prisoners, they ought to pray for their conversion, and to try by their example to impress firmly on them the fear of God and His love; they must never hear any details of their past life in the world.

"Those in the infirmaries, or in visiting dungeons, should speak consoling and edifying words to help them to support their troubles in a spirit of faith and submission to the will of God."

The Sisters of Mary and Joseph are bound to recite daily the "Office of the Holy Spirit;" they are to spend much time in prayer, and to have a great love for our Blessed Lady, St. Joseph, and all the Saints. They are to endeavour "to be perfect;" for, continues the Rule, "Let your life be in honour of the Holy Spirit, a continual act of pure and perfect charity. Be full of zeal, and embrace by desire the salvation and perfection of all the world; have generous courage to suffer all, to do all, and to undertake all for the glory of God, and the salvation of your neighbour."

"Live without desire and without design; give up yourselves to the most loving providence of God.

"Love the interior life of Jesus as much as zealous employments will let you.

"In great trouble and danger hope with a great confidence, not that God will console and deliver you, but that by you and in you His most holy and loving Will be done.

"Be nothing to yourselves; be all to God."

With these and other beautiful words the Sisters of Mary and Joseph are encouraged to advance in their arduous vocation.

This Congregation is governed by a General Superior, who is always the Bishop of the diocese in which the Mother-House is situated. A priest is appointed by him to govern, and under him again a Mother-General. Many of the large female prisons in France are under the charge of these Sisters. The great general prison of St. Lazare, in Paris, is presided over by them with admirable skill. They have also the refuges for those leaving prisons, and for preservation, as mentioned in the Rule. Their habit is simple—a black dress and veil, and underneath the black veil is one of blue, which distinguishes them from other religious.

Thus, while sin brings its victims to these sad places of earthly expiation, so love brings his victims also to suffer with them, that together they may enjoy a full and free eternity.

## CONGREGATION OF THE BLIND SISTERS OF ST. PAUL.

ALTHOUGH this Congregation is a very small one, and possesses but one house, the very fact of its existence is so remarkable, and its place among the religious Orders of the Church is so *unique*, that we bring it forward to notice.

All the other Orders of the Church have the salvation of others in view; whether the religious be hidden behind a *grille* to spend her life in prayer, or whether she go to and fro in the busy world, the object is the same, to devote herself for the salvation of others. The Sisters of St. Paul have a somewhat different aim; their design is to give the blessing of the religious life to those who otherwise would be cut off from it.

The way in which this Congregation sprang into existence was as follows: A lady, named Mademoiselle Bergunion, had devoted herself to works of mercy, though apparently without an idea of becoming a religious. In 1837 she opened an *ouvroir* in Paris for young girls, whom she taught to work, and also instructed in their religious duties. These young girls slept in the house, and were quite under her care. In 1851, three young blind girls who were homeless were brought to her; she took them in, others quickly followed, and without any wish on her part the house became gradually filled with blind women and girls. Soon the idea of founding an Order for the blind presented itself. Mademoiselle Bergunion found among her pupils numbers of souls most desirous of devoting themselves to God's service, and of being numbered among those more especially His own. Blindness was, however, an insuperable obstacle to entering any religious Order, and therefore a new Institute was wanted. Accordingly, Mademoiselle Bergunion, with the assistance of some ecclesiastics, began to train some of the blind to the religious life, and finding the plan succeeded perfectly, she laid her design before the Archbishop of Paris, without whose approbation and guidance the community could never be erected into a Congregation. The Archbishop examined the undertaking and gave his sanction. The foundress and several others then made their vows. The community increased and is now a numerous one. It is composed of two classes—the blind Sisters and the *Sœurs voyantes*, or the Sisters who see; these latter devote themselves to the assistance of the others, and to the performance of those various duties which are impossible to the blind. Their life of charity is perhaps greater because it is so hidden, for none but God and His angels can witness the thousand little self-denials the service of the blind Sisters must entail upon them. Attached to the convent is a blind asylum for girls, and the blind religious impart to the children the knowledge they have acquired. The peculiar methods of reading and writing, the most delicate and elaborate kinds of needlework, music and singing, together with various sorts of useful industrial work, are taught. The blind Sisters and these children have the care of the large convent garden, and are often busily employed in pulling up the weeds, which they learn to distinguish by touch from the plants.

Thus the time of the religious is passed between prayer and work. There is something to our minds most touching in the foundation of this Order; of all the afflictions by which certain classes of our fellow-creatures are, as it were, set apart from the rest of the world, sealed with a more than ordinary mark of suffering, there are none who call forth our deepest sympathy so much as the blind. One of the curses of the olden law fell on those who did them wrong, and we need not recal the Gospel lessons of Divine compassion and tenderness to them. And then, in some sense, they are all marked out for the religious life; no need of *grille* for them, for a perpetual cloister shuts them in from the fair bright world around. But if hidden for ever from its loveliness, at least they miss the other and darker side of the picture. If they cannot see a sunny smile, or watch a saintly countenance, they are spared the sight of those dark and deadly passions which so often disfigure the human face. And then, if their mind has no images of earthly beauty to dwell on with delight, perhaps with less distractions, with more intensity, they can soar towards the uncreated Beauty, which it hath not entered into the heart of man to conceive.

And the Blind Sisters of St. Paul have endeavoured to improve to the uttermost the lesson of their affliction, and by giving up much of the enjoyment yet left to them, endeavour to press forward to a higher aim and brighter crown. They have chosen St. Paul for their especial patron, in remembrance of his miraculous blindness, and strive, like him, to wait in patience till the scales shall fall from their eyes. Instances of their cheerfulness and perfect resignation to the Divine Will may be found in the following incidents. One New Year's Day—a time set apart throughout France for *congratulations*—the Chaplain of the Convent entered the recreation room and found the Sisters in earnest conversation. He asked what it was all about. "Oh!" they replied, "we are counting up the graces and gifts for which we have to bless God, and as you may imagine, Father, we have not nearly finished," and among these gifts they reckoned their *blindness.* On one occasion the doctors expressed an opinion that if one of their companions underwent an operation she would be cured. It was done, and she regained her sight. It was immediately proposed to send her elsewhere, lest the contrast with their own fate should tempt the blind to discontent. But it was a mistake; the blind Sisters and pupils both declared that though they were glad for their companion, they were equally contented for themselves. Thus has the love of God calmed in them eager earthly wishes; they are content to lose sight of the things of earth, content to wait a little while till on their astonished gaze shall burst the glory of the Beatific Vision.

## CONGREGATION OF THE HELPERS OF THE HOLY SOULS.

It seems almost a strange thing that it should have been left until our own days to found a Congregation especially devoted to the Holy Souls in Purgatory. The devotion has indeed been a favourite one in many religious communities; the Order of *Loretto*, in particular, cherished it and regarded it as one of the ends of their Institute. But, apparently no religious body had devoted themselves by name, and in an entire manner, till the Congregation of which we are about to speak took its rise. It was founded by a lady named Mademoiselle Eugénie Smet, a native of Lyons. She was devoted to the service of God and the poor, but had no thought of becoming a religious. On All Saints' Day, 1853, she was kneeling before the Blessed Sacrament exposed on the Altar, when the thought struck her of having an association of prayers for the souls in purgatory. On All Souls' Day while in thanksgiving after Communion, another thought impressed her, that while so many religious Orders existed for the wants of the Church militant, there were none for the Church suffering, and it seemed to her as if God asked her to fill up this void. In terror she shrank back from the prospect, and she implored our Lord by His Five most Holy Wounds to give her five marks that this idea came from Him, and was not an illusion. The signs she asked for were—

First, that the Holy Father should approve of the idea without the intervention of a Bishop; secondly, that the Bishop of the diocese should approve of it; thirdly, that five of her friends should be willing to join her; fourthly, that it should spread rapidly; and fifthly, that some priest then unknown to her should have the same inspiration, and direct the undertaking. One after another her requests were granted; five of her friends came forward anxious to join; they all happened to be rich, and on reckoning together the sums they would bring, the total was a large one. This did not please Eugénie; she knew that God loves best the works that begin in poverty and difficulty, and she knelt before her crucifix, saying with simplicity, "Oh, my Lord! we shall never succeed, for we are too rich!" Very shortly afterwards her friends, one after another, changed their minds and went into other convents, and then five others came forward to her aid, none of whom brought any money; still Eugénie hesitated, till at length it occurred to her to consult the saintly *Curé d'Ars*, from whom she believed she should learn the will of God, and she besought him to consider the project on All Souls' Day, 1854. He complied, and said to her afterwards, "It is a work that God has long since desired;" and he further assured her that the idea of founding an Order devoted to the Holy Souls came directly from the Sacred Heart.

The work then was commenced in Paris, in January, 1856. The other tokens she had asked for came one by one. It is an unusual thing for Rome to grant the brief of authorization to a Congregation except through the request of a Bishop; in this instance it was given to a priest, and without any hesitation. But difficulties and trials of various kinds assailed the rising community; when news of these was brought to the *Curé d'Ars*, he smiled, saying, "She reflected well before she took her resolution. She prayed, consulted others, and weighed well the sacrifices she would have to make; she had all possible security—what did she further want? She only wanted crosses; now she has them. Tell her that these crosses are the flowers which will soon turn to fruit." Gradually the Congregation grew into form, and it was decided that the Sisters should unite works of mercy to their prayers; they were to visit the sick, and especially the dying, to assist them in their last agony, to prepare the corpse for burial, and when the poor have no other friend, they were to follow them to the grave. They were to recite daily the Office for the Dead, and all their prayers and works were to be offered for the relief of the Church suffering. Their motto was to be "To pray, to suffer, and to work for the souls in purgatory."

They decided on choosing the Rule of St. Ignatius for the foundation of their own Rule and Constitutions; and the Curé d'Ars, on being told this, exclaimed, "They could not have chosen better." And when he heard of the loss the community had sustained in the death of Monseigneur Sibour, he said, "A community founded on the Cross need not fear wind, rain, or storms; these trials show clearly how much this work is pleasing to God.

You cannot doubt that your troubles and sacrifices have already done service to the cause of the suffering souls." Fortified by the advice of him whom they looked on as a saint, the Helpers of the Holy Souls have gone stedfastly on in their work of devotion: they have now a large community in Paris. Their work is hidden, and their reward unknown on earth; they do not know when a soul is set free and goes to enjoy the beatific vision; they do not know how the desolate and forgotten souls are rejoicing in their charity; only on the eternal shore will they fully understand the greatness and the beauty of their calling.

It is appropriately that we end our little volume with an account of this Order.

We have traced, though briefly and imperfectly, the spirit of charity in religious Orders; for it is the same love of God flowing out into love for men that animates the cloistered and the active religious, and which has reached in its onward course the Church suffering.

Briefly and imperfectly, we repeat, has the task been done, for the subject on which we wrote was of the works of God; and to record in fitting words how He can fashion the hearts of men and make our weak human nature strong, noble, and heroic in self-abnegation, is indeed a difficult, if not an impossible, task. No invention of men, nor merely human system, could have survived so many shocks, or influenced in all ages and in all circumstances so many minds—only the Creator of hearts could so have controlled them; and it seems to us impossible to trace the course of religious Orders without perceiving them to be the work of His Divine Majesty.

# LIST OF CONVENTS IN GREAT BRITAIN AND IRELAND.

| NAME. | OBJECT. | NO. OF HOUSES. |
|---|---|---|
| Benedictines of the Perpetual Adoration | Perpetual Adoration | 2 |
| Sisters of the Assumption | Perpetual Adoration | 1 |
| Sisters of the Assumption | Education | 1 |
| Canonesses of St. Augustine | Perpetual Adoration | 1 |
| Benedictines | Contemplative | 5 |
| Sisters of St. Bridget | Education | 4 |
| Brigittines | Contemplative | 1 |
| Carmelites | Contemplative | 14 |
| Sisters of Charity of St. Vincent de Paul | Active | 8 |
| Sisters of Charity | Active | 12 |
| Sisters of Charity of our Lady of Mercy | Active | 1 |
| Sisters of Charity of St. Paul | Active | 23 |
| Ladies of Charity | Active | 1 |
| Sisters of the Holy Child | Education | 7 |
| Poor Clares | Contemplative | 4 |
| Poor Clares Colletines | Contemplative | 2 |
| Sisters of our Lady of Compassion | Active | 3 |

# LIST OF CONVENTS.

| NAME. | OBJECT. | NO. OF HOUSES. |
|---|---|---|
| Dominicanesses | Contemplative | 1 |
| Dominicanesses of the Third Order | Active | 5 |
| Sisters of Penance of St. Dominic | Active | 4 |
| Sisters of the Holy Family | Active | 2 |
| Franciscans of the Third Order | Contemplative | 1 |
| Franciscans of the Third Order | Education | 2 |
| Franciscans of the Immaculate Conception | Active | 5 |
| Sisters of the Sacred Heart | Education | 4 |
| Oblates of Mary Immaculate | Active | 1 |
| Faithful Companions of Jesus | Education | 11 |
| Sisters of our Lady of Loretto | Education | 14 |
| Sisters of St. Louis | Active | 1 |
| Sisters of Jesus and Mary | Active | 1 |
| Sisters of the Holy Name of Mary | Active | 1 |
| Sisters of our Lady of Mercy | Active | 96 |
| Sœurs de la Miséricorde, or Nursing Sisters | Active | 1 |
| Sisters of Nôtre Dame | Education | 11 |
| Sisters of our Lady of the Orphans | Education | 1 |
| Little Sisters of the Poor | Active | 2 |
| Sisters of the Presentation | Education | 47 |
| Sisters of Providence | Active | 4 |
| Redemptoristes | Contemplative | 1 |
| Sisters of the Good Shepherd | Active | 6 |
| Trappistes | Contemplative | 2 |
| Sisters of the Holy Union | Education | 2 |
| Ursulines | Education | 5 |
| Ursulines of Jesus | Education | 4 |

| NAME. | OBJECT. | NO. OF HOUSES. |
|---|---|---|
| Institute of the Blessed Virgin | Education | 4 |
| Sisters of the Visitation | Contemplative | 1 |
| Total of Contemplative Communities | | 36 |
| Total of Active Communities | | 294 |

## ORDERS OF WOMEN IN THE COLONIES.

Sisters of Charity, Sisters of Mercy, Sisters of Loretto, Sisters of the Sacred Heart, Franciscans of the Immaculate Conception, Sisters of Our Lady of the Orphans, Sisters of St. Joseph.

# LIST OF ORDERS AND CONGREGATIONS OF WOMEN.

Religious of the Perpetual Adoration.
Sœurs de St. Agnese.
Sœurs de St. Aignan.
Sœurs de St. Alexis.
Sœurs de St. Ambroise.
Sœurs de St. André.
Sœurs Angéliques.
Annonciades de Dix Vertus.
Annonciades Célestes.
Annonciades de Lombardie.
Annonciades Recluses.
Filles de l'Assomption.

Religious of the Assumption.
Augustines.
Canonesses of St. Augustine.
Augustines Converties.
Augustines de St. Catherine des Cordiers.
Augustine Dames de St. Cyr.
Augustines Dechaussées.
Augustines Hospitalières.
Augustines de l' Hôtel Dieu.
Augustines de St. Marie.
Augustines de St. Marthe.
Augustines de la Récollection.
Religieuses de St. Basile.
Congrégation des Beátes.
Béguines.
Benedictines.
Benedictines de Bourbourg.
Benedictines de Cologne.
Benedictines de Fontevrault.
Benedictines de Montmartre.
Benedictines de Nôtre Dame.
Benedictines de Nôtre Dame de la Paix.
Benedictines de Nôtre Dame de St. Paul.
Benedictines de la Sainte Trinité.
Benedictines de Val du Grâce.
Bernardines.
Bernardines de Sang Precieux.
Bethléemites.
Blind Sisters of St. Paul.
Brigittines.
Religious of St. Bridget.
Filles de la Calvaire.
Sœurs de St. Camille.

# ORDERS AND CONGREGATIONS.

Capuchinesses.
Carmelites.
Cellites, ou Sœurs Noire.
Sœurs de la Charité de St. Vincent de Paul.
Sœurs de la Charité d'Evron.
Sœurs de la Charité de St. Louis.
Sisters of Charity.
Sisters of Charity of St. Paul.
Filles de la Charité.
Ladies of Charity.
Sœurs de St. Charles.
Sœurs de St. Charles à Nancy.
Chartreuses.
Sœurs de l'Instruction Charitable.
Sœurs de la Sainte Chrétienne.
Sœurs de l'Union Chrétienne.
Sœurs de la Doctrine Chrétienne.
Sœurs des Écoles Chrétiennes.
Sœurs de l'Instruction Chrétienne.
Sœurs de l'Institution Chrétienne.
Sisters of the Holy Child.
Poor Clares.
Poor Clares Colletines.
Pauvres Clarisses dites Urbanistes.
Dames de St. Clotilde.
Cistercians.
Religieuses de Corps de Christ.
Religieuses de la Crêche.
Filles de la Croix.
Sœurs Marianistes de la Croix.
Filles Dieu.
Sœurs de la Mère de Dieu.
Hospitalières de Dijon.

Congrégation des Dimesses.
Dominicanesses.
Dominicanesses of St. Catherine of Sienna.
Sisters of Penance of St. Dominic.
Tiers Ordre de St. Dominique.
Hospitalières de St. Esprit.
Sœurs de St. Esprit.
Sœurs de la Faille.
Sœurs de la Sainte Famille.
Religieuses Feuillantes.
Chanoinesses de Noli de St. François.
Pénitentes de St. François.
Pénitentes de St. François de l'Étroite Observance.
Sœurs Grises de St. François.
Sœurs du Tiers Ordre de St. François.
Sisters of the Third Order of St. Francis.
Franciscans of the Immaculate Conception.
Récollectines de St. François
Oblates de St. Françoise de Rome.
Fillopines ou de St. Philippe Nevi.
Sœurs de la Foi.
Filles de St. Génévièye.
Religious of the Sacred Heart.
Religieuses de Verbe Incarné.
Oblates of Mary Immaculate.
Religieuses Humiliées.
Chanoinesses de St. Jean de Jerusalem.
Chanoinesses de St. Jean l'Evangéliste.
Religieuses de St. Jérôme.
Faithful Companions of Jesus.
Filles de l'Enfance de Jésus.
Filles de l'Enfant Jésus.
Filles de Jésus.

Vierges de Jésus.
Sœurs de St. Joseph l'Apparition.
Sœurs de St. Joseph de Cluny.
Filles de St. Joseph.
Hospitalières de St. Joseph.
Sœurs de St. Joseph.
Sœurs de St. Joseph au Puy.
Sœurs de Marie et Joseph.
Hospitalières de St. Lazare.
Sœurs de St. Marie Madelaine.
Religieuses de la Pénitence de la Madelaine.
Religieuses Madelonnettes.
Sœurs de St. Marie.
Sœurs de la Bienheureuse Vierge Marie.
Filles des Sacré Cœurs de Jésus et Marie.
Filles des Sacré Cœurs de Jésus et Marie de Louvencourt.
Sisters of our Lady of Loretto.
Sœurs de St. Marie de Lorette.
Sisters of the Holy Name of Mary.
Sœurs de St. Marthe.
Religieuses de St. Maur.
Sisters of our Lady of Mercy.
Religieuses Mimimes.
Tiers Ordre des Mimimes.
Sœurs de la Miséricorde.
Sœurs de la Miséricorde de Jésus.
Religieuses de Nôtre Dame de la Miséricorde.
Sœurs de la Nativité.
Sœurs de la Nazareth.
Chanoinesses de Nôtre Dame.
Congrégation de Nôtre Dame.
Sœurs de Nôtre Dame.

Sœurs de Nôtre Dame des Anges.
Sœurs de Nôtre Dame l'Auxiliatrice.
Sœurs de Nôtre Dame de Compassion.
Sisters of our Lady of Compassion.
Sœurs de Nôtre Dame de Charité.
Sœurs de Nôtre Dame de Chartres.
Sœurs de Nôtre Dame de Grâce.
Sœurs de Nôtre Dame de l'Immaculée Conception.
Sœurs de Nôtre Dame de la Présentation.
Sisters of our Lady of the Presentation.
Sœurs de Nôtre Dame de Refuge.
Religieuses de Mont Olivet.
Sisters of our Lady of the Orphans.
Religieuses de la Pénitence.
Little Sisters of the Poor.
Religieuses Prémontrées.
Dames de la Propagation.
Sœurs de la Providence.
Sœurs de la Providence de Dieu.
Sœurs de la Divine Providence.
Sœurs de St. André de la Providence.
Hospitalières de la Providence.
Sisters of Providence.
Sœurs de la Purification.
Religieuses Redemptoristes.
Sœurs de St. François Regis.
Dames de Marie Reparatrice.
Dames de la Retraite.
Sisters of the Christian Retreat.
Dames de St. Roch.
Sœurs du Saint Sacrament.
Sœurs Sacramentines.
Sœurs de la Sagesse.

## ORDERS AND CONGREGATIONS.

Dames de Bon Sauveur.
Chanoinesses de Saint Sauveur.
Dames de Bon Sécours.
Sisters of the Holy Sepulchre.
Religieuses Servites.
Filles de Nôtre Dame de Sion.
Sisters of the Good Shepherd.
Helpers of the Holy Souls.
Dames de St. Sophie.
Religieuses Théatines de l'Immaculée Conception.
Sœurs Trappistes.
Religieuses Trinitaires.
Sœurs de la Trinité.
Tiers Ordre de la Trinité.
Dames de la Sainte Union.
Ursulines de Paris.
Ursulines de Toulouse.
Ursulines de Bourdeaux.
Ursulines de Lyon.
Ursulines de la Présentation.
Ursulines de Jésus.
Ursulines sans Clôture.
Religieuses de Vallombreuse.
Filles de la Vierge.
Filles des Sept Douleurs de la Sainte Vierge.
Filles de St. Thoma de Villeneuve.
Sisters of the Institute of the Blessed Virgin.
Sisters of the Visitation.

\* Pains have been taken to make this list complete; but the number of Orders in the Church are so numerous, that it is very possible some may have been omitted.

**THE END.**

www.ingramcontent.com/pod-product-compliance
Lightning Source LLC
Chambersburg PA
CBHW020317240426
43673CB00039B/835